I0188197

THE PREACHER'S LIBRARY

The aim of this small collection of books is to help preachers in the basic problems of their task of proclaiming the Christian Gospel under modern conditions. *The Living Word* by Professor Gustav Wingren of Lund and *The Theology of Dietrich Bonhoeffer* by Professor John D. Godsey are published in this Library at the same time as this book.

A GOSPEL WITHOUT MYTH?

Bultmann's Challenge to the Preacher

by the same author

THE IMAGE OF GOD IN MAN (out of print)

translator of

INFANT BAPTISM IN THE FIRST FOUR CENTURIES

by Joachim Jeremias

by Rudolf Bultmann

THEOLOGY OF THE NEW TESTAMENT (Vols. I and II)

ESSAYS—Philosophical and Theological

JESUS CHRIST AND MYTHOLOGY

about Rudolf Bultmann

DEMYTHOLOGIZING AND HISTORY

by Friedrich Gogarten

MYTH IN THE NEW TESTAMENT

by Ian Henderson

THE CHRISTIAN MESSAGE AND MYTH

by L. Malevez, S.J.

AN EXISTENTIALIST THEOLOGY

by John Macquarrie

THE SCOPE OF DEMYTHOLOGIZING

by John Macquarrie

A GOSPEL WITHOUT MYTH?

BULTMANN'S CHALLENGE TO THE PREACHER

DAVID CAIRNS

Professor of Practical Theology
Christ's College, Aberdeen

SCM PRESS LTD

BLOOMSBURY STREET LONDON

FIRST PUBLISHED 1960

PRINTED IN GREAT BRITAIN BY
ROBERT CUNNINGHAM AND SONS LTD
ALVA, SCOTLAND

To

EMIL BRUNNER

Theologian, Preacher and Evangelist

in gratitude for his friendship

CONTENTS

PREFACE

THIS book is an attempt to evaluate Rudolf Bultmann's theology, and in particular its challenge to the preacher. The first part is less directly addressed to that task than what follows, and it may be that some readers will do well to start reading at the second part. Yet the first part has also its relevance, since Bultmann's claim to produce a myth-free gospel and theology rests upon his belief that Martin Heidegger has provided him with the non-mythological and adequate concepts which can govern both theology and preaching. My first three chapters contain a sustained attempt to refute this belief.

The term 'myth', which Bultmann uses so freely is an ambiguous one. In this book I have generally followed his usage, employing the term to describe that type of thinking which employs concepts inadequate to their objects, and does so naïvely, without consciousness of their inadequacy. It is, however, my conviction that no concepts are wholly adequate to describe the transcendent realities of revelation, and that we must therefore continue to use terms which are in part inadequate, though with consciousness of their inadequacy. Only once or twice have I given to the term its everyday meaning, as describing events which did not, in fact, happen, or persons who never existed; and then I have drawn attention to the sense in which the word was being employed.

In almost every case I have used my own translation of passages quoted from German or French language authors. I have tried, however, wherever possible to give the full reference to the English translation, where one exists.

It remains for me to express my thanks to various friends who have helped me; above all to Professor Ian T. Ramsey of Oxford, whose careful criticism and suggestions have very much improved the book from its first draft; to Professor T. F. Torrance of Edinburgh University who first suggested the theme to me; to Professor D. M. Mackinnon, Dr Ronald Hepburn and the Rev Neil Alexander, of Aberdeen University, whose encouragement and advice have meant much to me; and to Dr John Macquarrie, of Glasgow University, who most kindly put his Glossary of Heidegger's terminology at my disposal.

And since we often learn most from those with whom we disagree most emphatically, asking ourselves, 'If you can't accept this teaching, then what have you to put in its place?', I would wish to record my appreciation of the stimulus received from the thought of the great writer with whom this book principally deals.

DAVID CAIRNS

Part One

I

PREACHING, THEOLOGY AND PHILOSOPHY

1. Introduction

RUDOLF BULTMANN is not only an eminent New Testament scholar, he is also a preacher of the gospel who takes his task with the utmost seriousness. And, as a preacher, he has one paramount gift, the gift of sensitiveness to what his hearers may be thinking. As you read his sermons, you can hear the question which is in the back of his mind: 'Supposing there is a man who has just come into this church; a man with little or no religious background; how much of all this that I am saying will have any meaning to him? As he listens to me, is he all the while saying to himself, "Try as I may, I simply cannot believe that"? Or is he quite unable to attach a meaning to my words? Do they seem to him pure myth, or even worse, mumbo jumbo?'

It is because Bultmann is so acutely aware of this situation that he has entered upon his ambitious project of demythologizing and existential interpretation which has cost him—and his critics—so much toil and sweat, if not also blood and tears. And when we see the enormous labour he has put into the controversy, and the undesirable notoriety it has brought him, and the theological odium it has aroused, let us remember that his main aim has been the spread of the gospel, a motive which must make us respect him even if at times we are most critical of his reasoning.

Bultmann is convinced that the Bible contains large elements of myth, which modern man is simply unable to accept literally, try as he may. In fact, however, such an acceptance is not necessary, indeed it is contrary to the real intention of the sacred writings. The mythical material can and must be reinterpreted, and reinterpreted in existentialist terms; to be more precise, in terms discovered by the philosophical analyses of Martin Heidegger. Only when this has been done will this material be able to express adequately, and in a way that modern man can appropriate, the challenge of the Word of God.

By thus boldly declaring his indebtedness to the work of a particular philosophy, Bultmann has faced the world once more with a problem which is as old as the Christian faith. He has made us ask yet once again what is the relationship between preaching, theology and philosophy. Must theology and philosophy be mortal enemies, as both Tertullian and Luther thought? If so, since both disciplines make a claim to truth, one of them at least must be wrong in that claim.

We can see how inevitably the problem arose for the first Christian preachers and theologians. Here were men utterly convinced of the paramount importance of what they had to say. They had a message about *the* decisive event of all history, an event in which the heart of the universe had been revealed. They knew that the stamp of uttermost reality was set on Jesus Christ, and that none but the highest place in the universe would do for his throne.

But they did not make these claims in an unpeopled world. The philosophers and the wise men had each their own teaching, and the mystagogues had their own schemes of salvation. Men's minds were full of concepts that belonged to Stoicism, Gnosticism, Philonism, systems either philosophical, theological, or else rankly mythological. And so we find St Paul in his famous address at Athens using language which is recognizably Stoic, while John in the prologue to his Gospel uses the logos concept which he would probably not have used in that place unless it was already intelligible to the Greek world. Later we find Athanasius describing the work of Christ as the gift of incorruptibility to man, while Clement of Alexandria speaks of the Christian as the true Gnostic whose character is impassible. What is the meaning of such language? Does it necessarily imply a subservience of Christian faith and theology to the systems of thought whose terminology it borrows? If such a usage involves not the certainty but the possibility of disloyalty to the Christian revelation, what is the danger signal? Can philosophy open a man's mind to accept the gospel? Can it close his mind to the gospel, or make him see it, as it were, through distorting spectacles? Can a gentlemen's agreement be worked out between philosophy and theology? If so, on what terms? Will it depend on an amicable partition of territory? Or, to change the figure, must theology allow the philosopher, like a ploughman in a field, to do the preparatory work without which no lasting theological harvest can be reaped? Does theology mediate between philosophy and preaching? Can the philosopher tell the preacher what to preach, or how to express what he has to say? All these questions rise up and face us as we read Bultmann's work. And it is only fair that I should indicate to the reader the standpoint from which this book has been written, and the views here to be developed on the relations between preaching, theology and philosophy. Some of these views will naturally only become clear towards the end of the discussion, but to some extent the ground can be cleared already. The themes now to be handled are of primary importance. They deserve (and have often received) a much fuller treatment than the necessarily perfunctory consideration which alone is possible within the confines of a single chapter. But it is only fair to the prospective reader that I should attempt to indicate, if not to vindicate, the standpoint from which this book has been written. At the end of the chapter tentative answers to some of the questions here propounded will be offered, and the special place claimed by Heidegger and Bultmann for the former's philosophy will be indicated. Thus we shall be prepared for the next chapters, in which this claim is submitted to a careful examination.

2. *Preaching and theology*

Theology exists because there has been a revelation of God in Christ, and because there is preaching today about the revelation. Theology is thus meant to be a norm for preaching, but it is itself subject to another norm, the revelation of God in Christ. Its aim is to keep preaching true to the revelation of God.

But at this point two facts must be taken into consideration.

First, it is harder for us to answer the question, 'What is this revelation?' than it was for our ancestors who believed in verbal inspiration. For we realize that it is impossible, strictly speaking, to identify revelation with the written words of the Bible. We realize that when we speak of these written words as the revelation, we are talking in a general rather than in an exact sense. This was true always, for revelation is always a personal act of God, a personal relationship between him and the believer, and therefore never simply to be identified with a written text. But the old doctrine of verbal inspiration implied such an identity, it implied the infallible correctness of every word of Scripture. Where the sacred writings took the form of narrative, it was assumed that this was an exact transcript of past fact; where the content was doctrinal or moral, it was assumed that the teaching was all equally binding on mind and conscience, except in cases where one dispensation had been replaced by another, as Old Testament sacrifice had been replaced by the death of Christ. It was thought possible and right to preach the full Christian doctrine from any passage of Old or New Testament, and this was done by the elaborate use of allegories. The spiritual and historical insight of individual teachers and preachers has always to some extent prevented this from becoming too mechanical a procedure, but it cannot be denied that the advance of modern historical scholarship has worked a radical change and, among other things, has made the necessary correction of preaching by the norm of revelation a more complex and difficult affair than our ancestors thought. For it is no longer possible simply to affirm the identity of revelation with the text of Scripture. The words of the different writers of both Testaments can now no longer be thought of as in themselves revelation, but must be conceived of rather as various witnesses to the revelation which God gave to them in personal encounter as they went through life, a revelation which found its consummation in Christ, and which is renewed again in the contemporary encounter of God with the believer who hears the word in faith. We find God revealed to us by means of the words of these past witnesses, and not without them, but he is more than they are; he is our contemporary.

In the Bible we have historical accounts in the usual sense of the word historical—accounts of events that happened. But the link between revelation and the narrative of past event is seen to be less simple and direct than it was once assumed to be in the days of verbal inspirationism. All the gospel writers bear witness to one whose life was a historical fact, but it is clear that St John, for example, while preserving some primitive historical traditions, is more concerned to portray the decisive place and significance of Jesus in God's purposes for men than to give an account of what he did. Thus, while history in the ordinary sense of the word remains important, the place of witness in the Bible is more central than used to be realized, and the revelation itself—or himself—is the centre to which the converging arrows of witness point.

The second fact which we must consider is this. Theology must respect both the original witness of those who stood nearest to the primary revelation, and were summoned by God to testify to it; and after them it must reverence the classical formulations of the church theologians. But it has also the task of continually restating the content of revelation in the ever-changing situation of our times, and in discussion with modern hostile doctrine, or misunderstandings and misrepresentations of the gospel. So while it is controlled by the original teaching and preaching of the Church, it is not slavishly limited by them. It bears witness to the same revelation, but in the context of a different world from that of the first century, and must be expressed in its relation to different currents of secular thought. Yet this must never imply a mere swimming with the secular tide.

So we see that both theology and preaching have one supreme loyalty and one only, loyalty to the revelation of God in Christ. Whatever their relation to philosophy, their norm lies in this revelation, and that must remain true despite the difficulties which, as we have indicated, arise nowadays in appealing to this norm. And theology is meant to act as a subsidiary norm, itself under the revelation, and controlling the content of preaching, helping preaching itself to keep loyal to revelation. It will be later seen, however, and has already been hinted, that theology, and even preaching, to a lesser degree, can make a certain use of the concepts of contemporary philosophy. The significance of this will be noted below, but it in no way detracts from the truth of the principle enunciated above.

3. Theology and philosophy

How is theology related to philosophy? No satisfactory answer to this question can be found so long as we talk of philosophy in general terms, allowing to it the prestige we accord to a scholarly discipline whose findings could only be called in question by our denying the claims of rationality itself. To speak of philosophy in this way is to ignore the fact that there are a number of ways of conceiving the task of philosophy, and accordingly a number of different, and often conflicting, 'philosophies'.

For the purpose of this inquiry we may distinguish two main classes of philosophy. We shall have to ask later whether there is room for a third.

A. The first class consists of a number of 'philosophies' which are all, more or less, in competition with each other. All of them have, however, one characteristic in common. Each of them has as its foundation a certain imaginative vision of human existence and its background in the world. Each of them is the expression of one existential interpretation of reality.[1]

[1] In this context I use the word 'existential' in no technical sense, but rather to indicate an interpretation which is no mere matter of theory, but one that involves an active orientation of oneself in one's world, and an attitude of feeling towards it. Bultmann occasionally uses the term thus.

It would not be true to say that all modern educated men understand their existence in the world in the same manner. It is hardly possible to conceive of two philosophers more different from each other in their existential interpretation of man's relation to his world than the German Karl Marx and the Italian Giovanni Gentile. In such philosophies it is the existential vision and outlook which is fundamental, rather than the system which is built up on it. The reasoning in the system does not find its conclusion in the imaginative vision; rather is it dependent on it as its presupposition. To the believer in a philosophy of this kind, his intuitive vision seems axiomatic. Emil Brunner has suggested that each of the main types of philosophy of this systematic kind starts from an undoubted and important element in the cognitive situation; the subject or the object, or the unity of subject and object in feeling.[1] Whether this classification be correct or not, it remains true, I believe, that the various philosophies are expressions of varying existential interpretations, and that if the underlying existential interpretation be shaken, the philosophy no longer seems convincing.

The Christian thinker has no ground for quarrelling with the mere fact that other thinkers make existential interpretations of the nature of man in his world, for undoubtedly he is himself committed to an existential interpretation of his own nature and place in the world, though not to an interpretation taken over from any alien system. The most important difference between the Christian thinker and his non-Christian interlocutor in this respect is that the Christian believes that a decisive act of revelation has taken place, and allows this belief to exert a radical influence on his existential vision. The non-Christian philosopher of the type under consideration usually assumes that his existential vision is the result of an insight which is purely human.

Although the various philosophies are expressions of various existential outlooks on the world and on man, there can be no doubt that the detailed study of such a philosophy has often the power to convert a man from another outlook to its own. This may simply be the result of the fascination of a system which seems to swallow up and account for all reality, and this completeness may suffice for a time, or permanently, it may be, to hide the incapacity of the philosophy to account for certain facts of which common sense is aware. Such seems to have

[1] Emil Brunner (with special reference to philosophical anthropology), *Gott und Mensch*, Tübingen, 1930, pp. 74-5 (Eng. tr.: *God and Man*, SCM Press, London, 1936, pp. 141-5); (with special reference to ethics), *Das Gebot und die Ordnungen*, Tübingen, 1932, pp. 19-29 (Eng. tr.: *The Divine Imperative*, Lutterworth Press, London, 1937, pp. 34-43).

been the fascination of Hegel's system, an intoxication which seems this century to have been followed by a revulsion no less complete.

'Conversion' is a suitable term to use for such a change, for it is a change in our fundamental conception of ourselves and our world which is here being described. What happens in such changes is by no means necessarily to be considered irrational, for the study of a philosophy may awaken a man to the significance of one or more of the great realities. Thus Plato's Socrates awakened men to the dignity of moral obligation, and to the shoddiness of the sophists' philosophy of power. And Kant awakened his generation to the dignity and supreme value of the good will, and the unbridgeable gap between duty and interest, while Hegel gave men an insight into the cosmic power of reason.

It will, however, surely be admitted that there are certain philosophies with which Christian faith and thought will be in more or less clear contradiction. For example, there can be no truce between it and crude materialism, or Gentile's idealism, or Hegel's; or the younger Ayer's Logical Positivism, though it must be admitted that there are great elements of truth in most of these philosophies. The Christian thinker, believing that a once-for-all act of revelation has taken place, will rebut the claim of the Hegelian who asserts that Christian faith only says less clearly, and in picture-language, what Hegel expounded clearly in concepts. And any philosophy which avers that theological statements or the utterances of faith are nothing but expressions of emotion, any philosophy which denies the possibility of revelation, or of transcendence, or of the quasi-personal confrontation of God and man, cannot logically be accepted by a Christian.

On the other hand there are philosophies whose affinity with the Christian outlook is closer, which either decide some of these issues in a sense similar to the Christian sense, or at least leave these issues open. It will frequently be found that the exponents of these philosophies have been influenced by Christian environment and upbringing, or are actually themselves Christian believers. This does not necessarily imply an unreasoning submission to external authority; all it need imply is that the Christian faith has influenced more or less profoundly their existential understanding of themselves in their world. So their interpretation seems to themselves as axiomatic and immediate as do the other interpretations to their various advocates. There may well be a number of Christian philosophies, whose difference among themselves comes naturally, not from their leaving room for Christian faith, or from their common presupposition of it, but from their varied interpretation of their subject matter. A philosophy which coheres with the Christian existential imaginative vision of the world may thus be just as rational as philosophies which express visions that differ from the Christian one.

What is the difference between Christian philosophy and Christian theology? The difference lies not so much in their presuppositions as in their subject matter. Christian theology deals with the revelation which culminated in Christ, while Christian philosophy deals with the many problems of man's life and knowledge which are common ground between him and other philosophers who do not accept the revelation. It is natural that there will be certain ground where the two disciplines overlap, and there it may be that the interest of philosophy is more theoretic, and more given to detail, while the interest of theology will be more directed towards the revelation, and determined to safeguard the points where it may seem to be in danger. For example, both Christian and non-Christian philosophy will be interested in a doctrine of history, and eager to work out its detail. The interest of Christian theology here will be directed rather to certain crucial points; for example, it will resist any doctrine of history which seems to it not to lay sufficient emphasis upon the factual character of past history, and tends to dissolve this into nothing more than existential significance. The interest of theology in such a matter depends upon the fact that history's character as a record of past events alone can give it that concreteness which can serve to draw the line between it and fiction. For revelation demands something more than fiction as its vehicle. The influence of the Christian philosopher's faith upon his thinking will be greatest in those matters which lie nearest to the realm of revelation; it will diminish to vanishing point as the matters studied grow more remote from that centre.

Sometimes it is more help to give a concrete example than to talk in the abstract. Examples of Christian philosophy in the modern world are to be found in A. E. Taylor's *Faith of a Moralist*[1] and Professor de Burgh's *Towards a Religious Philosophy*.[2] It is clear that if a Christian philosophy is thus possible, its acceptance may make easier for the philosophically-minded student the acceptance and retention of that imaginative outlook on man and his place in the world which is implicit in the Christian faith. For such a philosophy helps him to understand his faith and its implications better, and gives him more of an intellectual purchase upon it. To say this is not to imply that before a man can

[1] London, 1930. [2] London, 1937.

become a Christian, he has to accept or work out for himself a Christian philosophy. The Christian gospel has its own power to go direct to a man's conscience, and with its acceptance, he will already possess the rudiments of the Christian existential outlook on himself and the world.

Discussion between the Christian philosopher and the exponents of other competing philosophies is certainly possible. To the Christian thinker his own interpretation of reality has its own luminosity, and any assertion which declares it to be false will naturally meet with resistance from him. Yet his controversy with the representatives of other philosophies is not limited to such resistance. He will examine their rival constructions, and ask them whether these do not in some degree fail to give an account of important realities of experience which common sense must universally acknowledge.

Examples of this type of reasoning can be found in de Burgh's discussion of the philosophies of Spinoza and Gentile.[1] Here it is argued that while Spinoza was assured by personal experience of the possibility of moral liberation by the way of knowledge, yet that experience seems irreconcilable with the principles of his metaphysics. 'If time be but an aid of the imagination, which vanishes for clearer vision in eternity, what real significance can we attach to the transition from a state of ignorance and vice to that of virtue?' Further, 'Moral experience is inexplicable on the basis of Spinoza's metaphysic. He could neither account for the fact of vice, nor, granting the fact, for the victim's liberation from enslavement.'

Gentile's idealism, on the other hand, breaks down in the epistemological field. It so deals with the act of thought that the thinker can think only as the transcendental, never as the empirical ego. Hence no account can be given of the obvious fact that Croce and Gentile, to take an example, are different thinkers.

Whether these particular criticisms are in themselves cogent is a matter for the specialists to decide. The point to be made here is the obvious one, that this general type of criticism with its appeal to common sense is a perfectly legitimate one in the hands of philosophers criticizing each other. And while the Christian philosopher will convince other Christians if he can point out that elements in a philosophy are in irreconcilable conflict with the Christian outlook, he can go further and carry with him philosophers who do not share the Christian outlook if he can succeed in this second type of argument.

[1] De Burgh, op. cit., chs. IV and V.

A treatment of Dr Bultmann's own philosophical interpretation of reality along these lines will be attempted later in this book.[1]

At this point we may turn to the question whether a philosophy can make a man see the Christian faith, as it were, through distorting spectacles. Since the prestige of Christianity in past days has been great, there has never been a dearth of men who claimed that they represented its true genius, and yet quite clearly failed fully to open their minds to it. The cause has usually been that they held a world-view which forced them so to misrepresent Christianity, and were not clear-sighted enough, or brave enough openly to avow the fact that their viewpoint was not the Christian one.

A most interesting example of such distortion is to be found in Emerson's famous address to the divinity students at Harvard in 1838. Here he talks about the moral sentiment which makes the soul of man divine, and whose cultivation brings a man into harmony with the whole universe. This message about the divinity of man was proclaimed by Jesus. 'He said, in this jubilee of sublime emotion, "I am divine, through me God acts, through me speaks. Would you see God, see me; or see thee, when thou also thinkest as I now think." '[2] It was the crime of Jesus' immediate and later followers to assert, 'This was Jehovah come down from heaven, I will kill you if you say he was a man.'

Emboldened by his transcendentalist philosophy to go behind the only historical sources, Emerson is thus able, without textual evidence, to affirm what Christ must have said. Historical Christianity, he avers, has become corrupt, ritualistic, authoritarian, and forgetful of the divinity in every man. Thus misrepresenting in a pantheist sense the Christian doctrine of the image of God in man, Emerson is quite unable to appreciate the Christian doctrine of revelation, and the doctrine of Christ's person, and is audacious enough to rewrite history to suit his own philosophy. Doubtless much of the Christianity with which he was acquainted may have been formalistic and dead, and there may have been some excuse for his rebellion. But the point has been sufficiently made that his idealism made him incapable of a true understanding or appreciation of Christianity.[3]

[1] I am quite aware that he denies having such an outlook (see *Glauben und Verstehen*, Vol. I, Tübingen, 1934, p. 31. He has one, all the same.

[2] Emerson, *Miscellanies*, 4th ed., London, p. 105.

[3] See also H. R. Mackintosh, *Types of Modern Theology*, London, 1937, pp. 42-3.

'A man has only one mind, and one half of it will inevitably colour, or help to colour, the other half. A glaring example is the obstinate attempt Schleiermacher makes, as we shall see, to argue that the will of God and the nexus of

At an earlier point in this chapter it was conceded that theology, and even to some extent preaching, makes use of concepts of contemporary philosophy. And the promise was made that some explanation of this fact and its implications would be given. Does this borrowing of concepts mean that theology is in some way subordinated to philosophy? We shall concede that at times the language used by theology belongs to systems which are by no means wholly sympathetic to the Christian outlook.

Probably the first, and certainly the most famous, of all such borrowings occurs in the book of the Acts, where St Paul in his sermon in Athens quotes from the Stoic poet Aratus, and uses a certain amount of Stoic terminology. It is clear that in so doing, his aim is to reach a point of contact with his hearers, and this passage has caused some distress to modern theologians who dislike the idea of a point of contact, and the possibility of admitting that the heathens could have known something of the true God. Some of them have gone so far as to suggest that the sermon was not successful, and that Paul here learnt a salutary lesson, and never afterwards used this method of approach. They draw attention to his words in I Corinthians, 'And I brethren, when I came to you, came not with excellency of speech or of wisdom, declaring unto you the testimony of God. For I determined not to know anything among you save Jesus Christ, and him crucified.'[1] This they declare to represent a change in Paul's preaching approach to men, and his resolution to tamper no more in future with natural theology.

Unfortunately for them there is no trace of such a change of heart in Paul's other writings, so we may well ask whether this passage really has this significance. Not only is there evidence in an earlier passage in Acts[2] of Paul's outlook being the same as is recorded in the Athens sermon,[3] but also the letter to the Romans expresses clearly the same views.[4]

But this affirmation that God has manifested himself to the Gentiles, and this use by Paul of Stoic concepts, does not in any way imply the

natural causation are only two names for the same thing. Because God is immutable, there can arise in him no new purpose. . . . What relation, except that of antagonism, does this thought of an immutable cosmic process have to the Biblical view of the world as wholly, and at every moment, in the hand of a God who is free and almighty? At this point, as at some others, Schleiermacher has lost sight of the Absolute Power that, for prophets and apostles, resides in absolute love and holiness; and what has hidden it from him is his impersonal philosophy.'

[1] I Cor. 2.1. [2] Acts 17.22-31. [3] Acts 14.15-18. [4] Rom. 1.16-32.

subordination of Christian preaching, faith, and theology to an alien philosophy. Paul did certainly believe that there was enough of truth in Stoicism to give point to his introduction. If there were not behind the Stoic philosophy a true self-manifestation of God, then the use of Stoic language would have been useless for a Christian sermon.

But when we examine the sermon we make a most interesting discovery. The language used is partly Stoic, and would be recognized as such by its hearers. But the thought underlying the language is not Stoic, but Hebrew and Christian. By the use of Stoic language, Paul does not dip his standard to the Stoic philosophy. The norm of truth here is not the Stoic concept of the universal logos, but the Biblical conception of God the creator.

Here I cannot do better than quote a study of this passage from Max Lackmann's scholarly *Vom Geheimnis der Schöpfung*, a work which has not yet had the attention and respect that it deserves.[1] Commenting on the words 'For in him we live and move and have our being', Lackmann writes: 'Paul uses Stoic formulas and concepts'. These, he continues, point back to Plato's thought of the world-soul as the first mover. And in these formulas the Godhead is regarded as the reason and soul which fills and moves the whole world. 'This does not however mean that Paul does homage to Greek pantheism and the world-soul. As the apostle used his formula "*ἐν Χριστῷ*" and "*ἐν θεῷ*", so here also, following Psalm 139.5, and Jeremiah 23.24, he uses the thought of a Creator's hand enfolding and upholding every creature. We are upheld by the effectual presence of a God who is thought of as a person and not as a substance. With this application and transformation of Greek thoughts of God and the creation, Paul makes us realize once more that even the untruth of heathen theology draws its life from the truth of the true God of Israel and of the Church of Christ. By using the heathen theological formulas, Paul bends them back into obedience to the Spirit of God, to whom in truth they belong.'

What we have indicated at length with relation to this passage, could also be shown with reference to John's use of the logos concept in the prologue to his Gospel. It is indeed true that the concept of the logos in John is chosen partly because it has a kinship with Greek teaching, but here too the content of the concept is taken from the context of Hebrew thought, not Greek thought. Karl Barth has said that there is a fundamental lack of seriousness in theology's use of philosophical concepts. This is perhaps unfortunately put, since it

[1] Max Lackmann, *Vom Geheimnis der Schöpfung*, Stuttgart, 1952, pp. 255-6.

suggests, what is certainly not Barth's meaning, that theological thinking is necessarily less strenuous and disciplined than philosophical thinking. But Barth is right, as indicating that within Christian theology philosophical concepts are used rather as illustrations than as governing norms; the weight is laid preponderantly, not on the illustration, but on the reality which the theologian seeks to communicate. Each time he uses a philosophical concept, he is to be imagined as saying, under his breath, 'It is thus, if you will have it', 'if I may so put it'. And frequently the fact that he uses a number of such philosophical concepts one after another, indicates the way in which he is conscious of the partial unsatisfactoriness of all of them, and his unwillingness to take any one of them wholly seriously within his discipline.

Certainly, as Dr James Brown has indicated, in his attempts to describe God's sovereignty Karl Barth uses philosophical concepts with a careless abandon. If he were taking them wholly seriously, this would mean that he was involved in contradiction. Yet in the end, what Barth wishes to say is quite clear to the careful reader.[1]

If the case here put is valid, we can understand how the Christian theologian can and must use contemporary philosophical language, and yet in so doing, can avoid falling under the tutelage of an alien philosophical system. Further, we might say where the danger of such a tutelage arises. It will arise when the concepts begin to alter the content of the faith which uses them, rather than themselves being 'bent back', in Lackmann's phrase, into the service of the Christian revelation. It is not always easy to tell the exact point where, from the Christian point of view, such a distortion begins. We shall later have to ask whether Bultmann's own reading of the gospel has in certain points been influenced illegitimately by concepts from the existentialism of Heidegger.

B. There is a second type of philosophy with which Christian faith and theology have to deal. Its relationship with preaching is much more indirect. In this philosophy no imaginative vision of man's existence and the world is necessarily presupposed. The work here done is critical, and we may therefore call this 'the critical philosophy'. Such a philosophy waits until it has statements of faith, or theological statements and work before it, and then it examines them. Its most prominent contemporary form is the linguistic philosophy, whose exponents have often been influenced by the study of scientific thinking.

[1] James Brown, *Subject and Object in Modern Theology*, SCM Press, London, 1955, ch. VI, esp. p. 150.

They have found that a verification method, so valuable in science, has a relevance in much wider fields, though its form and rigour are by no means the same in every field. One of the main questions of the linguistic philosophy today is accordingly what relevance this method can have in the field of religion, and if it is relevant, what form it can take there. There is a difficulty here, alongside and out of these questions arises the challenging suggestion that if a statement makes claim to truth, we must be able to specify certain conditions which would 'falsify' it, or at least render it much less likely to be true. And, since the Christian is expected to say of God, 'Though he slay me, yet will I trust in him', and faith is defined as a holding fast to God in face of whatever may happen, it looks as if faith could not satisfy the verification principle. And if faith cannot do so, then neither can theology, for Christian theology builds upon the findings of faith. Here is a problem which the critical philosophy in its linguistic form has posed to Christian thinkers, and it has led them to see better what Christian commitment is, how it is much more than assent to what can be observationally verified.

This philosophy further investigates the language and the reasoning found in works on theology. It inquires whether the analogies found there are able to bear the weight that theologians ask them to carry, and since many theologians seem positively to delight in antinomy and paradox, it asks what criterion they have for distinguishing between sheer contradiction and sublime paradox and mystery.

All this work is necessary, and the theologian cannot but welcome it. And, once these questions have been asked, he must himself do the best he can to answer them, thus himself entering into the field of critical philosophy. There are times when he must examine, on his side, the suggestions of the critical philosopher as to what the real meaning and reference of theological statements is. And at times he will have to resist these often well-meant suggestions, as endangering the claim to truth which theology can never renounce without committing suicide. Most theologians would, for example, reject Professor Braithwaite's well-intentioned interpretation of the significance of religious language.[1]

In relation to paradox, the theologian must admit that *sheer* paradox is simply nonsense. But he may, in certain situations, be compelled to reject what he believes to be rash and premature resolutions of paradox, situations where he is convinced that for the time being he is forced to

[1] R. B. Braithwaite, *An Empiricist's View of the Nature of Religious Belief*, C.U.P., London, 1955.

hold two positions, each of which seems to be vital, yet which are hard to reconcile with each other. That such a reconciliation at some level is possible, he must surely believe, unless he is prepared to say a final good-bye to reason.

What can the Christian theologian hope to achieve as a result of such discussion and reflection along with the critical philosopher? It would be too much to hope that he could demonstrate to a man who does not share his fundamental Christian world-outlook that this outlook is true, for this would be to destroy the distinction which Christian theology has always drawn between faith and sight. On the other hand, he may hope to make a good case against anyone who argues that he is talking complete nonsense, and may even aim at eliciting the concession that 'If there be a revelation such as you affirm, then this is the kind of way you will have to speak theologically about it.'

It is true that there is no clear-cut line of demarcation between the critical type of philosophy and the first type of philosophy which we mentioned, which may be actually hostile to Christian faith and theology. For behind a critical philosophy there may lie the conviction or suspicion that theological statements, and statements of faith have no claim to truth at all. This is obviously the case in A. J. Ayer's *Language, Truth and Logic*. Such a conviction implies an existential view of man in his world where there is no place at all for the transcendent realities of religion. But this marginal uncertainty does not alter the fact that there are these two kinds of philosophy of which we have spoken, and that the Christian thinker has to deal with both. Therefore, at one remove, both kinds have also an influence on the language of preaching, though the norm of both theology and preaching is the revelation in Jesus Christ.

C. It is claimed that there is a third kind of philosophy, which is clearly different from the two mentioned above. The first type might have been described as constructive, in the sense that it implies a whole world-outlook either friendly or hostile to the Christian faith. The second type is not thus constructive, but purely critical, and so essentially neutral. And now the claim is made that there is a third type which is more than critical, and yet at the same time essentially neutral. It does not start from any particular view of the world, but from that everyday understanding of being which in some measure we all possess. It purports to deal with a different sphere from that of theology, or any of the other scholarly or scientific disciplines. *They*, it is claimed, belong to the ontic sphere, the sphere of particular facts and experiences. *It* is concerned with the ontological sphere, in particular it deals with the fundamental structure of human personal being (*Dasein*), which can be disclosed only by a certain type of rigorous penetrative philosophical analysis, the phenomenological method, whose task it is to lay down the pattern that all ontic disciplines must follow, in so far as they are activities of human personal being. The reference here is, of course, to the study of ontology as Heidegger practises it, of which we shall have to speak in later chapters of this book.

The claim to penetrate to this deeper level is not made by the philosophies of the first type we have considered. Indeed they do not possess the concepts 'ontic' and 'ontological' in the sense which Heidegger has given to the words. The suggestion is sometimes made that Heidegger's thought may be useful to Christian theologians because of its kinship with Biblical thought, and indeed because of its origin in Christian sources in Augustine, Pascal and Kierkegaard. But if this suggestion is taken seriously, it will mean that we regard Heidegger's as a philosophy of the first type, and akin to Christian thinking, because its understanding of man in his world has been profoundly influenced by Christian faith and thinking. Both Heidegger and, I believe, Bultmann would claim that it depends not on anything so haphazard as a historical origin or on the vision of this or that particular Christian, but rather on the rigorously systematic phenomenological method.

Heidegger indeed has such confidence in his method that he declares that any scholarly work in theology will have to build on the ontological foundations laid down in his important work *Being and Time*.[1] This claim is accepted by Bultmann. Clearly, both these writers believe that Heidegger's work is neutral in the sense that it is not the expression of one possible existential interpretation of man in his world, while other interpretations might have led to other ontologies. It is, they aver, both necessary and authoritative, and valid for all future time, though Bultmann is apparently not quite so sure about its finality as Heidegger.[2]

[1] The English translation by John Macquarrie and Edward Robinson will be published by the SCM Press in 1961.

[2] Bultmann, *Kerygma und Mythos*, Herbert Reich, Evangelischer Verlag, Hamburg-Volksdorf, vol. II, p. 193.

In recent years five volumes have appeared in Germany entitled *Kerygma und Mythos*, edited by H. W. Bartsch, and published as above, vol. I in 1948, vol. II in 1952, vol. III in 1954, vols. IV and V in 1955. They contain important contributions to a very lively theological discussion originated by an Essay by

But, whatever their differences both thinkers are quite satisfied that on the ontological level, no ontic issues are foreclosed by the analyses of 'Time and Being', and Bultmann is quite certain that here a gentlemen's agreement is offered by Heidegger to the Christian theologian and believer, who will be able to do his own proper work at perfect liberty in spite of his ontological dependence on Heidegger.

It is further suggested that this system supplies the concepts which must be employed if modern man is to understand the gospel and its claim upon his will. Even at this early point we may suggest a misgiving. For when we have read the exceedingly obscure and unconvincing pages of Heidegger on the ontological structure of guilt, we may well find ourselves asking whether modern man, any more than ancient man, is in need of such 'help' before he can know what guilt is, and in what circumstances he should feel guilty, and when he should not. And if the man in the street can tell without Heidegger's assistance when he is rightly termed guilty, then will not such knowledge suffice also for the preacher who is to address him, and the theologian who is to write for the preacher?

4. Conclusions

It will now be possible to give tentative and provisional answers to some of the questions put at an earlier stage in this chapter. Can a philosophy open or close a man's mind to the gospel, or make him see it through distorting spectacles?

If the first type of philosophy be considered, we may recall that there have been philosophies of this kind with recognizable Christian affinities. But if a philosophy in this class is hostile to Christianity, it clearly can close a man's mind to the faith, or distort it for him. It cannot of itself, even if sympathetic, open a man's mind fully to Christianity, though by removing ideas hostile to our faith, or by working out in its own field some of the implications of a Christian outlook on man and the world, it may make faith more thoroughgoing in its expression.

A critical philosophy, on the other hand, should neither directly help nor hinder a man in believing. But in so far as a man, while believing, may have puzzles about certain specific claims, it may

Rudolf Bultmann entitled 'Neues Testament und Mythologie', which is printed at the beginning of vol. I. This volume, with some omissions and an addition, has appeared in an English version by R. H. Fuller, published under the title, *Kerygma and Myth*, SPCK, London, 1954.

strengthen his belief by showing him that in fact he has been considering certain doctrinal assertions in a naïve and uncritical way. A man's faith may be made easier when he sees that 'impassible' or 'omnipotence' or even 'person' in a trinitarian formula has to be given an interpretation other than that which a first glance might suggest.

And yet there can be no doubt that in effect a critical philosophy may shake a man's faith, when the formulations of it which he previously accepted are now called in question, or even declared meaningless. If his previous religious experience had been sufficiently profound, he might well have been able to face such criticism without flinching. But in fact our experience can nowhere be wholly isolated from our interpretation of it, least of all in this field, so that the critical philosophy can undoubtedly have the effect of shaking faith, though when the matter has been thought out, faith may be more stable than ever before.

With regard to the third type of philosophy, if it exists, it ought not to have any distorting or disturbing effect on faith. On the contrary, while it could not be claimed that this philosophy obviates the need for the leap of faith, it may be able to clear away irrelevant hurdles, and allow a man a clear run at the essential one!

The question remains whether Heidegger's special work really does perform the function claimed for it. The question may be kept in mind whether a reformulation of the Biblical message under his guidance is really so unprejudiced as is supposed. If it should turn out that what we have before us is not a third type of philosophy, but yet another sample of the first type, and one inconsistent with the Christian outlook, then even this claim would have to be rejected, though it might still be conceded that this philosophy had given us important insights, and accordingly had done a real service to faith incidentally.

Can there, then, be a gentlemen's agreement and partition of territories between theology and philosophy? With reference to the first type of philosophy, the answer is 'Yes', if the philosophy be a Christian one, or if it leaves open such issues as the Christian faith declares should be left open, if it is to have space enough to breathe. Otherwise the answer will be 'No'.

With regard to a critical philosophy, the answer is that a gentlemen's agreement is necessary and inevitable, the partition of territories being, however, not a useful figure here, since the function of the philosopher is to criticize and to help the believer and the theologian to get their thinking straight.

With regard to a philosophy claiming to be of the third type, the answer will be, 'Yes, if such a philosophy is really neutral, and if the ontological and ontic sphere can really be kept apart, in such a way that ontological decisions really leave ontic issues open.' Otherwise, the answer will be 'No'. Does theology mediate between philosophy and preaching? Can the philosopher tell the theologian what to say, and through him, the preacher? With regard to the first kind of philosophy, the answer will be 'If the philosophy is hostile to Christianity, certainly not'. If the philosophy is not hostile, the philosopher will not want to tell the theologian what to say; he will leave him free in his own field. But he may be able to provide him with useful categories which give the preacher an inroad into the unbeliever's field. In so far as the philosophy is critical, the philosopher may help the theologian, and indirectly the preacher, to get his own ideas clear, and at the worst will have to rejoin, 'Whatever you want to say, you have not yet succeeded, in my opinion, in saying it intelligibly.'

With regard to the third type of philosophy, if the discipline of ontology, as Heidegger understands it, is really possible, and really neutral, then the philosopher will be able to influence and change the *language* which the theologian and the preacher use, but will neither change nor wish to change the *content* of what the preacher and the theologian say, which will continue to have as its supreme and sole norm the revelation in Christ. That this is the correct view of Heidegger's function in relation to theology and preaching, is the belief of Rudolf Bultmann. If, however, the claim to neutrality can be shown to be false, then, in proportion to its falsity, the philosophy will not only be influencing the language of preacher and theologian, but also the content of their message. And this will not be a harmless mediation between philosophy and preaching, undertaken by theology, but a dangerous one, which deprives it of its true norm in the revelation.

We must now turn to a closer study of Heidegger's *Being and Time*, in order to evaluate his claims for his own work, and see whether we have here in truth an instance of a third type of philosophy which can at the same time control the language of Christian theology and preaching, yet leave them free for their own work. Does Heidegger enable us to understand what the Bible is really driving at? Does he enable us to grasp what theological language really means? Can he help us in these ways to put fresh life into our preaching?

II

HEIDEGGER, CRADLE OR CUCKOO?

1. Introduction

SINCE Bultmann accepts the claims of Heidegger that all future scientific theology must base itself upon his work, it will be necessary to give in this chapter some account of *Sein und Zeit*,[1] Heidegger's chief work, in which this claim is made. Only sufficient will here be said about the book to make intelligible the claim of Heidegger, and the criticism of it which we shall offer of that claim. Further, our brief account of Heidegger will be oriented so as to make intelligible Bultmann's own comments about Heidegger's philosophy and his own relation, as a theologian, to it.

2. 'Being and Time'

Only the first part of this important work has been published, and as it appeared as long ago as 1927, it is doubtful if it will ever be completed. The work is an inquiry into the meaning of being in general, but the volume published deals with personal being, emphasizing its temporal, historical, character.

A word is necessary at the outset on the phenomenological method employed by Heidegger, though there must be a more thorough discussion of it later. The use of this method was a striking characteristic of the philosophy of Edmund Husserl, who coined the phrase 'To the things themselves!' His conviction was that, in the various fields of philosophical research, a standpointless study of the phenomena would disclose their ontological structure. This is also Heidegger's belief, though he is of the opinion that this structure does not easily show itself, and, for reasons which will become clear later on, actually conceals itself. In Heidegger's opinion, the discipline of ontology, that is, the study of being and its structures, is only possible because the

[1] *Sein und Zeit*, by Martin Heidegger: Halle.a.S., 1927, henceforward cited as *S.u.Z.*

phenomenological method is valid. The book is full of examples of this method. Heidegger starts with the examination of a particular phenomenon, and once he has got it clearly in view, discards what in it appears to be superficial or misleading, inquiring all the time what is the ontological structure underlying it, without which it would not be possible.

The book is extremely obscure, full of specially invented terms, and there will be few who can claim to have Heidegger's system at their finger-tips. In writing this chapter I have been faced by a difficulty: whether to place before the reader who is not willing to undergo the stern discipline of reading *Sein und Zeit* for himself, even a brief and telegraphic account of its arguments. I have decided, however, to retain only the bare minimum necessary for the understanding of the criticism later to be made of Heidegger's claims for himself, and Bultmann's claims for Heidegger. Only thus has it seemed possible to avoid completely discouraging any who are very interested in a critical and philosophical study of Bultmann's theology, but are not willing to follow the extremely complex detail of the Heideggerian system.

Man's being, Heidegger tells us, is of such a character that he is always embarked on a project—always already on the way to something. Such projects are not merely examples of the structure of man's purposive activity. It is this structure which *all* man's activity possesses, and he owes it to this ontological structure that he can have purposes at all. Further, man's being is always being-in-a-world, and here something more than spatial inherence is meant. Spatial inherence is only one expression of this inherence. Man cannot be regarded in abstraction from this world, nor this world in abstraction from him. If the attempt is made to do so, then the 'broken pieces', 'man' and 'world' are so misinterpreted that they can no more be fitted together again than the broken fragments of Humpty Dumpty's shell! Man is always in his world, and his world is open to him, and he to his world; each of them interpenetrates the other. Because of this openness he can know his world, and also project himself in it, act in it. Indeed, knowing is one particular type of project.

The question is next asked, 'Who is it that exists in-the-world?' Philosophers have generally answered 'the self', and have regarded this self as a special kind of substance, which retains its identity in spite of its changing characteristics. But Heidegger regards this as a mistake, and in a sense, a deliberate mistake. It is part of a perverse flight from our own authentic being, in which, inevitably, we are all involved.

There is an inevitable tendency for man to run away from his authentic self, and one of the ways of doing this is to regard himself as much as possible as if he were a thing. What exists in-the-world as personal being (*Dasein*) is not, as the philosophers have thought, a substantial self, but primarily and most commonly an existent in an inauthentic mode of personal existence, which Heidegger calls *Das Man* ('One'). This is a kind of Mrs Grundy, full of chatter, mediocrity, and superficiality. Heidegger does not conceive of 'One' as unreal; it is very real, but it is personal being in an inauthentic mode. We are thus driven to ask what is the authentic existent which is to be contrasted with the inauthentic 'One'. To discover the authentic counterpart of 'One', Heidegger has recourse to the phenomenon of anxiety, for he believes that when this phenomenon is subjected to the scrutiny of the phenomenological method, this scrutiny will disclose the hidden authentic personal existent.

Under further examination it is perceived that anxiety is distinguished from fear; for fear is directed to 'some object out there in the world', whereas anxiety is felt for my own self as a being with certain possibilities of which the ultimate and final possibility is my own death, the inevitable future cessation of my own being. This is that finally inescapable destiny from which the inauthentic and impersonal mode of being is incessantly in flight. 'One' never dies, but lives in an anonymous immortality of a kind. Authenticity is achieved in so far as I am able in anxiety to realize that my own being is a being-unto-death, and to grasp that prospect and accept that destiny with resolve.

A further inquiry undertaken at this point by Heidegger is the investigation into the undifferentiated structure of personal being, which, as it were, underlies all its different embodiments. This also is revealed to the phenomenological inquiry by a study of the phenomenon of anxiety. Here three things are revealed to me.

(1) My being is seen to be already 'thrown' and abandoned to the world. We note that this is a disclosure linking me to my past.

(2) Anxiety also reveals my being as possibility, as freedom to choose authentic or inauthentic existence. This disclosure links me to my future.

(3) There is an almost invincible tendency to choose inauthenticity. My personal being dissipates itself in an inauthentic mode of commerce with the things in the world. This characteristic Heidegger calls 'fallenness'. This fallenness links me with the present; it is the mode in which I am present with the outside world now.

This threefold unity, this structure of personal being, which marks my being as temporal, and makes possible the inauthentic and authentic modes, is called by Heidegger 'care'. We must note that this use of the word, like that of 'fallenness', is highly technical.

Having thus sketched out his conception of authentic personal being, Heidegger next asks whether there is in fact and experience any confirmation of the truth of this interpretation. He believes that there is, and proceeds to the phenomenological examination of conscience.

As we have seen, everyday existence is an inauthentic mode of personal being, and so the achievement of authenticity, if it is to be possible, can only come about by means of a reversal of the choice of inauthenticity which has previously been made. For, as the reader will remember, there is an inevitable tendency for personal being to run away from its authentic mode; it is always already fallen. The phenomenon which enables us to reverse this choice of the inauthentic is the call of conscience. Conscience is a silent call; it does not say anything to us. Who is it that is called? It is personal being, living in the far country of inauthenticity—the country of 'One'. Who is it that calls? Here no theological, psychological, or sociological explanations are to be permitted. The one who calls us is our own authentic personal being, calling us back to our own most authentic possibilities. The very fact that the call seems to come from above us and beyond us, is a sign of how far we have wandered from our authentic selves. To this call there corresponds a possibility in us of hearing and understanding and following it, a willingness to have a conscience. The call neglects and passes over Mrs Grundy in contempt, thus silently annihilating her and her noisy and evasive interpretations, and her chatter about the world.

And to what are we called? We are called to recognize and to shoulder our guilt. Here a new phenomenological investigation begins, since Heidegger is convinced that our everyday interpretations of guilt are far wrong. The outcome of this investigation is that guilt, ontologically considered, is a negativity in our personal being, which is the origin of all culpable particular acts. For the act cannot have culpability given to it by something external, but arises from our very self. This negativity is rooted in our very being, a negativity due to our thrownness, that limits all our possibilities. We did not make ourselves, but had to take over our destinies. Further, our possibilities are limited by the past. When we take over responsibility for this personal being which has been wished on us from without, we become guilty. At this point we must break off our skeleton outline of *Sein und Zeit*.

3. An explanation of some terms

In Heidegger's philosophy we often come across the four terms, 'existential' and '*existentiell*',[1] 'ontic' and 'ontological'. Let us start with the term 'existential' as we find it in the phrases 'existential interpretation' 'existential analysis'. The existential analysis is the task undertaken in *Sein und Zeit*. It is an analysis of the meaning of personal being in general. Being-in-the-world, care, temporality, and so forth are the ontological structures which Heidegger believes to underlie personal being (*Dasein*), and these structures, it is claimed, must be disclosed before the meaning of personal being is rightly understood. As Dr Macquarrie has pointed out,[2] they play in relation to personal being and our knowledge of it, a role in some respects similar to the categories of Kant's philosophy in relation to the constitution of phenomenal objects and our knowledge of them. The existentials, or ontological structures of personal being are a kind of framework within which all particular or ontic facts must fit. The realm investigated by the existential analysis is the ontological; the realm of the various sciences, and of all human experience, is the ontic. Theology must be reckoned among the sciences, being a discipline which deals with the ontic from start to finish.

We may ask, what it is that constitutes an existential? Is it a pattern which is universally found in ontic experience? For example, do we call 'care' an existential because it is universally and identically present in all instances of personal being? The answer is, 'No; rather is it a structure that lies beneath all manifestations in ontic personal being, and manifests itself in different ontic phenomena'.[3] Were the ontological structure of personal being not care, these varying phenomena would not be possible. And as it is with care, so it is with all the existentials; they are the grounds of the possibility of ontic phenomena.

For Heidegger an existential analysis indeed starts with the ontic; for where else but with experience could any such investigation begin? But it seeks to disclose the underlying ontological patterns. It is a theoretic and highly sophisticated pursuit. It must be distinguished from an *existentiell* understanding or interpretation. An *existentiell*

[1] I apologize for the adoption of this German term, which appears inevitable.

[2] John Macquarrie, *An Existentialist Theology*, SCM Press, London, 1955, p. 61.

[3] *S.u.Z.*, p. 199. The sentence in inverted commas gives the gist, not the exact words, of Heidegger's argument.

interpretation is implied by every intelligent decision made by a man in the choice of one possibility rather than another, for every such decision implies some implicit understanding of his own nature and place in the world. But an existential analysis tells us what are the possibilities within which all human choices are made.

In Heidegger's opinion the phenomenological method is the only way in which we can arrive at an existential understanding. With the possibility and validity of the phenomenological method, therefore, stands or falls the possibility of distinguishing between ontic and ontological levels of being, and consequently the possibility of the existential analysis.

4. Heidegger and the phenomenological method

Heidegger, as we noted above, did not invent the phenomenological method, but adopted it from Husserl, his old teacher and predecessor in the philosophical chair at Freiburg. Husserl claimed that his method was free from all presuppositions and wholly without prejudice, saying, 'We take our start from that which is prior to all standpoints; from the whole realm of that which is given in perception, before theoretic thought has got to work on it; from what can immediately be seen and grasped.'[1]

Neither of these thinkers is, however, satisfied with mere description. Both go on to discuss what they believe to be implied by what is perceived, but is not itself directly given to perception. And here, while each claims validity for his results, they part company in their conclusions, a fact which the older man was not slow to indicate, by his disapproval of the younger man's results.[2]

The phenomenological method, then, claims to disclose and to exhibit the ontological structures underlying phenomena, and makes the claim that its disclosures are universally valid. Like all other philosophical reasoning, it hopes for, and aims at, final agreement with its interlocutor, expecting to convince him. In his transcendental deduction of the categories, Kant sought to show that they were both constitutive of objects and necessary components of our knowledge of them. Heidegger does not believe that in the field of the existential analysis proof is possible, but his terms 'exhibit' and 'disclose', clearly

[1] E. Husserl, *Ideen*, quoted by de Waelhens, *Philosophie de Martin Heidegger*, Louvain, 1946, (henceforward cited as *de Waelhens*).

[2] *de Waelhens*, op. cit., p. 16.

imply the expectation that at some point in the discussion, the conclusions of the phenomenological method will be 'seen' or 'manifest' to both parties in the debate.

But now comes a difficulty peculiar to Heidegger's system. As we have seen, his doctrine of inauthenticity prepares him for the experience of a strong and stubborn resistance on the part of the interlocutor to the results of the existential analysis. Time and again he draws our attention to the fact that a general assent will not be given to some conclusion of his,[1] and his line of argument at such points is always much the same, 'If what I have said about the camouflaging and self-deceptive powers of "One" be true, then this is exactly what we should expect to find.' To this his critic will retort, and not without logical justification, 'Yes, but surely you are here assuming exactly what you set out to "exhibit", namely that your existential analysis, including your teaching about "One", is true, and this is the very point at issue! Another, and more likely reason for my disagreement with you, is that your analysis is faulty and your phenomenological method unsuited to the subject to which you are applying it, namely, personal being. And further, even if the deceptive powers of "One" be the reason why I disagree with you, you are still in the unfortunate position of having failed to convince me, and a thousand like me. And so how are you going to make good the validity of your existential analysis, which you hope to make the acknowledged prolegomenon of all the special sciences.'

Heidegger is not unaware of these difficulties, and sets about further attempts to verify his theory by reference to the experience of his interlocutors. It seems that at one point he attempts a 'genetic' verification of his teaching. If, for one reason or another, a theory meets with a stubborn, or even indignant resistance on the part of its critics, its author may be able to undermine that resistance by pointing out, and, by its means, accounting for, a number of puzzling and hitherto apparently unrelated facts of common experience. A classical example of the genetic justification of a theory is to be found in Freud's *Introductory Lectures on Psycho-Analysis*,[2] where he explains by means of the hypothesis of repression into the subconscious such puzzling phenomena as psychological forgetting, dream symbolism, and 'Freudian' slips of speech. Here there was, on the part of the public, a somewhat similar resistance to direct acceptance of Freud's theory, as we have found in the case of Heidegger's analysis. But, as will be seen,

[1] e.g. *S.u.Z.*, p. 311.

[2] London, 1929, ch. I.

Heidegger cannot make anything like such a strong case for his theory as Freud.

The passage where Heidegger seems to attempt a genetic verification comes after his analysis of authenticity as the resolute choice of being-unto-death.[1] At this point he starts anew with a phenomenological study of conscience, which, as the reader will remember, he interprets as the silent call from authentic personal being to personal being dispersed in everyday existence. It would seem as if this were an appeal to an undeniable fact of experience, by referring to which Heidegger seeks to obtain indirect confirmation of his special doctrine of authenticity. But the trouble is that his analysis of conscience, while containing some profound thoughts, will be thought of by many readers as perverse in many respects.[2] Thus what is offered is not the confirmation of a theory by reference to unmistakable facts of experience, such as Freud was able to offer, but merely a second and equally questionable reading of a second area of experience to confirm the questionable interpretation of a first; in fact, an assertion in support of an assertion.

At this point de Waelhens offers a penetrating criticism: 'We feel obliged nevertheless to note that . . . we do not see in the existential philosophy as Heidegger conceives it any difference between a theory and the bearing of witness. Theory is an interpretation of facts, and the bearing of witness is also an interpretation, since the predominance of "One" excludes from the start any direct assent (on the part of the interlocutor).[3] And the witness has to be read into the facts rather than read out of them.'[4]

One question which the critics of Heidegger's ontology persistently ask, is the following, 'Are the results of his existential analysis, in particular his special doctrine of authenticity, not really the results of his ontological investigation, but rather its presuppositions? Has he steered his phenomenological investigation so as to obtain the desired results?'

Heidegger is too subtle a thinker not to be aware of this difficulty, and in a very important passage[5] comes back and back to it. At one point he asks, 'Does not a particular ontic conception of authentic existence, a factual idea of personal being, lie at the base of the ontological investigation which we have just carried through?' And then he goes on roundly to state, 'That is in fact the case,' and emphasizes

[1] *S.u.Z.*, p. 266-7. [2] See pp. 48-50, below.
[3] Words within brackets not in *de Waelhens*.
[4] *de Waelhens*, op. cit., p. 151. [5] *S.u.Z.*, p. 310 ff.

that 'this fact must not be denied, nor, as it were, wrung from us as a concession, but must be understood in its positive necessity, which results from the particular subject-matter of the investigation.'[1]

To explain Heidegger's line of thought at this juncture, it is necessary to recall what he has said at several points earlier in the book, that it is of the character of personal being that it is continually projecting itself, embarked on a voyage. This constant pattern in all the activities of personal being appears also in the activity of thinking. Before we can ask a question, we must have some notion of what the answer is, to guide the direction of our inquiry. And the ontological inquiry is no exception. We must have some implicit conception of being, which grows out of our everyday understanding of being, before we can ask the relevant ontological questions. Heidegger tries to show that the line which his thought has taken is not guided by prejudice, but by the very nature of the subject-matter. But his attempt to do this consists merely in a repetition of the line of his argument.

His difficulty is obvious. He has claimed to start from that everyday understanding of being which in some measure we all possess,[2] but these very words remind us how unpromising a start this must be for his analysis, for the chief concern of everyday existence, in his opinion, is to mislead us. And so we find him yet again asking the question whether his interpretation of authenticity 'does not have an ontic conception of existence as its basis, which may be possible, but does not need to be convincing for everyone'.[3]

How does he meet this doubt? As we have said, he attempts to show that the line of his argument is necessitated by the subject-matter. But his attempt to do so consists in yet one more repetition of the line of his argument. He asks whether there is any more authentic possibility of being-in-the-world than the facing of our own death. But this is precisely the point where he can only bear witness that so it appears to him, and there are many who will assert that in all the existential analysis there is no more questionable point than Heidegger's teaching about the content of authenticity. What if, as Christian thought would indicate, authentic personal being were the response of man in love to God and to his fellow human beings? It is very possible, as de Waelhens has claimed, that there may be a number of different readings of human nature and that, whatever presuppositions we may start from, we shall be able to find confirmation of our particular viewpoints from experience read in the light of our presuppositions.

[1] *S.u.Z.*, p. 310. [2] *S.u.Z.*, p. 312. [3] *S.u.Z.*, p. 312.

To sum up. The question still remains unanswered whether Heidegger's analysis starts at the right point, and moves in the right direction, i.e., is necessitated by the subject-matter; or is guided by some prejudice or foregone conclusion. Those who differ from him in their views on personal being may well feel that the latter is the case. Others may ask whether, in this matter, there is any right direction to go; while yet others will feel convinced that there is a right direction, but that no general agreement can be hoped for on this issue, since the phenomenological method is here inapplicable. It might well be asked whether there is even one everyday understanding of human personal being. When one thinks of Cardinal Newman, to whom the existence of God was more luminous as a fact of experience than the existence of his own soul, can we agree that he, and, say, Bertrand Russell, have the same fundamental interpretation of personal being to start from? Surely the relationship to God cannot be added on to one's conception of personal being as a postage stamp can be stuck on an envelope, without altering its whole ontological structure and one's understanding of it at the same time!

5. *Bankruptcy of the phenomenological method in this field*

The aim of these last pages has been to cast a doubt on Heidegger's application of the phenomenological method to personal being. The reason for this doubt is the conviction that no generally agreed ontology of personal being is possible, since the different interpretations offered are always dependent on various conflicting sets of presuppositions. And Heidegger's analysis of personal being is no exception to the rule.

Emil Brunner has enunciated a principle of great importance which is of the highest relevance in this context. He has called it the 'law of the closeness of relation' (*Gesetz der Beziehungsnähe*). It runs thus, 'The nearer that anything lies to the centre of existence where the whole is at stake, that is, man's relation to God and the being of the person, the greater is the disturbance of rational knowledge through sin. The further anything lies from this centre, the less the disturbing factor makes itself felt, and the less the difference between the knowledge of the believer and that of the unbeliever.'[1] The disturbance will be at a

[1] E. Brunner, *Offenbarung und Vernunft*, p. 378 (Eng. tr.: *Reason and Revelation*, SCM Press, London, 1947, p. 383.) In applying the 'law of the closeness of relation' in this, or any other particular instance, I would wish to avoid the extremely offensive suggestion that the interlocutor can differ from my position only because of sin in him.

maximum in theology, at a minimum in the exact sciences, Brunner continues, and non-existent in the realm of the formal. Therefore it is senseless to talk of a Christian mathematics, but meaningful and necessary to distinguish the Christian conception of freedom, of the good, of community, and above all, a Christian conception of God from every other conception.

If this law holds, then it is clear why Heidegger's existential analysis betrays marks of presuppositions which do not bear the mark of necessity or universality, and it is equally clear why a reality as central as personal being is not to be approached by the phenomenological method, which can expect the universal assent of careful thinkers. Something of this difficulty has indeed been seen by Heidegger, and allowed for in his doctrine of resistance. But the resistance is more stubborn than he realizes and in our opinion its causes are not what he believes them to be. The phenomenological method may do well in fields where there is little disagreement between believers and unbelievers, but here, we submit, it is inapplicable.

6. *Ontology and theology in Heidegger's thought*

What is Heidegger trying to do in this book? He sets out to give us an ontological analysis of personal being, telling us what it is to be a man. And his assumption is that this investigation can be carried out at the ontological level, without interfering with the autonomy of the particular sciences, of which he reckons theology to be one.[1] For all these disciplines deal with the ontic level. To theology Heidegger assigns the task of elucidating the relationship of man to God, and while he acknowledges that theology's task is to operate within the presuppositions of faith, his assumption clearly is that since ontology is prior to theology, his existential analysis is competent to say what man's being is, before ever the question of the relation of man to God is raised.

The manner in which Heidegger allocates the themes to ontology and theology can be illustrated by a particular instance. Expounding the concept of ontological fallenness,[2] he tells us this lies within the field of the existential analysis, and is an essentially ontological structure of personal being, and has nothing to do with the ontic question of whether man is in the state of integrity, or is fallen in the religious sense of these terms; matters which are the concern of theology.

[1] *S.u.Z.*, pp. 10-11. [2] *S.u.Z.*, p. 179.

It is clear that if there is to be a 'gentlemen's agreement' with which the theologian and the ontologist can both feel safe and contented, a great deal will depend on the possibility of defining clearly the difference between the ontic and the ontological, and delimiting the spheres of each. It is also clear that the work of the ontologist will have to be purely formal and neutral, in the sense that no questions are decided by him, even unconsciously, which may compromise the autonomy of faith and theology. For example, the existential analysis will have no right to suggest an ethical ideal, or to give moral content to the doctrine of inauthenticity or authenticity.

In general, theologians do well to be chary of dependence on secular philosophical systems. There is, for example, the famous example of the influence of the philosophy of Aristotle on Roman Catholic theology. This influence Protestant thought holds to have been on the whole unfortunate. Here a double defence may be made by the Romanists; first that St Thomas radically deepens and alters some of the chief Aristotelian concepts and, secondly, that it is not the whole Christian revelation which is re-stated in the terms of a secular philosophy, but that the revelation is added intact to a structure of thought built up by the natural powers of reason in those fields where reason has a competence of its own.

There is, however, a more recent and exemplary warning for Christian theology, of the dangers of dependence on a secular philosophy. I refer to the Hegelian types of theology which were fashionable both on the Continent and in this country during last century, whose results are generally agreed by Christian theologians to have been disastrous.

7. The Ontic and the ontological, a breakdown of barriers?

Let us now try rather more closely to examine the relations between the ontic and the ontological in this system. Are their spheres kept, as Heidegger would wish, safely isolated from each other? It must be confessed that this is one of the most intricate problems connected with Heidegger's thought; and yet it is of the highest importance that we should not leave it untouched, for the conclusions which we reach here will help to determine our whole response to his claims to provide an ontological preface for all theology.

When we ask the ontological question, 'What does it mean *to be*, what is the significance of being?', and when we examine personal beings with Heidegger, we find a complex of structures which he calls 'the existentiality of personal being'. Looking through *Sein und Zeit* we find many such structures. First, being-in-the-world, with its three components, the world, the being who is in-the-world, and the inherence of that being in the world. Then there is 'care'. And there is 'being-along-with-other-persons'. All these, with other similar structures, are existentials.

Here, though ourselves more than suspicious of the phenomenological method in this field, we may agree that the search for such existentials is not obviously doomed from the start to fatuity. Personal being does seem to some extent to answer to Heidegger's description of it as 'care', inasmuch as it is always related somewhat as he suggests to past, present and future, while at the same time there are very different ontic expressions of this ontological pattern in actual life. We would agree also that all personal being is being-in-a-world and being-along-with-other-personal-beings, two further existentials mentioned by Heidegger, though the ontic modes of such being vary very widely.

If so, then as Macquarrie has well put it,[1] the ontological underlying structures will define the horizons within which ontic possibilities will fall. And there may well be a partial and approximate agreement between Christian and non-Christian thinkers as to these structures. Indeed such agreement would not be a very startling result.

But it is with regard to the detailed working-out of the scheme that our doubts rise, and finally harden into convictions that Heidegger's system will not do. The place where the incompatibility most clearly declares itself is perhaps the discussion on fallenness, inauthentic and authentic being, for it is here that his distinction between ontic and ontological, *existentiell* and existential, appears to break down.

We remember that for Heidegger, the sphere of the ontic should be of interest only in so far as it provides the starting point of an existential analysis, or confirms the results of one. If it is to keep within its bounds, the analysis will make no suggestions concerning which modes of being, or which actions, are morally valuable, and which are worthless or reprehensible.

The official position of Heidegger's existential analysis is that fallenness is an existential, while authenticity is a particular (ontic?) mode of it. On p. 130 of *S.u.Z.* Heidegger unmistakably tells us that authenticity is an *existentiell* modification of 'One', which is a fundamental existential. And on p. 179 we are told that, existentially interpreted,

[1] John Macquarrie, *An Existentialist Theology*, p. 34.

authenticity is a modification of fallenness. Thus, officially, fallenness is for Heidegger an existential, an ontological structure underlying the ontic possibility of authenticity. When a man makes resolute choice of his own authenticity as being-unto-death, he is still ontologically fallen. This enables Heidegger officially to regard fallenness as neutral. He says 'The ontological existential structure of fallenness would be misunderstood if one were to give it the significance of a bad or lamentable ontic property.'[1]

Possibly, however, there is confusion here in Heidegger's mind, and not merely obscurity in his text. The reason for this assertion is as follows. It will be agreed that while our attitude to an existential should not be anything but neutral, our attitude to an ontic fact, especially when it is a particular human choice, will often be emotionally and morally coloured.

Now, for all his official attempt to be neutral in the matter of fallenness, Heidegger's close linking of it with inauthenticity, and the terms he uses in connexion with it, such as 'gossip' and 'mediocrity', and the way in which he describes how Mrs Grundy is jealous of anything which exceeds her own powers, make it clear that he regards 'fallenness' with high disfavour. It is, indeed, predominantly regarded by him as bad, and therefore, as ontic.

On the other hand, if inauthenticity be looked upon by Heidegger with disfavour, authenticity is clearly looked on with favour. This may be technically in order, in so far as authenticity has officially in his system an ontic status. But this ontic status then ought to lift it outside the scope of the existential analysis. For the only legitimate place for the ontic in such an analysis is that it should function as the starting point for the discovery of ontological structures. But in a sense authenticity is the goal of Heidegger's whole enterprise, and it provides the basis for an ethic[2] which is full of content, an ethic of an aesthetic, romantic and tragic character.

Heidegger's language is reserved, and so this conclusion is not at once evident, but the kind of morality that arises out of this clear-sighted resolve in face of one's own death is the kind of morality which tends to be adopted where God is no longer believed in. It reminds one of the aesthetic morality of the sagas as we see it exemplified in such figures as Sweyn Asleifson of Orkney and Burnt Njal of Iceland. And we remember that they belonged to a day when the ancient gods were

[1] *S.u.Z.*, p. 176.
[2] Though naturally this is not worked out in detail.

dead and the light of Christianity had scarcely tinged the northern horizons. We find a morality of this sort hinted at in Wagner's *Ring*, and in some of our profounder humanists of today, who feel compelled to adopt a naturalist philosophy. Such a morality of protesting individual integrity and open-eyed despair is perhaps a natural alternative for a man who, like Heidegger, denies the transcendent in the commonly accepted sense of the term, and asserts, if not the non-existence of God, then at least his absence.

In fact then Heidegger's fallenness is not a formal, ethically neutral existential of all personal being. It is clearly, at least on some occasions, regarded in his system as one of two mutually exclusive ontic possibilities for men. As Christians we may think that there is much to be said for Heidegger's aversion from sham and convention, though we may feel that there is a certain amount of arrogance in his distaste for the majority of his fellows. But what can Christian thought make of the other ontic possibility—the clear resolve in the face of death as one's ultimate possibility, which makes all human projects finally futile? Surely the relation between this and a Christian view of authenticity is that of a clear alternative. If the one be true, then the other is false.

If these arguments are valid, then we clearly must reject the claim that theology must accept the work of the existential analysis, and the arguments that only by such acceptance will 'its statements be able to make a claim to conceptual intelligibility'.[1]

8. Heidegger's account of conscience

Let us now go on to examine Heidegger's analysis of another important concept, conscience. Here no attempt can be made to reproduce the closely articulated and technical exposition of the author. Conscience, Heidegger tells us, is a very ambiguous phenomenon,[2] differently interpreted by different thinkers; and this might lead us to give up in despair any attempt to examine it by our phenomenological method. But this very ambiguity is a sign that we have here a fundamental phenomenon of personal being. And he goes on to study it with a view to laying bare its existential implications.

Such an ontological investigation of this ontic reality is, he continues, prior to any psychological description of the experiences of conscience, and also prior to any attempt to explain conscience in biological terms. But it is also far from any requisition of this phenomenon for the

[1] *S.u.Z.*, p. 180. [2] *S.u.Z.*, p. 268.

purposes of theistic proof or as a sign of an immediate awareness of God.[1]

Now let us be clear what is happening here. An ontic phenomenon is being analyzed by the phenomenological method, and both naturalistic-reductive explanations and theological apologetic interpretations are being magisterially warned off. In the end, what Heidegger produces is an interpretation of conscience in terms of the self, where there is no place left for God and for what is usually called the transcendent at all. Now, many Christians would claim that no adequate interpretation of conscience can be given, except on the assumption that man is confronted by the Absolute Thou. Conscience is indeed not directly the voice of God, since its content may be very mistaken. It may, therefore, be a mishearing of his voice, but unless he were speaking, I for one, do not see how we could hear the call at all. At this point in the existential analysis, then, it is evident that Heidegger is not laying down the formal presuppositions of all theological interpretation. What is happening is that certain fundamental ethico-theological questions are being settled in a manner hostile to Christian theology. The cuckoo, in short, is already installed in the nest.

It is worthwhile asking at this point if any valid arguments are brought forward by Heidegger against theistic interpretations of conscience and obligation. There is one descriptive sentence in his analysis of conscience which could not be better put. 'This call,' he writes, 'is certainly not ever planned or prepared, or willingly uttered by ourselves. On the other hand the call most certainly does not come from another who is with us in the world. The call comes out of me, and yet above me.'[2] How admirable this is as a description of that singular combination of autonomy and heteronomy which is one of the distinguishing marks of moral obligation! We shall agree with Heidegger that moral obligation cannot be grounded in the command of any other human person, nor, as Durkheim would have us believe, in the interests or the command of any number of persons banded together in human society. Nor can the call of conscience come from any existent of a non-personal character. But surely the alternatives are not exhausted, when we have taken into consideration all these explanations, and with them that to which Heidegger believes he has shut us up if these are excluded, namely, that the perceived element of heteronomy is due to the fact that my true self which calls me is hidden from me by my fallenness, and that it calls me back to my authentic

[1] *S.u.Z.*, p. 269. [2] *S.u.Z.*, p. 275.

possibilities. Why should conscience not be related to the call of a personal character from One who stands in a quite singular relation to me, not identical with myself, but nearer to me than any finite being?[1] I would claim that a position like this is one that many theists would be unwilling to surrender, though there are doubtless very crude formulations of it which would on philosophical grounds be unacceptable. And yet Heidegger has arbitrarily rejected it. There is no logic in the exclusion; there is just no room in his system for this possibility. The cuckoo does not need to argue with the hedge-sparrow chicks. It just shoulders them over the edge of the nest.

9. Heidegger's account of guilt

In Heidegger's phenomenological analysis of guilt,[2] something extremely odd takes place. As an ontic phenomenon, guilt, one would say, is a characteristically religious magnitude, being inseparably attached to our relation to God and our relation to other persons. In his analysis of it to disclose its ontological ground, Heidegger manages at the same time to discredit these religious overtones in guilt, on the grounds that they belong to the everyday superficial mode of our self-understanding. In such everyday interpretations, guilt is described as the absence of something, and 'something', says Heidegger, is obviously not an existent of the type of personal being, but has rather the character of a thing, an object. Now it is part of the etiolated self-understanding of everyday existence, that personal being should mistake itself for a mere thing, an object amongst objects.

Further, Heidegger suggests that guilt, seen as relating to other persons, is not seen in its true nature, but belongs to the superficial conventional sphere of activity in which we live with other persons.[3] So that which is disclosed at this level cannot be the real ontological foundation of guilt. Here we take note of Heidegger's individualism. It is true that he asserts that being-with-other-persons is an existential of human personal being, and that he allows that there is not only a fallen form of this mode of being, but an authentic one.[4] But of this authentic form of existence-with-others he says almost nothing. It is the return to oneself which for all intents and purposes constitutes authenticity for him, and the relation to others is almost entirely

[1] 'Nearer' because there is no human being who stands so close to my personal being that my true freedom can be equated with surrender to his will. Yet the Christian must say of God, *Cui servare est regnare*.

[2] *S.u.Z.*, pp. 280-9. [3] *S.u.Z.*, p. 283. [4] *S.u.Z.*, p. 264.

considered as a decadent mode of existence, which provides a lurking-place in which we can hide from our authentic being. Here then, we have a non-Christian view of man. For in Christian doctrine, personal being is linked up, not only with one's neighbour's being, but also with that of God, and only in love of God and our neighbour is authenticity to be found. The attempt to find an ontological fallenness which contains the ground of the possibility of actual ontic fallenness is itself probably a hopeless enterprise, but certainly it has not been made easier by Heidegger's belief that man's being can be truly described without taking into account his relation to God.

Here, under guise of an unprejudiced ontological analysis, Heidegger discredits those interpretations of ontic guilt which are characteristically religious and Christian, relating us to God and to other men. Surely it is not only in what might be called technically the superficial spheres of personal relation to others that guilt is evident, but in that very moment when our own and their authentic being is disclosed to us, in the moment when we know that we have failed them, have sinned and come short of the glory of God, his image in them and in ourselves.

In the end, Heidegger reveals what is, in his view, the ontological structure of guilt, which lies at a deeper level than ontic guilt, and then defines the horizons of its possibility. The guilt which is an existential of personal being consists, we are told, in the fact that we have to enter upon life, taking over, as it were, a fate for which we are not responsible. Personal being, Heidegger tells us, always consists in the actualization of one possibility, and therefore precludes the actualization of other possibilities, which have been surrendered. This negativity is the ontological foundation of guilt, which is said to have no morally deplorable character, but to be one existential constituent of man's being as engaged in the fulfilment of projects.

This so-called ontological guilt, however, is clearly not guilt at all, it is what Christians would call created existence, which we take over in the very act of living. It may well be the ground of the possibility of ontic guilt, but it is at the same time the ground of the possibility of everything else in human life, so why, for example, should it not be called ontological virtue? Here, surely is shown the bankruptcy of the existential analysis in so far as it claims to provide the framework within which all ontic phenomena of human life must lie.

10. Conclusions

So we see how unfounded is the claim that theology must accept the ontological groundwork of the existential analysis if it is to be a respectable, scholarly discipline whose statements 'will be able to make a claim to conceptual intelligibility'. The defence made by Heidegger and his Christian apologists is that there is no real conflict between his concepts and Christian concepts. His existential analysis, they aver, can provide a cradle[1] in which Christian theology can safely rest, for he is speaking of realities on the ontological level, while Christian thought deals with the ontic level. Heidegger has moved in on the ground floor, Christian thought lives on the first storey. But if, as I have been arguing, Heidegger is really laying claim to both ground floor and first storey, then Christians may well claim to have the right to throw both him and his furniture out on to the street. To change the figure, Heidegger's ontology is not a nest in which Christian faith and theology can be safely nurtured, but a cuckoo occupying that nest, which if it is not faithfully dealt with, will soon shoulder out the Christian fledglings on to the ground below.

The conclusion of our study of Heidegger is then as follows, the existential analysis does indeed possess an impressive and close articulation, and frequent psychological profundity. Yet, for all that, in so far as it claims to trace out the horizons of human possibility and dictate the form of all religious experience *a priori*, it has definitely failed to make out its case.

This does not mean that in rejecting these claims, we must assert that we have learnt nothing from it. It has given us many profound insights into the nature of personal being, and has shown us how inadequate for our understanding of persons are the categories suited to the understanding of things.

There may then be real benefit from cautious experimentation with some of Heidegger's ideas within the field of theology, and in the exposition of Biblical texts. But we must not be hypnotized by the magisterial claims of the analysis to be queen over the sciences.

Heidegger's claims to give *the* understanding of man's nature have now been before the public for a quarter of a century. These claims, which Bultmann supports, were criticized as long ago as 1931 by Brunner, Löwith, Kuhlmann and de Waelhens. It will be our task in the next chapter to examine in some detail Bultmann's advocacy of

[1] *K.u.M.*, I, p. 54 (Götz Harbsmeier).

this case. But our conclusion from the study of Heidegger's own work is the same as that reached by Brunner[1] and the other critics. Heidegger's existential analysis is not suited to serve as a kindly and uncompromising cradle for Christian theology.

[1] See especially E. Brunner, *Zeitschrift für Theologie und Kirche*, 1931, pp. 111 ff., and de Waelhens, *La Philosophie de Martin Heidegger*, p. 359.

III

HEIDEGGER WITH THE NEW LOOK?

1. Introduction

WE have already seen reason to reject Heidegger's claims for his own ontology. In this chapter our task will be to examine the work of two theologians, who claim to make a use of the existential analysis, and we shall try to ascertain the nature and degree of their professed and real dependence on it. The first and more important of these is Rudolf Bultmann. Had he not first made the link with Heidegger, it is unlikely that any other theologian would have done so, or that Heidegger's challenge would have excited so lively an interest in the theological world.

Here, as elsewhere in this controversy, we are somewhat hampered by the occasional and controversial character of Bultmann's theological writings. It is true that Heidegger's influence on him has been of long standing.[1] but a proportionately small part of his writings has been dedicated to this theme of his relation to Heidegger, and it is not altogether easy to establish what exactly he understands that relation to be.

2. Bultmann's own theory of his dependence on Heidegger

(*a*) The earliest exposition by Bultmann of his views on this theme is perhaps the most thorough that he has given us, and appears in an article called 'The Historical Character of Personal Being, and Faith', which was published in 1930.[2]

Here he accepts Heidegger's delimitation of tasks and fields of work for ontology and theology, a delimitation already familiar to us. Bultmann specifies the task of theology as the study of personal being in

[1] *Glauben und Verstehen*, vol. I, Tübingen, 1934 (hereafter referred to as *G.u.V.*, I) is dedicated to Heidegger 'in grateful memory of our time together in Marburg'.

[2] 'Die Geschichtlichkeit des Daseins und der Glaube', *Zeitschrift für Theologie und Kirche*, vol. X, 1930. Antwort an G. Kuhlmann, pp. 339 ff.

faith and unfaith, and calls theology a fundamentally historical discipline, because it not only starts from concrete happenings within the realm of personal being, but is interested in them all the time as such. Philosophy (ontology) studies its object with the aim of understanding the meaning of being in general.

Bultmann continues his exposition: Every theology depends on a philosophical system of concepts thought out before it starts its work, and even if it claims not to do so, it is still unconsciously in such a relation of dependence, or else it philosophizes on its own initiative, and its performance in so doing is correspondingly crude and naïve.[1]

He goes on to say that he does not wish his argument to become lost in abstractions. He will therefore illustrate his case by a study of the relation of one philosopher, Heidegger, to one theologian, Gogarten, and show by this concrete example the relationship of the ontological existential analysis to the ontic discipline of theology.[2]

Bultmann's problem is to accommodate Heidegger's thought on the ontological level, with Gogarten's on the ontic level, thus avoiding a conflict between them. Let us see how successful he is here. Like Heidegger, Gogarten, says Bultmann, attempts to reach an original understanding of history and historical being, in opposition to the common interpretation. But a conflict with Heidegger seems to be inevitable, for in Gogarten the concept 'being unto death' is not found at all, and in Heidegger, the concept of 'my neighbour' is not found, while for Gogarten it is precisely the encounter with the Thou as my neighbour which constitutes historical being. For Heidegger personal being is limited (*begrenzt*) by death; for Gogarten it is limited by the Thou. We do indeed find in Heidegger that the concept of 'the other' as 'one present-along-with-me' modifies the factual possibilities of my decision, but it does not play the part of an existential, giving to personal being its ontological structure. This function is reserved for the temporal character of personal being as being-unto-death. Heidegger holds that 'I see the other' because I am conscious of myself in resolve, facing my inevitable death. Gogarten does not mention death at all. He teaches that, faced by the claims of the 'Thou', I have the alternative possibilities of hatred or love thrust upon me. Only when I accept the claims of the 'Thou' upon me, do I see him as a 'Thou', and only then is authentic historical being present. Note that for Heidegger recognition of the 'Thou' is secondary to the grasping of our own authenticity in resolve, while for Gogarten the order is reversed.

[1] Op. cit., p. 343. [2] Ibid., p. 354.

Now, to the unsophisticated reader, it would surely seem that here we have a real contradiction. Here, he will say, are two competing existential analyses. Both may be false, certainly both cannot be true. But Bultmann is committed to denying this contradiction. His way out is to assert that Heidegger's 'resolve in face of death' is a purely formal, ontological concept, while Gogarten's 'decision to love' is the sole factual or ontic embodiment of this resolve. The ontological analysis, he avers, cannot approve or disapprove of this conclusion about the 'decision to love', for the latter is to be found at the ontic and not at the ontological level. Nor, for the same reason, can the existential analysis offer any objection to Gogarten's further proposition, that only he who knows himself loved in Christ is set free to love the human Thou in his turn.

In the last pages of the essay,[1] Bultmann still tries to maintain that there is no real conflict between Gogarten's position and Heidegger's, though the latter asserts that personal being is limited by death, and the former, that the limitation is exercised by the accepted claim of the 'Thou'. But here he has shifted his ground. He asserts that the man who does not love, sees the limitation as imposed by death, while the man who loves and believes, sees it as given by the 'Thou'. Here we must ask, have we not been provided with a new pattern? The ontological substructure, with the ontic filling, has been whisked away from us, and instead we are given an account on the ontic level, of the being of the unbeliever, and another account on the ontic level, of the being of the believer. The context, however, leaves it uncertain whether this is the case, or whether what is presented to us is the (ontic or ontological(?)) being of man as seen, and differently seen, by the believer and the unbeliever respectively.

Then a new device is employed. An attempt is made to approximate the two views by saying that even Heidegger has conceded that it is the limitation of the self that is important, and the question of what ontic phenomenon—death or the 'Thou'—limits it, is a matter of secondary importance. Further, death does also remain for the believer, and so, in a sense, limits him also, though for him it means grace, and not judgement. And faith sees that in death God meets the natural man, (as a Thou?), and also that when the natural man meets with God's revelation, it is nothing less than a death for him.

But surely, if Bultmann were satisfied that the ontological and ontic levels could be clearly separated, there would be no need for him to

[1] Ibid., pp. 263-4.

approximate these concepts of limitation by the 'Thou', and limitation by death, to each other. The fact that an attempt has been made to do so, though in so laborious and unconvincing a manner, is surely an involuntary confession of the instability, even the untenability, of the whole position. So we must end our discussion of this essay with the conclusion that this presentation of Bultmann's case in relation to the work of Heidegger and Gogarten, has proved a signal, though ingenious, failure.

At the close of our study of this first essay of Bultmann's it is, however, necessary to draw attention to the fact that this is still his official theory of the relation of theology to philosophy, and in particular of his own relation to the work of Heidegger, in spite of the severe criticism of philosophers like Löwith, Cullberg, Kuhlmann and de Waelhens, and theologians like Heim and Brunner.

(*b*) The next study which he gives of this theme is to be found in the first volume of his Essays, *Glauben und Verstehen*, in the third and concluding section of an essay called 'The Problem of Natural Theology'.[1] In spite of the very strange final pages of this essay, whose content was foreshadowed by some statements in the earlier work we have just mentioned, it must be considered as another attempt to formulate the official position, and so comes naturally next in our study, not only because it follows it in the time-order, but because, on the whole, it is an expression of the same viewpoint. In these pages Bultmann discusses once more the particular question of the relationship between theology and philosophy. As is common with him, he develops his own position in a kind of imaginary dialogue, bringing forward theses, and then adducing objections to them, until at the end he has arrived at the full statement of his position.

He asks,[2] 'Could one say that the relationship between the two disciplines of philosophy and theology is such that their subject-matter is different; that philosophy has unbelieving personal being as

[1] *G.u.V.*, I, pp. 305-12.

[2] In the earlier part of the concluding section of this essay, Bultmann has been claiming that theology must allow philosophy (and he means Heidegger's existential analysis), to dictate to it its main ontological content, and thus theology takes over the results of the existential analysis. There is not the space here to deal with this passage in detail, but the careful student will probably agree that Bultmann has by no means proved here that Christian theology must submit to the contention that these concepts mean exactly for it what they do in the work of Heidegger. All that he has done is to demonstrate the more pedestrian conclusion that Christian theology uses terms which are not gibberish to the secular man; that is, that there is sufficient common ground for these statements to have meaning for secular man.

its theme, and theology has believing personal being? But surely philosophy, he rejoins, claims to deal with personal being as such, and must claim to disclose the ontological structures which render possible both the act of faith and the act of unbelief. In any case, believing and unbelieving personal being do not stand over against each other like two material objects that have nothing in common. Theology speaks of the historical character of personal being, of its power of understanding, and of decision, and clearly by these terms it means the same phenomena of which philosophy also treats. Thus it acknowledges that one can speak of personal being as such, and that the structures of personal being which philosophy discloses are valid also for believing personal being. And indeed the claim of faith is not that justified man is man with new demonstrable qualities, something totally different from unjustified man, but it affirms that justified man is man acquitted.

A second suggestion is put forward only to be rejected. We cannot say that the philosophical analysis is completed or corrected by the theological one, as for example, by the suggestion that not 'care' but love is the fundamental core of human nature (Koepp's suggestion).[1] Philosophical analysis will not admit such a claim; its picture can only be rejected or accepted as a whole.'

A third suggestion. Could it be suggested that theology discovers a phenomenon of personal being which is invisible to philosophy. Such a phenomenon might be faith, or unbelief. But, as we saw, philosophy ought to be able to disclose the existentials which make acts of faith or unbelief possible. But the theologian, on his side, could not admit that unbelief is merely an occasional act of personal being; he asserts that unbelief is the fundamental constitution of personal being! Here, then, a threatening fact appears, which would seem to bring the disciplines of philosophy and theology into sheer contradiction on the subject of personal being. For does not Christian theology claim that the essential character of fallen personal being is unbelief? And philosophy, it would seem, does not see this at all! But philosophy, continues Bultmann, *does* see it, only, 'for it, this phenomenon is freedom, the original freedom, in which personal being constitutes itself'.[2] And philosophy on its side sees the phenomenon of faith, but 'only as a lost, senseless possibility'. Thus far Bultmann.

Now, let us pause for a moment to take stock. We can hardly avoid the conclusion that this phenomenon, seen by philosophy as 'freedom,

[1] Dr Macquarrie's attempt in part to rewrite the existential analysis might also come under this criticism of Bultmann's.

[2] *G.u.V.*, I, p. 310.

the original freedom in which personal being constitutes itself', is the resolute decision in the face of death, which for Heidegger constitutes authenticity. And the faith which philosophy sees as 'a lost, senseless possibility', is what the Christian theologian sees as authenticity, true historical being. Thus theologian and philosopher, by Bultmann's own account of it, are in violent conflict as to what constitutes authentic personal being. What then can have happened to the gentlemen's agreement[1] and peaceable division of territories of which we heard a little time ago? Here, with a vengeance, is a reversal of the position mentioned earlier in the essay!

At this point we must put a question of method. On what grounds, we must ask, has confidence, a moment ago so complete, been now withdrawn? Would Heidegger agree to this last-moment indictment of his results? Would he not at once retort, as Bultmann has just suggested that he would, 'Take me not at all, or all in all'?

If what Bultmann here says in his argument is true, then it is quite clear that Heidegger's existential analysis, with its claim to total acceptance by theology, is by no means the neutral and impartial investigation that Bultmann has claimed it to be. Was it neutral up to a point? Did it suddenly, or gradually, diverge from neutrality? To such questions we have surely the right to demand an answer, but no answer is offered us.

But Bultmann does not seem to see the intellectual difficulties into which he has got, since a few pages later, at the end of the essay, he says, 'Since there is no other personal being than this being, which constitutes itself in freedom, the formal structures of personal being, which are disclosed in the ontological analysis, are "neutral", that is,

[1] In a long, carefully reasoned, and hostile article ('Offenbarungstheologie und philosophische Daseinsanalyse' *Z. Th. K.* 1958/2, pp. 201-53), Hellmut Haug has attempted to establish the impossibility of a gentlemen's agreement between Heidegger's existential analysis and the theology of Rudolf Bultmann. Haug discusses and rejects two mutually contradictory attempts of Bultmann to dovetail Christian theology and the existential analysis. He certainly makes a damaging case against Bultmann, but how it is to be answered is Bultmann's own problem rather than ours, since we have rejected the competence of Heidegger to write an ontological preface to every theology. Haug writes as a wholehearted supporter of Heidegger; seldom can the printed page have given expression to such supreme confidence that the last word about the constitution of human nature has been said. If Haug's claim to represent Heidegger is valid, then the mask is off, and the neutrality of the latter's ontology is seen to be a fiction. For on the basis of the existential analysis Haug denies the possibility of a transcendent revelation through historical fact. Haug's conclusions are however not so decisive as he believes, since they are not the result of a rigorous, legitimate and universally persuasive phenomenological method. The denial of the possibility of revelation is only the natural result of the relationship to God having been left out at the beginning of the investigation.

they are valid for all personal being,'[1] a statement which Emil Brunner has described as 'the fundamental error'.[2] Bultmann is able to make this claim, only because he believes that Heidegger's system is built up on the 'original interpretation of personal being'. But that is the very point in debate; he has himself (apparently unconsciously) conceded only a few pages back, that Heidegger is by no means so securely founded.

The question at stake is not whether there is one kind of personal being, or more, but whether there is one kind of interpretation thereof, a neutral one, or whether there are not at least two, a believing interpretation, and an unbelieving one.

If, then, we turned to this second essay in the hope of finding a more convincing exposition of the official position of Bultmann, we must confess that by this essay confusion has only been worse confounded.

We come now to the more incidental passages in which Bultmann indicates the relation of faith and theology to ontology. These two passages are better known than the earlier two, since they both occur in the more recent Kerygma and Mythos discussion, and luckily they can be treated more briefly.

(*c*) The first of these passages occurs in Bultmann's famous first essay, 'New Testament and Mythology'.[3] It will be remembered that here Bultmann argues in favour of an 'unmythological existential interpretation' of the New Testament message. He offers us such a version of the condition of man as unbeliever, and another of the condition of man as believer. What of the transition from the former condition to the latter? Here the New Testament, in speaking of the saving act of God in Christ, indubitably, says Bultmann, uses mythological language, with its statements about pre-existence and atonement. But, he asks, can this mythology too not be reinterpreted in non-mythological terms? He argues that, in a sense it can, though there must still be talk of a decisive act of God in Christ, and if that be regarded as myth, then this minimal element of myth remains.

But now comes the further question. What if even the talk about an act of God be in itself mythology in a far more radical sense, a sense to be specified in the following sentence? What if the Christian faith itself be reducible to a symbolical expression of truths already accessible

[1] *G.u.V.*, I, p. 312.
[2] Brunner, *Mensch im Widerspruch*, Berlin, 1937, p. 556 (Eng. tr.: *Man in Revolt*, Lutterworth Press, London, 1939, p. 545).
[3] *Kerygma und Mythos*, I, pp. 15-48. Henceforward the volumes in this series will be cited as *K.u.M.*, I, II, etc.

to mankind in general, as indeed Hegel and Yorck von Wartenburg and Dilthey suggested it was, so that the notion of an action of God becomes in principle unnecessary? It is at this point that Bultmann throws out the question whether Heidegger's existential analysis is not a secular philosophical representation of the New Testament view of human existence. Here is the passage: 'Above all, Martin Heidegger's existential analysis of personal being appears to be nothing other than a secular philosophical representation of the New Testament view of human existence, man existing as a historical being, in "care" about his own existence, on the basis of "anxiety", continually in the moment of decision between the past and the future, faced by the question whether he is to lose himself to the world that lies "present-to-hand", the world of "One", or whether he is to win authenticity in the surrender of all security, and in unconditional surrender of himself to the future. Is not man thus understood also in the New Testament? When it is occasionally objected that I interpret the New Testament with the categories of the Heideggerian existential philosophy, I am afraid that my critics are wilfully closing their eyes to the actual problem before them. I mean, that we should rather be concerned with the fact that philosophy from its own standpoint sees the truth of what the New Testament is saying.'[1]

It may be that Bultmann is expressing himself carelessly here, but the whole force of the argument lies in the suggestion that Heidegger, without accepting the fact of a revelation or saving act of God, has been able, by means of the existential analysis, to arrive at *the same conception of man* as the Christian faith.

It is this disturbing fact, and no merely formal ontological statements, which, we are assured, should be worrying Bultmann's critics. There is no mention here of ontic and ontological levels, and no comforting talk of a gentlemen's agreement. And though Bultmann here merely puts out a question, the whole way he continues his argument suggests that this interpretation of the passage is right, though as usual, we shall see that he soon gets into difficulties, of which we shall speak in a moment. Philosophy is right, he claims, in its doctrine of man, and in its teaching about authenticity. But it is wrong in its belief that man can attain authenticity by his own efforts. For in all its struggles, his will remains a fallen will.[2] Then, finally, Bultmann concedes that philosophy's *conception* (*sc.* Heidegger's conception) of authenticity is

[1] Bultmann, *K.u.M.*, I, p. 33.
[2] So that after all a Divine action is necessary to restore him to authenticity.

distorted by the fact that it believes he can achieve it by his own efforts.[1]

Here is a concession, though not nearly so open as we would like to see, that Heidegger's interpretation of authenticity is divergent from that of the New Testament. But further, if Heidegger's conception is distorted, how can it serve as the ontological foundation for a Christian ontic concept? It is clear that what we have here are two conflicting ontic concepts. As Emil Brunner has said,[2] 'Christian concepts have this peculiarity that they cannot be cut adrift from the event of revelation, since they indeed all have this event as their object. One cannot make a philosophy with Christian concepts, concealing their origin, and claiming that it stands upon its own feet.'

In the passage quoted above Bultmann is forced, against his will, to travel at least part of the way towards the conclusion that the attempt to cut man's being adrift from the relation to God and to God's act in Christ has led to a falsification in Heidegger's ontological doctrine of man. This I believe to be the right conclusion, but it is contrary to Bultmann's official position.

(*d*) The last exposition and criticism of Bultmann's view of the relation of the existential analysis and theology deals with some critical remarks by F. K. Schumann,[3] one of the acutest of all the participants in this discussion, and with Bultmann's reply to him.[4]

Schumann's argument, in brief, runs thus: It is highly questionable if a neutral existential analysis is possible. Such is doubtless Heidegger's aim, but all the way presuppositions influence the line of his thought. For example, there is the presupposition that it is possible to analyze man's being without taking into consideration his relationship to God. An existential analysis would have a completely different colour, or might even turn out to be impossible, if we came to the conclusion not only that man has ontically a positive or a negative relationship to God, but that the fundamental relationship to God belongs to man's being as such, as the Biblical conception of man's existence in the image of God implies.

To this Bultmann replies: Certainly the existential analysis implies the presupposition that we can analyze personal being without taking into consideration the man-God relationship. 'But is an analysis of human personal being in relationship to God at all a meaningful

[1] *K.u.M.*, I, p. 37.
[2] E. Brunner, 'Theologie und Ontologie', *Z.Th.K.*, p. 120.
[3] *K.u.M.*, I, pp. 190-202. [4] *K.u.M.*, II, p. 194.

possibility, when the relationship God-man can only be an event in the concrete encounter of man with God? A pure analysis of personal being cannot take the man-God relationship into its purview, because it abstracts from the concrete encounters in which existence from moment to moment realizes itself. But by neglecting it, it leaves room for it.' When the existential analysis speaks of man's historical character, it discloses a character of personal being which faith and faith alone understands as man's relationship to God.

Let us consider this answer to Schumann. The most important assumption here is not reasoned at all. It is the assumption that the relationship man-God, since it is actualized in an event, belongs solely to the ontic sphere, and has no ontological significance. But we must point out that *all* events are ontic, and yet some of them have ontological significance. If none had, Heidegger's analysis would never get started. The relationship with other men is only actual in ontic events, and so is the relationship with the world. And 'One' and existence-in-the-world are two of the main existentials in the analysis upon which Bultmann is building. Why then may the same not be said for the relationship man-God? True, for God, the relation to us is not necessary; he would be God whether we existed or no. But it is a thoroughly tenable position that man is, among other things, and above all other things, essentially a being responsible to God. His whole being exists in act of response, positive or negative, to God. From God he cannot escape. That means, that the relation to God might be called an existential of human personal being, to which innumerable ontic phenomena of human life bear witness, since it is the ground of their possibility. Though we too on our side would have to admit that this cannot be *demonstrated*.

There is one further disastrous result of Bultmann's dependence upon Heidegger, which we must notice here. He asserts that the relationship to God, being confined to the ontic sphere, is without special ontological significance of its own. What then are the categories, or existentials in terms of which our experience of God is to be interpreted? The answer is, quite baldly, those existentials which are suitable for the interpretation of personal being *with God left out*. Bultmann has said in the controversy with Schniewind: '. . . Of course a philosopher, so long as he is speaking philosophically, cannot speak of God's action, since he is not speaking at all of a concrete event, which takes place between persons, but can only show what is the significance of personal happenings in general. But in so doing, he may be able to help theology to find the right concepts for talking unmythologically about God.'[1]

That means nothing else than this, that the concepts used to describe the human I-Thou relation can be applied univocally to the I-God relation. Dr Bultmann appears in his theological thinking, at times at least, to have no inkling of the fact that our relationship to God is different in any way from our relationship to our human neighbours. In an acute essay written as long ago as 1931, Gerhardt Kuhlmann[2] asks whether theology has not as its object a reality which is the only true transcendence, whose ontic character is of a quite singular kind. We conclude that Dr Bultmann has, for most of the time, little real awareness of one of the essential tasks of theology, its problem of expressing the transcendent in terms of human concepts. He has little understanding of what Professor Ian Ramsey has described in modern terms as 'the singular logic of religious statements'.[3] This blind spot has led him to the belief that mythological language can wholly be reinterpreted in existential terms, and he owes this blind spot to his dependence on Heidegger.

Our conclusion concerning Bultmann's official theory of his own relationship to the work of Heidegger, is that he holds with great determination to the partition of the field between Heidegger's philosophy and the work of the theologian. But the confusions into which this fidelity leads him are obvious at every turn. Not infrequently he uses language which implies that faith sees the true nature of that of which Heidegger's analysis offers another and contrary account. And, lastly, Bultmann's attempt to use Heidegger's ontological foundation only escapes obvious bankruptcy because he believes that the concept of personal relations can be lifted without modification from the human sphere, and used univocally to describe man's relation to God.

Such is Bultmann's official theory; how does he apply it in practice?

3. Bultmann's actual relationship to Heidegger in practice

In conclusion we must now consider Bultmann's picture of unbelieving existence and existence in faith, which he claims as samples of existentialist Christian interpretation. We must then compare them

[1] *K.u.M.*, I, p. 124. [2] 'Krisis der Theologie', *Z.Th.K.*, 1931, pp. 126-7.

[3] There is however a very startling paradox to be observed here. At other times Bultmann is so aware of the difference of theological language from all other language, that he interprets its *existentiell* statements in a manner which actually destroys their truth-claim (see ch. III).

with Heidegger's account of the conditions of human existence which he describes as inauthentic and authentic. And we shall be forced to ask ourselves, is Bultmann's picture, by any conceivable stretch of imagination, describable as the theological ontic 'filling' of the formal structure of Heidegger's philosophical ontological picture?

The following is a short summary of Bultmann's Christian demythologized existential picture of inauthentic existence, of human existence without faith,[1] and existence in faith, authentic existence.

This world is the world of transitoriness and death, not because of its intrinsic nature, as the Gnostics thought, but because of sin, for which men are responsible. Sin and death are traced back to 'the flesh', which is not man's nature as such, but the sphere of that which is usable, transitory and at our disposal. The man who lives 'according to' this sphere, making it the basis of his life, lets himself be deceived by it, and becomes its slave, living from the seen rather than from the invisible, whether he does so frivolously, and as a slave to passion, or legalistically. Life is constituted (*getragen von*) by care; every man is directed by his care, his intention towards some object, some goal, and every man relies on the flesh, the visible sphere of things, for security.

But such security is in fact radically unattainable, and by acting as if it were in our reach we 'lose our life', and become victims of the external world, and, as a result this world, which could be for us a gift received from the Creator's hand, acquires the character of enmity, and obtains the mastery over us.

Since the visible world is transitory, he who places his trust in it becomes the victim of transience and death. Under this servitude men try to secure themselves against each other. Envy, anger, jealousy and quarrelling spring into being, but also convention and bargaining, current judgements and standards obtain a stranglehold over us. And thus arises the bondage to fear which burdens mankind.

But a true life would be one lived in dependence on the invisible, which is beyond our power to control, a life where all self-created security has been surrendered. And this is the life of faith, a life that becomes a possibility for man when he trusts in God's grace, and believes that the unknown, which is beyond our powers to control, comes to meet man as love, and brings to him his future. The man who thus opens himself to God's grace has his sin forgiven. He trusts

[1] *K.u.M.*, I, p. 27, and *Theology of the New Testament*, vol. I (Eng. tr.), chs. IV and V.

in God alone, and not in the world. This is no gesture of asceticism, but it means that he knows that the world no longer matters, nor do our possessions in it, be they few or many. We are crucified to the world, and it is crucified to us, for we know that we can have all from God's hand.

And this is eschatological existence, existence as a new creature. The life of the future is already actual. The new nature which we receive is not a nature that would guarantee our salvation, however licentiously we lived. Nor is it a nature which could be preserved only by an anxious asceticism. We have it, yet not as a magical substance. It is rather a possibility which lies open before us, to be realized by continual decision. Thus far Bultmann.

When we look at these statements we must affirm that there is much in them that rings true to the New Testament, and especially to St Paul. And the latter half, in particular, is a moving description of life as seen by the Christian, the life of Christian freedom. But on a second reading we find awkward questions rising in our minds. In the Bible, surely, the one supreme figure is God, and the great distinction is between him and his will on the one side and, on the other, everything that sets itself up against him. God in his purity, love and holiness is in the centre of the picture. There are places in Bultmann's analysis where these concepts seem to be replaced by others, which belong rather to the philosophy of idealism than to the world of Christian experience. We have the concepts of the invisible and the visible, the eternal and the transitory, that which is not at our disposal and that which is at our disposal. It is true that in the Bible God is described in most of these terms, but they are all subordinated to the God who is more than them all, and never adequately expressed in terms of any of them. Now in certain sentences of Dr Bultmann's account this idealistic distortion has its corresponding reflection in the teaching about the world and man. He says: 'Since the visible world is transitory, he who places his trust in it becomes the victim of transience and death'.[1] But surely this is not Biblical teaching! The Bible tells us that since man in his rebellion against God makes of this transitory world a use which is contrary to God's will, using it to assert his own independence of God, he becomes enslaved to it, he inherits death, which is not mere transience, but alienation from God which, if carried to its uttermost degree, will be worked out in its final consequence. And though sometimes 'the flesh' for Paul means the outward and

[1] *K.u.M.*, I, p. 28.

visible, surely its central significance for him is 'that which sets itself up against God'. And further, 'convention and bargaining, current judgements and standards' do not play so important a place in New Testament theology as they do in this account. Do we see here the cloven hoof of Heidegger's 'One'? It is my general impression that in Bultmann's preaching, which we have later to examine, this weakness does not manifestly show itself. Heidegger has had a more marked bad influence on him as a theologian than as a preacher!

But, in spite of these criticisms, the important issue at the present moment is not to find fault with this picture of man's being, which is approximately Christian and Pauline. The important issue is that we should display beside it the comparable Heideggerian picture of man in his inauthenticity and authenticity. So let us recall what this picture was, let us sketch out in briefest outline what Heidegger has written on this theme, and let us 'look here upon this picture and on this'.

As the reader will recall, for Heidegger personal being is considered as being either authentic or inauthentic; so we may compare his picture of inauthentic existence with Bultmann's sketch of man without faith. For Heidegger the sphere of inauthenticity is the sphere of the impersonal, the conventional, to which men surrender themselves because of their unwillingness to acknowledge their own authentic being. Thus they fall under the alien dictatorship of 'One', seeking refuge from the prospect of their own death, for 'One', like the old soldier, never dies. 'One' gossips without understanding, is ever seeking without coming to an understanding of the truth, for it does not desire truth. 'One' is jealous of whatever is profound or original, or whatever excels its own dull mediocrity. Dispersed in 'One', personal being misunderstands its own true nature, and mistakes itself for an object, a thing out in the world. And this misunderstanding is in a deep sense purposive, for it is an evasion of the tragic truth.

Heidegger holds that authentic personal being is discovered by a resolve to be oneself, a willingness to hear and answer the call of conscience. Thus we recognize that we are at the disposal of forces over which we have no control, and learn to take responsibility for the lot that was wished on us by destiny. In such an act, continually repeated, we accept our ontological guilt with clear-sighted resolve, and acknowledge the end to which our life must come, each one by his choices creating such values as may be possible in a world that is fundamentally heedless of him, his projects, his standards and values.

Thus he is freed from the tyranny of the spectral Mrs Grundy to whose conventional standards he is ever in danger of being enslaved, and to whose gossip he is still tempted to listen, as worthy of respect!

If this picture be a fair delineation in very brief compass of those parts of Heidegger's sketch of human personal existence which are the counterparts of the New Testament account supplied in demythologized form by Bultmann above, then we must ask a further question. Is it conceivable that Heidegger's sketch can in any way be considered as the ontological preface to the theological account given by Bultmann? Does Heidegger here define the horizon of possibilities within which the theological particularizations of Bultmann must lie?

Surely one has only to display these two accounts side by side, to see that this is an impossible thesis to maintain. What we have here are in fact two different and conflicting accounts of authentic and inauthentic existence. Common to both of them is the statement that human existence is divided into two kinds, in the one of which the self is alienated from its authentic being, and in the other of which this alienation is in process of being overcome. In both descriptions the flight from authenticity involves bondage to an external power which tyrannizes over personal being. But this is almost the total extent of the agreement, unless we take also into account the Heideggerian distortions in Bultmann's formulation of man's relation to God noticed above. But the differences are far more striking, and now we must examine these.

It is common knowledge that in astronomy the planet Neptune was discovered because of certain observed, but hitherto unaccountable variations in the path of the planet Uranus. Thus the invisible outer planet made its influence felt long before it was discovered. In a similar manner one has the impression that in Bultmann's account of man, the category of the invisible and the transcendent is working powerfully from the start, even before it is actually mentioned. It is against the invisible and undisponible that man directs his more and more panic-stricken efforts to find security in what is seen. This category is wholly missing in Heidegger. Bultmann would doubtless say that this is as it should be, for his own study is ontical, while Heidegger deals with the ontological, and God is an ontical theme, so that Heidegger cannot deal with him. But the place of God or the invisible is not left vacant in Heidegger, as would be the case if Bultmann were right. Its place is taken by our own authentic being, from which we are in flight. It would be nonsense to say that the Heideggerian resolve to be oneself in the face of death is the ontological structure, and the Bultmannian 'relation to the invisible' is its ontical filling.

Further, in Heidegger's system there is certainly a slavery to 'One', which in his scheme takes the place held in Pauline theology by 'existence under the law'. But there can be little doubt that if St Paul were confronted by Heidegger's philosophy, he would say that Heidegger's authenticity bears more clearly the marks of law and death than the conventional morality of 'One'. Surely the resolve to be oneself in the face of death bears the clear marks of lostness and despair. In short, Heidegger's whole scheme is a nightmare parody 'below the death-line' of the Christian scheme. This is its true character, and not the comfortable tenancy of the ground-floor, while Christian faith and theology look out complacently from the first-storey windows!

And this is the only sense in which it can with truth be said that 'Heidegger's existential analysis is only a profane philosophical representation of the New Testament view of human personal existence'.[1] In fact, it is not possible to make use of the existential analysis as a prolegomenon to theological studies, and in fact Bultmann does not do so. The fact that he thinks he does is a fundamental contradiction in his work.

When one first considers the relation of theology to Heidegger there seem to be, in the abstract, three possibilities. First, that the Christian theologian should fully accept Heidegger's claims.[2] Secondly, that he should accept Heidegger's work up to a certain point and, after that point has been reached, call all his results in question. Thirdly, that he should make a merely eclectic use of Heidegger's concepts, ascribing what seems true and illuminating in them rather to Heidegger's natural insight than to the perfection of his phenomenological method.

I have tried in the first section of this chapter to show that the first alternative turns out to be a cul-de-sac. Bultmann believes that he has chosen it. But in fact, while his theology has marks of existentialism, it is not fully based on Heidegger. It seems to be a mixture of Christian-Pauline, idealist and Heideggerian motifs. For this reason I have felt justified in including Bultmann's work in a chapter entitled 'Heidegger with the New Look'. The second alternative is the one chosen by Dr John Macquarrie, in his book, *An Existentialist Theology*. To an examination of this position we must now turn.

[1] *K.u.M.*, I, p. 33.

[2] In the field of psychotherapy L. Binswanger claims in like manner to base himself on Heidegger. But in fact he brings in other ontological notions of Buber's and his own.

4. Macquarrie and the phenomenological method

Dr Macquarrie's is a book for which we must be grateful. There is no other theological writing in English or in German which has so grappled with the work of Heidegger. Most of the critics are content with brief summaries. But Macquarrie has entered this tangled and difficult country, and pioneered there, tracing out the frontiers where it marches with the land occupied by Bultmann, taking his own compass-bearings, making his own measurements, and hacking his way through the tropical undergrowth of verbiage and difficult concepts. So that even where criticism of him is here made, it is accompanied by a deep sense of gratitude for those paths cleared, and compass-bearings taken. The criticism here offered will not attempt to evaluate the book's many virtues, but will confine itself mostly to questions dealing with the problem of method.

Our first question will be: Does Macquarrie accept the claims of Heidegger's existential analysis, to be an ontological preface to all theology?

There are two passages where he seems to commit himself to this position. In the first,[1] he says that the theologian is committed to presuppositions which 'are ontological; that is to say, they consist in a preliminary understanding of the being of the entities into which the inquiry is being made. For example, the theologian may ask, "What is man in his relation to God?" For the doctrine of man, that is to say, the content of the theological concept of man, he will go to the Christian revelation in search of his answer. But what about the "is" in his question? That already implies some understanding of the being of man—among other things, that the being of man is such that he can have a relation to God'. In the second passage, Macquarrie says that he is concerned to defend Bultmann on three grounds, the second of which is 'that since existentialism is especially concerned to analyze

[1] *An Existentialist Theology*, London, 1955, p. 6.

Clearly, Christians and non-Christians have much in common in their conception of man and his being, which makes discussion between them possible. But our answer to the assertion of the primacy of a neutral (?) ontology, must be that it is unacceptable, since the 'is' of man's being cannot be fully and rightly understood until it is realized as itself dependent on the relation to God. That is, man's being must be defined as *answering*, *created*, *responsible* being. These are not just qualities of man, these words describe modes of his existence, without which it would not be what it is. The first of these modes Heidegger ignores, the second and third he disastrously misinterprets. Our argument is that he does so because he starts with an ontic experience which has no place for God.

the constitution of the being of man, and since the theologian must make certain ontological assumptions about man, this philosophy stands in a special relation to the theologian's work'.[1]

Thus it would appear that Heidegger's claims are accepted by Macquarrie. We have seen that Bultmann accepts them, and Macquarrie informs us, so does Copleston, whom he quotes as agreeing that 'the problem of God is not raised on the plane of the phenomenological analysis of man' and explaining that 'the absence of God from Heidegger's philosophy is a mere circumstance attendant on his method'.[2]

But now comes the interesting point. Macquarrie quotes Copleston only to disagree with him. And he makes it quite clear all through his book that he intends in part to rewrite the existential analysis, and to give it a religious slant.

5. *Macquarrie's own version of the existential analysis*

Let us now consider the modifications which Dr Macquarrie proposes to make in Heidegger's analysis, in order to give it the 'new look'.

He says[3]: 'In religious faith, God is disclosed immediately with the self and the world. Heidegger teaches that in the original disclosure of *Dasein* (personal being), the self and the world are disclosed together. Religious thought must go beyond that, and assert that God is also disclosed—or rather discloses himself. In the light of that disclosure, the world is understood as creation, and the self as creature who may use the creation or be lost in it.'

What are we to make of this statement? It looks as if Macquarrie were saying that God himself appears in the existential analysis, disclosed by the phenomenological method. But in that case, what would become of faith? We shall see in a moment that this is not what Dr Macquarrie means; he is more cautious.

But it is interesting to note that Macquarrie is quite explicit, now as before, in his objection to Copleston, that he does not believe in a neutral existential analysis whose work is done before the concept of God can be introduced. In answering Schumann's pertinent question, 'Can there be a trustworthy analysis of human existence, which does not see that existence in relation to God?' he argues that Heidegger's

[1] *An Existentialist Theology*, p. 24.

[2] Copleston, *Existentialism and Modern Man*, Blackfriars, p. 18, cited by Macquarrie, op. cit., p. 73.

[3] *An Existentialist Theology*, p. 62.

analysis comes at one point very near to being a religious philosophy. Referring us to his next section, he says, 'It will be argued at that point that the existential analytic should *become* religious for its completion, and that God is disclosed with the self and the world, as has been already asserted.'[1]

In this next section, to which reference has just been made, Macquarrie deals with the phenomenon of 'anxiety'. Heidegger, he says, teaches that man is revealed to himself. To be a human person is to have some understanding of oneself. And the 'mood' (*Befindlichkeit*) which accompanies our consciousness of self discloses to us a truth about our being in the world. Mood 'lights up' being in the world, and discloses both the self and the world in their inseparable relation to each other.

The most significant of the moods by which man is affected, is that of anxiety, for it discloses man in his authentic being. 'Anxiety discloses to man that he is not at home in the world . . . Although Heidegger does not explicitly say so, we contend that at this point the existential analytic has brought us to the threshold of religion, and that the concept of anxiety demands a religious interpretation—and with it the whole concept of human existence. For in this fundamental malaise, which springs from man's very being, there is disclosed not only the self and the world, but also God. The disclosure does not indeed yield the explicit knowledge of God, but directs man to God as the ground of his being, in a way which will shortly be more fully described.'[2]

What is this way? It would appear to be more fully described on p. 76 where we are told that 'Anxiety does not itself disclose God, but discloses to man with his own being the possibility of God, and gives rise to his search for God'. Here Macquarrie appears to make use of a distinction between anxiety as an *existential*, and an ontic experience of religious awe, in which God may be directly revealed. 'Anxiety or dread, as we have considered it, is still a formal ontological or existential structure, a bare horizon of possibility, which has to be made concrete in some ontical or *existentiell* experience before religion proper emerges. . . . The distinction between the broad existential concept of anxiety or dread and the special religious concept of awe appears to me to be that whereas in anxiety the primary disclosure is of man's own being, while the possibility of God is lit up on the periphery, as it were, in

[1] *An Existentialist Theology*, p. 63 (italics mine). Reference to F. Schumann, *K.u.M.*, I, p. 198.

[2] *An Existentialist Theology*, p. 76.

awe the positions have changed, God's revelation of himself is central, while the being of man is now disclosed on the periphery'.[1]

Here, then, is an answer to our previous question. Anxiety, as analysed by Macquarrie, does not disclose God, but only a possibility of God, while God discloses himself only in a special religious experience. Macquarrie has thus contrived to define ontologically man's existence in such a way that it *can* have an experience of God, and is not, as seemingly in Heidegger's opinion, without an ontological possibility of such an experience.

But here we must ask why Macquarrie seeks at this point to amend Heidegger's analysis. Is it because the phenomenological method of Heidegger demands this addition? No suggestion of this kind is made, and we are left with the inescapable conclusion that at this point Macquarrie *sees* things in this light. And, of course, we would agree with him here. It is part of our theistic faith, part of our common Christian faith, for we believe that in some sense God is present to all men. But this we believe, not because of what any penetrative neutral phenomenological method presents us with, but as a part of our Christian faith.

Heidegger, however, will be quite unimpressed by these sentiments. Are we, accordingly, able to bring to bear upon him some train of reasoning, starting with the results of his phenomenological method on which he and we are agreed, and ending with our theistic conclusion rather than his own? No! He will have as good a right to his existential analysis, as we have to our theistic one. If the possibility of a theistic interpretation of anxiety has for a moment hovered before him, he has quite resolutely turned the other way, and refused to let what he calls 'the anthropological problem of the being of man in relation to God'[2] gain a precedence. Instead of regarding the relation to God as the fundamental characteristic of human personal being, Heidegger has deliberately chosen to rule out this transcendent reference. And Macquarrie is quite unable to offer to him, on the strength of the phenomenological method, any grounds why he should adopt an 'analysis à la Macquarrie', with an improved, and theistic, look.

The fact is, that Macquarrie has now cast the phenomenological method[3] to the winds, and is speaking as a Christian apologist, a right

[1] Op. cit., p. 77. One difficulty in this view is that it suggests that anxiety is an ontological *experience*. Surely, however, all experiences are ontic, though they may have ontological significance, as revealing underlying ontological structures.

[2] *S.u.Z.*, p. 190, n.

[3] We must not be misled by the fact that, with full justification, Dr Mac-

and proper thing to do, but a confusing thing to do, if you do not state that you have changed your approach, and that this is what you are now doing. We shall see the same pattern repeated when Macquarrie takes Heidegger to task over his interpretation of the phenomenon of conscience.

Next we must give Macquarrie's report of Heidegger's account of conscience, dealing only with those details which are needed for our immediate purpose, which, the reader will remember, is the discovery of the standpoint from which Macquarrie criticizes Heidegger, and on which he erects his new and improved existential analysis.

This is what Macquarrie says about Heidegger's account of conscience.[1] 'Conscience, therefore, on Heidegger's view, is the call of the self to the self—the authentic self to the fallen self. It belongs to the very structure of man's being as having a relation to himself. When he falls away from himself, the being of man becomes more or less split—an idea familiar to St Paul also, who conceived the life after the flesh as the strife of self against self.'

A few pages later we are told,[2] 'Our criticism of Heidegger concerns not so much his actual concept of conscience as the function which he assigns to it in making the bridge from fallen to authentic existence. Is conscience able to play the part, which, on Heidegger's theory, is demanded of it? If we can show that it is not, serious damage will have been done to Heidegger's argument at this vital point where it makes the transition from the analysis of fallen existence to that of authentic existence.'

Here, however, Dr Macquarrie must be reminded that for Heidegger, fallenness is not at all the same thing that it is for the Christian.[3] For Heidegger it is only an alienation from an authentic self, and has its place in a doctrine of man largely aesthetic in its standards. Heidegger is disgusted and repelled by everyday fallenness. But for the Christian, fallenness is revolt against God, the Creator and Father of our spirits. So that conscience, as Heidegger conceives of it, may well be able to achieve authenticity, as Heidegger pictures it. To him we might say,

quarrie also speaks of a phenomenological method at work within Christian theology. This is a method describing the objects known to faith, and within the purview of faith. It is different from the phenomenological method of the existential analysis of Heidegger, which claims to be standpointless, and universally persuasive.

[1] Op. cit., p. 143.

[2] Ibid., p. 147.

[3] Heidegger would, of course, agree that this is so, saying that his concept of 'fallenness' is the ontological precondition of the ontic fallenness studied by the Christian theologian. This view we claim to have dismissed.

as St Anselm did to his friend Boso, 'Thou hast not yet considered the weight of sin.'

In this context Macquarrie ingeniously introduces a distinction between ontological and ontic possibilities, which has no place in Heidegger's analysis at this point.[1] Here he argues that the transition from inauthentic being to authentic cannot be made by man's own efforts, for all that these can achieve are *ontic* possibilities. Conscience is, Macquarrie agrees, able to *disclose* to man his ontological possibility of authenticity. 'It cannot bring before him the *existentiell* possibility of authenticity for which he can decide. And it now appears that only some Power outside man, some Power not fallen as man is fallen, can bring to man this concrete possibility of regaining his authentic being. . . . Here for the second time we observe Heidegger's existential analytic approaching to the very frontiers of religion. His deep understanding of the fallenness of man, and of man's impotence so that responsibility already implies guilt, are factors in his thought which seem to demand for their completion a doctrine of God. On Heidegger's own view of man, it seems to me that man cannot lift himself, and that his authentic being can only be restored, if at all, from outside himself. Yet once again Heidegger does not cross the frontier when he reaches it, but turns aside to this unconvincing theory of the function of conscience as bridging the gulf from fallenness to authenticity.'[2] Again, says Macquarrie, the difference arises in the interpretation of anxiety. 'There [in the previous passage] Heidegger saw man disclosed in his facticity, adrift on the sea of what is, whereas the Christian sees man disclosed in his creaturely relation to God, the ground of his being.'

In comment on this passage, I would say that as Heidegger's conception of fallenness is superficial, so also is his conception of guilt trivial. For example, the ontological ground of factual guilt, as he describes it, has in my opinion nothing whatever to do with guilt as the Christian understands it.

Further we must ask Dr Macquarrie again, how does he propose to persuade Heidegger that conscience in his existential analysis is not able to play that part he assigns to it. Macquarrie starts with the Christian conception of fallenness and guilt, and tells us in language

[1] Here he is developing a hint given by Bultmann, *K.u.M.*, I, p. 37 and *Z.Th.K.*, 1930, p. 344, where Bultmann says that it is ontically impossible for a man to be justified in the sight of God, but ontologically this is a possibility. To say of an animal that it cannot be justified by works is nonsense, because righteousness is not an ontological possibility for a beast.

[2] Op. cit., p. 149.

coloured by existentialist terms that man is saved not by his own act, but by the act of God. But when he does this, he is speaking once more, not as a phenomenologist, but as a Christian apologist, and in the last pages of the paragraph quoted quite openly says so. 'The Christian sees man disclosed in his creaturely relation to God. . . . The Christian . . . turns again to the ground of his being, and finds that God supplies the power which he lacks in himself.'[1]

Thus in Macquarrie we do not in fact find an improved existential analytic using the phenomenological method, but a disguised Christian apologetic, according to which he rewrites Heidegger's existential analysis. But if this is so, then Heidegger's analysis has from the start much less prestige than Macquarrie is prepared to grant it, and is by no means able to lay the groundwork and foundation for theology.

It is admitted by Heidegger that all existential analysis must start from the ontic, and in this material must seek to disclose underlying ontological structures. But the trouble is that we arrive at different underlying structures according to what ontic experiences we start from! If we start from the ontic experiences of unbelief, it is not unnatural that we should arrive at ontological structures of human personal being which leave in fact no openness in man for an ontic experience of God. If, on the other hand our analysis starts from the ontic experiences of a believer, which include among them experiences in which he is convinced that God has actually disclosed himself to faith, it is not unnatural that we shall conclude that personal being is structurally open to such experiences of God. But this means that our ontology is never a neutral discipline; it is, in fact, always in part an extrapolation of our belief—or our unbelief. If this be so, then a neutral, rigorously scientific existential analysis is not possible. And rival existential analyses cannot refute each other logically, for they do not start from identical data, and the field they cover is not one where strict refutation is possible. In fact, Heidegger is no more a true exponent of the phenomenological method than Macquarrie. Each has his own set of presuppositions. Macquarrie's are Christian, Heidegger's non-theistic.

6. Conclusions

In concluding this chapter, it is only fitting once more to pay tribute to Macquarrie's book, and its clarity and ingenuity. If at various points

[1] Op. cit., p. 149.

I have felt bound to disagree with it, in many other respects I am in hearty agreement with it, and the course of the argument has led me to emphasize the points of disagreement rather than the others. The book opens up a large field of thought, and to have done so in the lucid and unambiguous language which Macquarrie commands, is to have done a great service to the Christian cause, whichever way the verdict of Christian opinion on Heidegger and Bultmann may finally fall.

In an earlier part of this chapter I tried to show that of the three positions that one could take up in relation to Heidegger, the first way, chosen by Bultmann, of affirming his claims, was not viable. Second comes Dr Macquarrie's position, that we should accept Heidegger up to a point, and then radically diverge from him. This way seems a definite improvement on Bultmann's, but suffers from a lack of coherence, adopting first the phenomenological method as valid, and then suddenly surrendering it, though perhaps not wholly consciously, for a method of Christian apologetic. The third alternative, which is that adopted in this book, is in principle to reject the phenomenological method in the sphere of the doctrine of man, and yet to be ready guardedly to accept and apply Heidegger's insights individually, and to allow oneself to be influenced by him in his criticism of crude substantialism in the same field. It may be asked what in fact has been achieved by this long and detailed discussion of Bultmann's and Macquarrie's version of existentialism. To this I would reply that only such detailed discussion can add anything at this late stage in the debate. And as long as the claims that Bultmann makes for Heidegger are not refuted, there is considerable danger for theology. I am convinced that even Macquarrie is taking Heidegger too seriously. In short, I wish to have the right on occasion, to snap my fingers at Heidegger's existential analysis, and to secure others in that right also.

And in view of the special theme of this book, we may remember that if Heidegger's claims are substantiated, then every B.D. student specializing in theology, will have to spend some weeks or months in mastering *Sein und Zeit*. To have shown that such labours are not really necessary, and that such effort and ingenuity as Dr Bultmann has expended in dovetailing his thought and Gogarten's into Heidegger's ontology are effort wasted; may perhaps be considered a service to theology, the handmaid of preaching and evangelism.

It is said that if a chalk line be drawn upon a slate, and a hen be forced to look at it steadily, it will rapidly pass into a hypnotic trance. Heidegger's existential analysis is in danger of becoming, in certain quarters, at least, the chalk line of modern theology. The writer of this book does not wish to suffer the fate above described, and if the case made in the second chapter and in this, has served, or can serve, to break the mesmeric spell for any fellow-mortal, the author will feel that his work has not been in vain.

Part Two

IV

MYTHICAL THINKING AND THE PREACHER

1. Introduction

THUS far we have been considering in the main Heidegger's claims for himself, Bultmann's acceptance of these claims, and his own professed and actual relation to him. Now we must examine more closely the actual results of the demythologizing project and the existential reinterpretation of the theology and preaching of Bultmann himself. We shall have to study the various difficulties which beset him, and his efforts to extricate himself from them, difficulties which mostly arise from his own philosophical presuppositions. When we reflect upon the matter, we shall find that few of these difficulties can in fact be laid to the blame of Heidegger. The first of the subjects for us to consider here is the demythologizing project and its startlingly unexpected effect on Bultmann's theology and preaching.

2. The demythologizing project: our initial sympathy and growing hesitations

Rudolf Bultmann is convinced that there is in the Bible much mythical material, whose true significance for our modern age can be disclosed only by an existential reinterpretation. This is familiar ground, and indeed there is no point in all his theology which has been more closely examined and scrutinized than his conception of mythical thinking.

In view of this discussion, which has already reached the point of tedium, might we not be spared the trouble of yet once again covering this ground, especially as some of the criticisms here to be offered agree with those of other writers? On second thoughts I am convinced that something still remains to be said on this subject from the special viewpoint taken up in this book. I remember rising very early, soon after sunrise on a summer morning in the Scottish highlands, and being astonished at something most unusual about the aspect of the familiar mountains, woods, and fields. At first I was unable to identify it, but soon realized that the strangeness was due to the unwonted, almost north-easterly, direction from which the level sunlight was shining upon all these features of a well-known landscape. My hope is that the already too familiar theme of mythical thinking may receive fresh light from the still too unfamiliar viewpoint which this book represents, the viewpoint of the preacher, the teacher, and the evangelist.

Let us therefore turn our thoughts to just such a situation. Anyone who has taught a Bible Class, or taken a Padre's Hour with the Forces, or discussed the Christian faith with scientifically-minded people, realizes that there are passages in Scripture whose inner meaning and relevance are anything but clear at a first glance. Honesty compels us to admit that we ourselves also find considerable difficulty in interpreting certain passages. Some of these raise the additional problem that their literal interpretation conflicts with the legitimate and established conclusions of modern science or history. And yet, while conceding that narratives like those of the Creation and Fall cannot be understood as recording historical or scientific fact, we are unwilling to jettison them. We believe that they have still much to say to us, that they have essential truths to tell us. Sometimes we are able to translate them into terms clearly less obscure, and to cast a flood of light upon them, both for our hearers and ourselves. And often we find that this translation is no longer, as was the literal version, in conflict with the assured results of modern science or history. Thus there is no theologian and probably no preacher, who does not in some degree employ an interpretative technique of this kind. And there is no theologian or preacher, who has thought deeply about his task, who is unaware of the problem.

Further, it is nearly impossible to read such a book as First Thessalonians, without being convinced that St Paul expected the almost immediate end of history with the coming of Christ, which would be accompanied by the resurrection of the dead. It may be that Paul was aware that his prediction of these events to which he looked forward was only a stumbling and stuttering expression of the ineffable, but the problem remains for us, how are we to interpret this expectation of his for ourselves and our contemporaries, two thousand years after the non-fulfilment of his hopes?

It is not enough to contrast the Hebrew way of thinking with the Greek, to the advantage of the former, and to say that while the Greeks believed in the immortality of the soul, the Hebrews always hoped for the resurrection of the body. The problem remains for us, if we find ourselves unable to take literally the notion of the second coming, as a coming literally to this earth, as an event verifiable to the sense-perception of these eyes,[1] then how are we to formulate the distinctive characteristics of the Biblical doctrine of the resurrection of the body? The result of our uncertainties is too often either that preachers feel themselves bound to give either a massively literal interpretation of the Biblical passages where concepts of this type occur, or else pass over in uncomfortable silence all areas of doctrine where such doctrines as the resurrection of the body are in question.

Bultmann has at any rate boldly grasped the nettle here, and whatever we may think of the way in which he develops his project, we should be grateful that he has not lacked the courage to make an attempt, where others have fumbled. With all of us, his demythologizing project should be able to count, accordingly, on a very sympathetic first hearing.

But when we read the list of what he considers mythical elements of belief found in the Bible, we are somewhat shaken. Among the New Testament contents which he relegates to the mythological shelf, there to await existential interpretation, are the following: the three-decker view of the universe, earth in the middle, heaven above, and hell beneath; miracle; demon possession; the belief that God guides and inspires men; the notion that supernatural powers influence the course of history; the belief that the Son was sent in the fullness of time; the pre-existence of Christ; the resurrection of Christ regarded as an event beyond and different from the rise of the Easter faith in the disciples; and the belief in the Holy Spirit, if that Spirit be regarded as more than 'the factual possibility of a new life realized in faith'.[2]

Surely something very strange has happened here! What is the criterion by which all these so different magnitudes have been judged mythical? At the one end of the scale Bultmann rejects as mythological the three-decker view of the universe, which clearly cannot be understood literally as a description of earth, heaven and hell. If ever such an interpretation was current, the scientific world-picture has made it impossible today. But at the other end of the scale we find Dr Bultmann mentioning in one breath with this (though a very long breath) the concepts of the pre-existence of Christ, and the reality of the Holy

[1] As the writer once heard it taken by an eminent Roman Catholic logician.
[2] *K.u.M.*, I, pp. 15-16, p. 31.

Spirit, considered as 'more than the factual possibility of a new life realized in faith'.

Here, we may retort, are conceptions taken from the very heart of theology. They in no way trespass upon those areas where the experimental sciences hold unquestioned sway. Therefore experimental science offers us no ground whatever for rejecting them.

No one has expressed more clearly the point that I am making against Bultmann than Emil Brunner, who writes, 'At one time he (Bultmann) contrasts the statements of the New Testament with the knowledge given by science, which, in so far as it is real knowledge—as, for example, that the earth is round, is simply our destiny. At other times he contrasts the New Testament statements with the thinking of modern man who has either a biological or idealistic conception of human nature. That modern man is more attached to one or other of these world-views; let us say—naturalism or idealism—is a fact, and that for this very reason the Christian understanding of man is a scandal to him, is intelligible. But here we have to do with questions of faith, or speculative world-outlook, which as Christians we have not to accept, but rather to oppose as wrong.'[1]

The situation is perhaps more complex than might appear. Christians are not obliged to support the Biblical picture of man or the world in every instance save where the scientific modern world view legitimately forbids them. There may have been advances in the understanding of man's nature, which do not have the compelling character of scientific truth, but which nevertheless may vindicate themselves by their interpretative power, and there are insights given us by the existentialist thinkers which may be included among these. But there are other concepts belonging to modern speculative world-views, which cut at the root of Christian belief, and the question may well be asked whether in this field Dr Bultmann has not made unnecessary and dangerous concessions. It was doubtless this conviction that more was being surrendered by the exponents of demythologizing than was demanded by the facts of the case, and more than the Christian faith could afford to lose, that led one eminent preacher to say recently that at first he had hailed Bultmann's proposals with enthusiasm, but that the more he saw of the project, the less he liked it!

And yet, with all this, the problem remains. There are elements of thought in the New Testament whose day has long passed; there are

[1] Brunner, *Dogmatik II*, Zürich, 1950, p. 313 (Eng. tr. of Brunner's Dogmatics is being published by the Lutterworth Press).

elements whose day can never pass. How are we to preach the great doctrines? To take everything that is said literally, to deal evasively with the issues, or to keep silent. Can Bultmann help the preacher here? He certainly needs help.

3. Bultmann's two definitions of mythical thinking: further indications of confusion

We have already[1] seen reason to suspect that there may be confusion in Bultmann's mind as to the definition of myth. Let us now examine his official definitions, which are two.

In his essay of 1941, 'New Testament and Mythology', which initiated the present phase of the discussion, Bultmann defined myth as follows: Myth 'is a mode of thought in which what belongs to the other world is pictured as belonging to this world; the divine as human, and the transcendent as immanent; in which, for example, God's transcendence is conceived of as spatial remoteness.'[2]

In a later essay, in answer to criticism, he proceeds to give another definition, which he apparently considers to be merely a repetition in other words of the first one. 'I use,' he says, 'the concept "myth" in the sense customary in historical science and comparative religion. Myth is the account of an event or happening in which supernatural, superhuman powers are at work, (and therefore it is often simply defined as the history of the gods).'[3] Thus it excludes certain phenomena and events from the known and familiar conditions and events of the world. 'Mythical thinking regards the world and world-events as "open"—open, that is, for the intrusion of transcendent powers, and thus not water-tight from the aspect of scientific thought.' Scientific thinking is the contrary concept to mythical thinking. It reckons with the closed sequence of cause and effect, presupposes the unity of the world, and regards the world and world-events as closed to all intrusions.

At this point it is necessary for us to comment that the two definitions of myth given above are not at all identical, though Dr Bultmann appears to think that they are, referring both times to his usage being that customary in comparative religion. In a word, the first definition is to be used to consign far the greater proportion of doctrinal state-

[1] See pp. 83 and 84.
[2] *K.u.M.*, I, p. 22 (footnote).
[3] For this whole passage, see *K.u.M.*, II, pp. 180-1. The sentences not in inverted commas give not the words but the gist of the argument.

ments about the transcendent, God, Christ and the Spirit, to the lumber-room of myth, there to await existential reinterpretation; while the second definition has the purpose of doing the same for miracle, at least, for miracle as it has been commonly defined and known in the days before Bultmann. Surely, we must conclude, this is too wide and indiscriminate a use of the term 'mythology'. Here it is being employed to cover the elements of primitive science which are impossible for modern man to accept while retaining his intellectual integrity. At the same time, it is being used to describe also certain other beliefs which are uncongenial only to certain speculative non-Christian world-views, e.g. the belief that God guides and inspires man. Then, thirdly, it is used to include language used of the transcendent. When we observe this, we must begin to feel that concepts are being used so carelessly, that the results are likely to command little intellectual respect.

We shall have to examine Bultmann's reasoning on myth on two very important points. Firstly, his relegation of doctrinal statements concerning God and the transcendent, to the mythical shelf. This we shall attempt in this chapter. Our discussion of his relegation of miracle to the mythical will be found in a separate chapter.[1] But first remembering the viewpoint of our particular study in this book, it is our duty to ask what is likely to be the result upon theology and preaching and evangelism of these two relegations.

4. The relevance of this relegation for preaching and evangelism

We concede, of course, that Dr Bultmann's relegation of certain elements of the gospel and theology to mythology, does not mean that he has no more use for them. He believes that behind mythical language there is a very real driving power, which comes from the fact that its real intention is very different from what it appears to be. Banished from the area of empirical reality, and not without reason, it is yet saying, in the wrong language, something extremely important about our human existence, and its relation to the transcendent, which can be translated, without remainder, into existential language.

But we must now ask, what are the theological and preaching results of this relegation, first in the sphere of miracle and secondly in the field of doctrinal statement? Firstly, then, the field of miracle. There can be little doubt that the banishment of miracle from the sphere of

[1] Ch. VI, 'Myth and Miracle'.

fact, and its 'reinstatement' in the field of existential significance, must lead to a radical scepticism about our historical sources in the gospels. If few or none of the mighty works of Jesus were ever really done, and if the real, though unconscious, purpose of the miracle stories related of him, is to indicate what God wishes to say to me through the (empirically quite undistinguished) story of his real life, then how much reliance can we any longer place upon the whole gospel story of that life? It has been acutely pointed out that if we remove all the miracle narratives from St Mark's Gospel, and if we remove also the attached teaching of Christ which seems to depend necessarily on the factual reference of the miraculous stories recorded, we shall have only a very meagre relic left. And it must be conceded, that the rejection of all the miracle-stories which at all exceed the analogy of our present-day experience, will lead to a radical scepticism, not only about the miracle-incidents of Jesus' life, but about the other incidents also, a scepticism which may even cause us to express the doubt whether anything worthwhile can be known about him. We recall in this connexion Bultmann's famous sentence in *Jesus*, that 'Almost nothing can today be certainly known about the life or personality of Jesus, since the Christian sources did not show any interest in these things, and, further, are very fragmentary and overgrown with legend . . .'[1]

There are certainly other reasons for Bultmann's historical scepticism about Jesus as well as his rejection of miracle. There is probably the New Testament scholar's experience of the various mutually contradictory interpretations of Jesus' life, and the distaste of a naturally fastidious man for the patronizing claims of the 'Life of Jesus' writers to an intimate knowledge of his inner life and consciousness. But chief among them must be the conviction on philosophical grounds, that the miracle stories must be rejected as mythical. And the consequence of this for Bultmann's preaching is, that his gospel may fairly be described as a gospel without the gospels. It is, therefore, probably no accident that there is in his sermons quite a lot about Jesus' teaching, but nothing at all telling us about the incidents of his life, or the qualities shown in his various dealings with men and women; with one exception only, in a sermon on the Miraculous Draught of Fishes, and here Bultmann tells us frankly that he regards the incident as a pious fiction.

Our conclusion then will be, that Bultmann's definition of mythical thinking, with a view to demythologizing and existential reinter-

[1] *Jesus*, Berlin, 1926, p. 12.

pretation, has here had quite the contrary result from that which was intended and hoped for. The aim intended was surely to bring Jesus and his challenge intimately before modern men, so that they might be forced to decide for him or against him. The actual result is to bring before modern man a gospel without the gospels, so that not without justification we may quote Mary Magdalene and say, 'They have taken away my Lord, and I know not where they have laid him'.[1] Instead of the living Jesus of the Gospels, we have an unknown Rabbi preaching the necessity of decision in face of the bare claim on his part that we should decide for him or against him. And we note that while it is the scepticism of Bultmann about the miracles which has had this result, the effect is to induce a scepticism not only about the miracles, but about the very figure of him whose message to us is 'He that hath seen me hath seen the Father'.[2] So that in the end it is the figure of the Father, and not only the figure of the Son that is obscured. How can this be preached? What is there here to preach?

2. Let us now examine Bultmann's relegation of doctrinal statements as mythological, with a view to seeing in this particular field the results for preaching, teaching and evangelism. Here again, we might at the first blush expect to give a welcome to teaching which might enable us, as modern men, to short-circuit the use of a number of concepts which today, one would think, can have little importance, and whose use to illumine points of doctrine today might suggest to us the words *obscurum per obscurius*—the interpretation of the puzzling by something still more obscure. But here, too, against our expectation we find that things are not quite so simple as they at first appeared to be.

Here we find Bultmann regarding the 'Sending of the Son in the fullness of time' as a mythical concept, and along with it the belief that 'This Son, a pre-existent divine being, appears on earth as a man, his death on the cross, which he suffers in the guise of a sinner, atones for the sins of men'.[3] We are therefore to conclude that all, or nearly all, of the statements of doctrine, by which preachers in the past have sought to awaken the love and gratitude of men for Christ in his work of salvation, are vetoed. Surely, here is a further crippling of the gospel. For are not such doctrines attempts, however imperfect and in need of mutual supplementation, to describe the meaning of the cross? One of the achievements of James Denney, in the field of atonement theory, was surely to show how absurd is the attempt in the face of a

[1] John 20.13. [2] John 14.9.
[3] *K.u.M.*, I, p. 16.

reality like the cross, to draw a distinction between the fact and the theory of it, the fact and its significance.[1]

But, we shall be told, the mythical concepts are being given up only to be replaced by an existential significance! We shall see in the next chapter how little confidence we can place in the sea-worthiness of this ark in which we shall be invited to take refuge. And, as preachers and evangelists, we should be very careful that we do not inflict a second crippling blow upon our gospel for the modern man, by rejecting concepts of atonement as mythical, until Bultmann has really driven his case home in such a way as to leave us no recourse but to agree with him. If he does make good his case against the doctrinal statements which have hitherto served the Church, then, however much the result may impoverish our theological thinking and our preaching, it will be our duty in the interests of truth to submit. But first let us examine the validity of his arguments.

5. Rejection of Bultmann's first definition of myth

I believe that we have good reason to reject Bultmann's veto on the doctrinal statements which theologians have hitherto used in speaking of God and the transcendent. And it will hardly be necessary to remind the reader that this is no merely theoretical subject of debate, but one which touches the very nerve of the faith and the preaching and teaching of it. The issue we are now to consider is therefore quite vital to the theme of the present book.

The reader will recall that the first definition of mythical thinking was that it conceived of the divine as human and the transcendent as immanent. One of the surprising characteristics of Bultmann's thinking at this point is, that he appears to grant the legitimacy of the term 'myth' only in cases where a thinker applies his concepts quite literally to the divine—univocally—and is totally unaware of the impropriety of so doing. Now, clearly, all our concepts are taken from the field of our everyday experience and, by definition, theology is a doctrine about God, or the transcendent. So it must surely follow that whether we realize it or not, our concepts are inadequate to this great theme. But Bultmann asserts that as soon as this inadequacy begins to dawn upon a thinker, the process of demythologizing has begun, and having begun, it must continue to the bitter end.

In response to the unanswerable objection that language must use

[1] James Denney, *The Death of Christ*, London, 1911, p. 86.

inadequate concepts to describe God, Bultmann writes, 'Now it is significant that those who try to maintain the inevitability of mythological language, in fact try to avoid mythological thinking, and understand the mythological concepts as admittedly indispensable pictures or symbols. They then obviously do not notice that they themselves are demythologizing, and that their own procedure refutes their claim. Who of them understands today the description of God the Creator in the sense of the myth? Or the words about God's throne, or about the heavenly session of Christ at God's right hand?'[1]

Bultmann's position on this matter can be summed up in three sentences.

(1) Mythical thinking exists, and by definition is unconscious of the inadequacy of the concepts which it applies to the transcendent.

(2) As soon as this inadequacy begins to dawn upon the thinker, the process of demythologizing has begun.

(3) Having begun the process of demythologizing, there can be no halting place for us until it has been carried through to the bitter end.

We can agree with the first and second propositions; it is the third which must be contested. In another passage, he says that once having started to demythologize, we must go the whole way with him, until we have expressed what we were trying to say in plain terms, without myth.[2] He concedes that mythical concepts may be *provisionally* indispensable, in so far as they refer to truths which cannot be expressed in scientific terms. But the adequate existential language, he insists, must be found for them. Indeed, he claims to place the men he criticizes in an inescapable dilemma, by asking them what is the meaning of the terms they are using. And if, in answer to his question, they take refuge in another symbol, he will ask what *its* meaning is, so that they are either condemned to an infinite regress, or to the discovery of a final unmythological expression.[3]

To anticipate for a moment the conclusions of a future chapter, we may point out that Bultmann believes he can afford to talk thus belittlingly of mythological language, because he is convinced that he has in the existential interpretation a set of categories which allow him to express transcendent truth with complete adequacy. And we find that, in his opinion, this existential interpretation is one which uses the terms suited to dealing with personal relationships between human beings. Here, unfortunately, it has escaped Bultmann's notice that the

[1] *K.u.M.*, I, p. 122; *K.u.M.*, II, pp. 185-6.
[2] *K.u.M.*, I, p. 21. [3] *K.u.M.*, II, pp. 185-6.

terms used of our relationship to other human beings cannot be used univocally, without stretching their meaning, to express our relationship to God. So that here, by definition, we have still use of inadequate concepts to describe the transcendent. Bultmann is still, according to his own definition, using mythological language, and must be invited to continue his demythologizing process till the bitter end.

In the end of his first essay,[1] Bultmann admits that he believes in 'an action of God in Christ, his decisive eschatological action'. This is the lynch-pin without which Bultmann's theology would topple into ruin. We must ask him whether the word 'action' here is used in precisely the same sense as when that word is used when applied to a movement or initiation of activity by a human being. The answer is, of course, that here the concept is used with an awareness of its inadequacy. Here, then, by Bultmann's definition we have a demythologizing which cannot be carried to the bitter end. If a reinterpretation (existential or otherwise) could here be found, which was not consciously inadequately describing a transcendent reality, would this not be proof that we were no longer talking about God, but only about ourselves?

If this be so, then surely the veto on partial demythologizing has been broken, and the action of past theologians vindicated. Following the example of the Bible, Christian thinkers down the ages have used figures adapted from the world of human experience, each of them in part suited to describe some aspect of the transcendent reality, and each of them inadequate and, if taken in isolation, in some respects false. The use of a number of these images together lessens the possibility of misunderstanding. The importance of this vindicated liberty for preaching should be emphasized.

It will be necessary at this point to anticipate in brief what is later said in our chapter 'The Flight from History'. Having denied the relevance for faith of the historical life of Jesus, and having rejected as mythical the figures which the New Testament and the Church have used to help men to understand what he has done for us by his life and death, Dr Bultmann finally asks himself, 'How do we see from the cross, that it is Christ's cross?'[2] And to this question he replies, that there is only one answer that we can give. 'We believe in it as saving event, because it is preached as such.' This strange and surely very unsatisfactory answer is the one to which his historical scepticism and his out-of-hand rejection of the mythological condemns him.

But if our arguments against him on these two scores concerning

[1] *K.u.M.*, I, p. 48. [2] *K.u.M.*, I, p. 41.

the historical and the mythological hold good, then the consequence will be that we are not, like him, left preaching in a vacuum. It certainly was not preaching of this kind which through the centuries has created faith. Nor, indeed, to his credit and his confusion, is Bultmann's own powerful preaching, preaching of this kind. What has created faith down the centuries was the preaching of men who preached Christ's death as saving event because they knew it *was* saving event, an event seen as the conclusion of a life which had no parallel among men, an event which the preachers were able in part to understand by means of concepts of atonement which, though confessedly inadequate, were yet not null and void.

6. Rejection of another argument of Bultmann's in favour of complete demythologizing

Another argument brought forward by Bultmann in favour of his radical project for demything is as follows. He claims that the New Testament itself, by its own character, urges on us the necessity of the task. The argument runs as follows: We find in the New Testament various statements, which, if taken literally, are mutually contradictory, but which, if regarded rather as expressing the New Testament understanding of human experience (i.e. as existential judgements), do not involve such contradictions.

As instances, Bultmann gives the following pairs of seeming contradictions; the conception of Christ's death as a sacrifice and as a cosmic event; the interpretation of his Person as the Messiah and as the Second Adam; the conception of the *kenosis* of the pre-existent Son of God and the report of the miracles by means of which he proves himself to be the Messiah; the conception of the pre-existent Son of God and that of the virgin birth; the belief in God the Creator, and the conception of the rulers of this world; and, above all, the fact that man is on the one hand conceived as a cosmic being, and on the other hand as an independent self, which, in decision, can gain or lose its authentic existence.[1]

The unprejudiced reader cannot but feel a certain artificiality in this list of antitheses. Many of them he would deny to be opposed to each other at all. But, with regard to some among the supposed contradictions, we can put forward a perfectly satisfactory alternative reason why these different concepts should be used within the Bible in dealing

[1] *K.u.M.*, I, p. 23.

with the same realities. For example, we have an excellent reason for saying why Christ should be regarded both as the Messiah and the Second Adam, why his death should be regarded both as sacrifice and as cosmic event, why God should be regarded both as Father and as King. The reason for these varying statements is, of course, that in speaking of transcendent realities, no one human concept is adequate, and the inadequacy of these concepts is not hidden from those who use them, so that there is no contradiction in the use of all of them at once. We shall have occasion once again, in our last chapter, to raise the question of these 'contradictions'—asking whether they *are* contradictions at all, and if they are not, whether their confessedly mythical or inadequate character really discredits them so completely as Bultmann would like to believe.

V

THE EXISTENTIAL INTERPRETATION

1. Introduction

IN Bultmann's theology demythologizing and the existential reinterpretation are connected as indissolubly as are dying and rising again in the Christian faith. We are told that the Christian message must submit to demythologizing in order to rise again to a new and more splendid life in the existential reinterpretation. We have seen how Bultmann considers that the preaching power of his views rests on the significance and validity of this 'existentialist' interpretation, an interpretation which in his opinion would not be compromised in the way that myth inevitably must be. But what *is* the 'existential' interpretation? With this question we have arrived at what is probably the most baffling and tantalizing problem in Bultmann's theology, or indeed in the whole field of modern theological discussion. The use of the word 'existential' has become fashionable in philosophy and theology since the time of Kierkegaard, but the distinction between the terms '*existentiell*' and 'existential' is of crucial importance in the work of Heidegger, to which Bultmann is deeply indebted. It might therefore be assumed that Bultmann's use of this highly technical pair of terms was the same as Heidegger's, but in fact this does not appear to be the case.

2. 'Existentiell' and 'Existential' in Heidegger and Bultmann

It is probable that in the use of these two terms Bultmann does not intend to deviate from his mentor more than is necessitated by the difference of his aim, and the difference of the medium in which he is working. But it is clear that while '*existentiell*' means the same for both men, 'existential' cannot possibly mean the same thing for Bultmann as it does in *Sein und Zeit*.

Heidegger, as we have seen, defines *existentiell* understanding as 'that understanding which leads us in our existence', meaning, in everyday language, the kind of understanding which lies, unformulated, behind our actions, and directs them.[1]

An existential understanding, on the other hand, is for him 'the analysis of the ontological structures of existence.'[2] Heidegger in his book is studying the ontic phenomena of personal being, in order to disclose the underlying ontological structures, and for him an existential interpretation is an interpretation with precisely this aim in view.

Now when we look at Bultmann's remarks about existential interpretation, we find a variety of meanings, but none of them is quite the same as this. It will be best to list the various meanings given by Bultmann to the term 'existential interpretation', giving a paragraph to each.

(*a*) The first definition is an important one in Bultmann's theology. We may put it thus, 'An existential interpretation is one which seeks to explain statements of faith and theological statements as being primarily expressions of man's self-understanding.'

Near the beginning of his first essay, Bultmann describes the true though unconscious purpose of myth as being disclosed in its existential interpretation. What the existential interpretation does is to translate the objectivizing language of myth into terms which express 'how man understands himself in his world'.[3]

Further, Bultmann tells us in the same passage, that . . . 'the real purpose of myth is to speak of a transcendent power which controls the world and man, but that purpose is impeded and obscured by the terms in which it is expressed'.[4]

From this we may guess that an existential interpretation, as here understood by Bultmann, leaves room for a doctrine of the world, as well as a doctrine of man, and also for a doctrine of 'the transcendent powers which lie beyond all that is to be found in the realm of human calculation and disposability.'[5]

This sense of the term 'existential interpretation' is so important in Bultmann's thought, that it is well worth-while giving it a somewhat closer examination. In his concluding essay in the second volume of *Kerygma und Mythos*, in the middle section entitled 'Demythologizing and Existential Philosophy', he says that in every inquiry we approach our theme with certain questions in mind, and that the right question with which to approach the Bible is 'the question concerning our human existence'.

[1] Heidegger, *S.u.Z.*, p. 12.
[2] *S.u.Z.*, p. 22.
[3] *K.u.M.*, I, pp. 22-3.
[4] Ibid., p. 23.
[5] *K.u.M.*, II, p. 183.

This is a vague phrase. It might mean that faith is self-understanding and nothing more, the function of revelation being at the best to 'trigger off' a new self-understanding in man. Were this the case, then theology, at the best, would be swallowed up in anthropology. This would be subjectivism with a vengeance.

But the phrase may surely mean that the right approach to the Bible is not that of the arm-chair critic, but the approach of the man who knows that his whole existence is at stake. In this case the existential interpretation may well include a claim to tell the truth about God.

There can be no doubt that Bultmann's intention is to give this latter sense to the phrase 'the question concerning our human existence', and not the first. Thus, when he describes Paul's conversion as a change in Paul's self-understanding,[1] he goes on to enlarge this statement by saying, 'Pauline theology is not a speculative system. It deals with God, not as He is in Himself, but only with God as He is significant for man, for man's responsibility and man's salvation. Correspondingly, it does not deal with the world and man as they are in themselves, but constantly sees the world and man in their relation to God. Every assertion about God is simultaneously an assertion about man, and vice versa. For this reason and in this sense, Paul's theology is, at the same time, anthropology.'[2]

Here we may note, before passing on to the next definition, that though theology is a special science and belongs, for Bultmann, to the ontic and not the ontological level of reflection, yet he believes that, in the sense above given, it should offer an existential interpretation.

(*b*) We may put the second definition thus: 'An existential interpretation is an interpretation of man in his world before God, which is possible for the educated man of today.'

In Bultmann's opinion there are three main types of thinking in the world. Two of them are legitimate, and one is illegitimate. The illegitimate type is mythical thinking, which erroneously expresses itself in the concepts of 'objectifying thought', which are suited to deal with the empirical world round about us. But the form of thinking which is legitimate within this field is scientific thinking, itself a more precise form of our usual workaday thinking. Scientific thinking lays claim to the whole of this field, and is bound in the end to oust mythical thinking from it. There is, however, a third kind of thinking, existential thinking, which, like scientific thinking, is legitimate within its own field. This is the field of personal relations and, Bultmann would claim,

[1] *Theology of the N.T.*, E.T., vol. I, p. 188. [2] Op. cit., pp. 190-1.

the field of our relations to God and the transcendent. Consequently, when mythical thinking has been reinterpreted in existential terms, all the conflict between it and scientific thinking has been removed. There can be no conflict between scientific thinking and existential thinking, because their fields are quite different, and mythological thinking has been warned off the field on to which it had trespassed.

Here we may notice that there is a link with the existential analysis of Heidegger. For Heidegger, in disclosing the ontological structures of personal being, claims to have defined the horizons of possibility for conceptual discourse about man.

Yet the link with Heidegger may not be so close as Dr Bultmann believes. If we look at Bultmann's rejection of various views as mythical, we shall find, indeed, that sometimes the criterion for rejection is that these views run counter to the Heideggerian existential analysis. For example, according to Heidegger, the whole application of the concept of substance to human nature is an error, and due to the deceitfulness of everyday existence (*Alltäglichkeit*). So any notion of grace as 'infused', or of the sacraments working *ex opere operato* is regarded by Bultmann as impossible for modern man to accept. But as I shall hint, a good deal of what is condemned as mythical is condemned, not because it is contrary to the teaching of *Sein und Zeit*, but because it is contrary to the particular brand of closed-circle thinking which Bultmann has espoused.[1]

(*c*) It is not, however, until his concluding essay[2] that Bultmann's clearest word on the existential interpretation is spoken. Here he writes, 'Fear of demythologizing may in part be based on the unquestioned presupposition that we must choose between mythology and science, the latter being that discipline which deals with human existence as if it were an empirical object. But is there no other language than the language of myth and science? Are sentences like "I love you" or "I ask for your forgiveness" spoken in the language of science? And, if not, is their language mythological? There is indeed a language in which human existence expresses itself naïvely, and there corresponds to it a science which speaks of existence without treating it like an empirical object.'

The reference in the last clause is clearly to Heidegger's existential analysis, which claims to disclose the structure of personal being, the kind of concepts suited to language about personal being, and the horizons within which such talk is meaningful. An existential inter-

[1] See our chapter on 'Myth and Miracle'.

[2] *K.u.M.*, II, p. 187.

pretation of myth will then be an interpretation in terms suited to deal with persons and inter-personal relations.

Bultmann continues, 'It ought to have become clear that demythologizing as existential interpretation, aims at clarifying the meaning of its statements, by freeing them from the concepts of objectifying thought, the thought of myth. But certainly it does not do this only to surrender them to the concepts of the objectifying thought of science. No, the purpose of demythologizing is to secure an understanding of scripture which is free from every world-picture projected by objectifying thought, whether the objectifying thought be that of myth or that of science.'[1]

Once more we draw the reader's attention to the fact[2] that when the statements of faith, or of the Gospel message, have been demythologized they will still remain statements of ontic truth. The fact that we use the terms 'existential interpretation' is apt to mislead us here, and make us think that the material on which the existential interpretation has done its work will itself consist of something so abstract as existential understanding (in Heidegger's sense of that word).

Bultmann has tried to give us some help here by indicating that some of his own essays are essays in existential interpretation.[3] This, then, ought to mean that these essays set out to give discussions which translate the gospel out of its outworn mythological formulations, and set forth its challenge in the personal categories in which all preaching —and theology—ought to be couched, in such a manner that conflicts with science are avoided. We have yet to offer a criticism of two of these essays in our discussion of the question whether Bultmann is rightly charged with subjectivism.

3. *The charge of subjectivism*

Before we go on to discuss this charge, we must make a few comments on Bultmann's first definition of existential thinking, which constitutes for him the true method in theology. In Bultmann's opinion, statements of faith, and also statements of the faith, are regarded primarily as expressions of man's self-understanding. We will agree that there is a

[1] *K.u.M.*, II, p. 187. [2] See above, p. 96.

[3] Bultmann, *Glauben und Verstehen* II, Tübingen, 1952, pp. 162-86, 246-61 (Eng. tr. *Essays—Philosophical and Theological*, SCM Press, London, 1955, 'Prophecy and Fulfilment', pp. 182-208, and 'The Christological Confession of the World Council of Churches', pp. 273-90). See *K.u.M.*, II, pp. 179-80, note 3.

remarkable interweaving in faith between our knowledge of God and our knowledge of ourselves. And in consequence, there is in theology, a remarkable interweaving between the doctrine of God and the doctrine of man. But we must ask ourselves whether in Bultmann's thought the true order is not reversed. Faith is surely in the first place a knowledge of God in his mighty acts, and only in the second place a self-understanding. There is in Bultmann so keen a desire to avoid metaphysic and speculation about God, that the whole doctrine of God is almost evacuated of content. And when the Holy Spirit has been demythologized into 'the factual possibility of a new life revealed in faith',[1] we are left asking why God the Father should not disappear in the same way?

It is in his concluding essay in *Kerygma und Mythos*, in the third section, 'On the Action of God',[2] that Bultmann tries most decisively to rebut this charge of subjectivism. Here, in shortened form, is the argument:

Behind all objections to demythologizing lies the fear that it will be impossible to speak of God's action, or that such talk will turn out to be no more than a pictorial description of subjective experiences. For is it not mythology to speak of God's action as an objective event encountering me? Bultmann's reply is, that when he speaks of 'the action of God', he means action in a fully 'objective' sense. But if God's action cannot be spoken of as a world-phenomenon, which can be perceived in abstraction from my actual involvement with it, then I can only speak of it by speaking of myself at the same time. To speak about God's action is to speak at the same time about my existence. As we live in space and time, an encounter with God for us can only be an event which at one time or another is 'here-now'. This event, in which I am here and now addressed, questioned, judged, blessed by God, is what is indicated when I speak of the action of God.

This event is not conceived of as an irruption or insertion in the stream of empirical events. It must be conceived of as an action *in* events, such that the closed series of events in the world is left unbroken. This is not pantheism, for pantheism identifies the series of world-events with God's action, since God, for it, is immanent in the world. The view Bultmann is advocating maintains that God from time to time acts and speaks, since the believer knows that from time to time he is addressed in the grace of God which meets him in the word about Jesus Christ. Faith in God does not arise as a general proposition that

[1] *K.u.M.*, I, p. 31. [2] *K.u.M.*, II, pp. 196-208.

there is an almighty Being. It can be expressed only in the act of submission to the act of God that compels me here and now.

But if God's action can be spoken of only when my existence is spoken of, if it be true that it cannot be ascertained apart from my active involvement in it, if it does not possess that kind of objectivity which can be established by scientific experiment, and scientific thinking; then the question arises whether we are not depriving the divine action altogether of objectivity as a reality lying beyond my subjectivity.

Bultmann retorts that there is a confusion here. From the statement that only the man who has been touched by God can speak about God, and from the fact that when he speaks of God he speaks also of himself, it by no means follows that God is not real apart from faith or the act of faith. Faith claims this transcendence, and to try to prove it would be treason to faith's own nature.

Take, he argues, an illustration from the life of a child.[1] In its actions it has an instinctive understanding of its own nature. Certainly this is not explicit: it is, in Heidegger's word, *existentiell.* It guides the child in all its actions and feelings. And at the same time the child understands its parents and teachers in its love, trust, feeling of protection, and obedience. This shows that the self-understanding we have is at the same time an understanding of other persons. It is not purely subjective, but has its objective correlate.

Now the same thing, Bultmann argues, is true of the self-understanding of faith. When I meet another and love him, I gain a new self-understanding, yet this only remains genuine when it keeps its relation with the other who encounters me. In the same way, my self-understanding in faith only remains genuine when I know God's grace as 'new every morning'. I can never put this self-understanding, so to speak, in my pocket and claim it as my own. I must receive it every day fresh from God's hand.

4. Appreciation and criticism of the above

This passage shows Bultmann at his best, and it demonstrates his eagerness to maintain the trans-subjective validity of the utterances of faith. This line of thinking is, of course, not new; it is to be found at the beginning of the first book of Calvin's *Institutes*, where the fact is emphasized that our knowledge of God and our knowledge of ourselves are correlatives.

[1] *K.u.M.*, II, p. 201.

There is, however, one point which must be made at this juncture. As was suggested in our chapter on 'Mythical Thinking and the Preacher', Bultmann seems not to notice that our concept of personal relations cannot be transferred direct and without change from our relation to our human counterparts to our relation to God.[1]

Even here, therefore, there is an inadequacy in our use of concepts, when we talk about God as 'Thou' and as 'Father'. Therefore, according to Bultmann's own view, we are either speaking mythologically if, like him, we do not realize the inadequacy of our concepts, or else, if we do, we are sliding down the slippery slope of demythologizing, a *descensus Averno* which can only stop when we have arrived at language which is purely existential and non-symbolic. And I fear that this means that we shall once more be inside the subjectivist circle which we so sincerely tried to avoid. Bultmann cannot have it both ways. Either our talk is about God, in which case it must certainly be inadequate to the reality and in that sense 'mythical'. Or else it is talk about ourselves, and ourselves alone.

5. Is Bultmann guilty of subjectivism?

There can be no doubt that if Bultmann is finally caught in the morass of subjectivism, it is not without a valiant struggle to reach firm ground. We must now deal with two of his essays, to discover whether, in our opinion, he is finally able to clear his feet or not.

(*a*) The first of these essays is entitled 'What is the Meaning of Discourse about God?'[2] Since theology is the discipline which speaks about God, the *logos* about *theos*, this essay is important as a guide to his views about the task of the theologian.

[1] See also *K.u.M.*, I, p. 124, where the same mistake is made. There Bultmann says that the philosopher, *qua* philosopher, cannot speak of God's action, because he does not speak about concrete happenings at all, which occur between persons. The philosopher can only show what personal happenings are in general. But just by so doing, he can help theology to find the right concepts for speaking unmythologically about God.

We must note that here God's action, as an ontic fact, is fitted into the ontological structure of 'personal happenings in general', as if the concepts which we apply to our relation to other human beings could be transferred without change of meaning to our relationship to God.

The point that we are making in the present chapter is different from the point made against Heidegger in our second chapter, and against Bultmann in our third. The gist of the contention there is that human personal being cannot be adequately defined if the relationship to God be left out. The point now at issue is that the categories or existentials adequate to deal with other human persons are *at the best* inadequate to cover our relationship to God.

[2] *G.u.V.*, I, pp. 26-37, 'Welchen Sinn hat es, von Gott zu reden?'

Since the theme handled is so important, it will be necessary to give a fairly full summary of the central argument of this essay. Here Bultmann says that if by 'speaking of God' we mean 'speaking about God', then the words have absolutely no meaning; for in the moment that we try to speak about God, we lose the object of our discourse. For the very concept 'God' means the omnipotent, all-determining reality. But when I speak *about* God, I no longer have this thought in mind, for then I am thinking of God as an object of thought, in relation to which I can be neutral, and about which I can make statements and conjectures which I am at liberty to reject, or to accept, if I find them illuminating. But there can be no standpoint outside of God. Nor can we speak of him in general propositions which are true in abstraction from the standpoint of the speaker. No more can one speak about love, unless such speaking is also an act of love, for every other kind of speaking about love puts itself outside of love.

But to speak of God from, so to speak, a platform of neutrality is not only senseless. It is downright sinful. Even if such a conversation about God arose from a desire for him, it would be sinful, for it would fail to grasp the true significance of our relation to him, and would entail our withdrawal from the absolute claim he lays upon us. Thus all talk *about* God is sin, and it is so even when in good faith we are compelled to dispute about God.

Now let us stop for a moment to consider what Dr Bultmann has said. There appear to be here two confusions.

In the first place, there is surely a confusion between an epistemological abstraction and a rebellion of will. Because speech about God involves the former, it does not necessarily involve the latter, and therefore is not necessarily sinful. This confusion gives to the whole essay a heated emotional tone, which cannot but strike the unprejudiced reader.

There is a second confusion which has almost graver results than the first, and which is to be found throughout both this essay and the other one to be considered by us, on 'The Christological Confession of the World Council of Churches'. This is the confusion between talk about God which has its origin in a concrete situation of faith, and talk which never gets beyond that. It is true that Christian theology must start from the situation of faith. But it is equally true that in that situation it is aware of a truth which has validity beyond that situation. Even apart from theology, faith itself always claims a trans-subjective validity for its affirmations. These are inspired by a special situation, but they refer to a God who exists beyond that situation, and they make assertions about him which claim to be significant and challenging for others who are in other situations. The whole Bible bears witness to experience of God which reveals his character in such a way that generation after generation may receive this witness, and learn from experience that it is true, and worthy of all faith. The same is true of preaching.

It is strange that this obvious point should have escaped Dr Bultmann, especially strange when he has himself elsewhere pointed out the confusion, when other people have been guilty of it.[1]

Bultmann continues[2]: Today our conception of reality is constituted by the world-picture which has dominated thinking since the days of rationalism. We regard something as real when we can 'place it' in the uniform system of the world, whether we conceive of this system in terms of causal materialism or teleologically, as does idealism. This world-picture is one which abstracts from our own existence, and we are apt to complete it by regarding ourselves as objects among the other objects in the world. Such world-views (*Weltanschauungen*) are welcomed by man, even when the place they allot to him is not an exalted one. For they allow him to flee from his own responsibility. And a world-view which claims to be a theistic one, or a Christian one, is not essentially better than any other, for here not only man, but also God, is regarded from outside, looked upon as an object, and as soon as we do this we give up the primary thought of God as the reality who determines our existence.

If such discourse about God and ourselves is illegitimate, then what can we say about our existence without falling into these errors? We can say two things:

(1) That we have responsibility for our existence.

(2) That our existence is absolutely insecure, and we cannot give it security. We cannot speak about our existence, because we cannot speak about God, and we cannot speak about God, because we cannot

[1] See *K.u.M.*, II, p. 198. 'From the statement that only the believer who knows he has been touched by God, can speak about God, and that therefore the believer, when he speaks of God's action, speaks also about himself, it does not in the least follow that God is not real apart from the believer or his act of faith.'

Here, further, it is imperative also to dissent from Bultmann's illustration about love (p. 26). If a man has known from experience what love is, it is possible to make affirmations about it, which are not themselves expressions of love, which yet can be recognized by others as true, and may even help them to enrich their own experience.

[2] *G.u.V.*, I, p. 31.

speak about our existence. But if we could speak with authority from God, then we could also speak about our own existence, and *vice versa*: Discourse about God, if it were possible, would at the same time be discourse about ourselves.

Are we to conclude, then, that the solution lies in Trappism and Quietism, in silence and inactivity? No, this would be an error, for such a decision would be as much our own decision as would be any garrulous activism, and therefore would be as godless as any talk about God which forgets his supremacy and claim upon us.

But if there were a compulsion laid upon us, not of a mechanical or emotional kind, but a compulsion quite singular, which at the same time was our true freedom, then we would at the same time be able to speak both of God and ourselves. And such witness would be the witness of faith. But we can never *know* that this compulsion is laid upon us, for to know is to range among the world of objects. We cannot even take the first steps to prove or make plausible the existence of the compulsion. Anyone who asks us for the grounds of faith will receive no answer, but will be told to believe. Even such discourse is discourse about God and, as such, if there is a God, it is sinful; while if there is no God, it is meaningless. And the decision whether it has meaning, and whether it is forgiven by the God who justifies the ungodly, is not in our hands.

Perhaps it will be a help to understand what Dr Bultmann is trying to say, if we remember the Pauline statement, 'Whatsoever is not of faith, is sin.'[1] Bultmann is trying to show that concrete statements about God made under the compulsion of faith are valid, if God exists, and that all discourse about God made without faith is both sinful and meaningless. If there is a compulsion of faith laid on me to speak of God, then my doing so will not place me on neutral ground from which I imagine myself free to say this or that about God, and therefore I shall not fail of my intention, to speak about God. My talk will really be about him. And, strictly speaking, such statements about God, on Bultmann's presuppositions, in so far as they are made in faith, ought to be clear of sin.

We will certainly agree that statements about God which forget his lordship over man and the universe, are sinful, and that the true knowledge of him is one which has its origin in faith. This is what Bultmann intends to say, but he has tried to give an epistemological proof of it, claiming that the very fact that we make a statement about

[1] Rom. 14.23.

God, proves that we have rebelliously separated ourselves from him. But this is just not true, for the statements about God originating from faith involve precisely the same abstraction as do the statements made by the rebel.

In another place in this essay,[1] Bultmann says that there are no general truths about God. It is hard to know what meaning he attaches to this term 'general truths'. It may be that light is thrown on the matter by another essay in the same volume, where he asserts that theology speaks of God in his particular determined relationship to the individual at any one time, and not of God in general in distinction from man in general.[2] But, as I have already suggested, these are not exhaustive alternatives. On the basis of the first alternative, no communication to others in other situations would be possible, while the second alternative suggests an attempt to pursue the study of theology after the manner of one of the experimental sciences. Theology lies between these two extremes; it deals with an experience in which a demand is laid on the will of the individual, and it makes statements which claim transcendence of the particular situation of the speaker, and aver their own truth of God in his relationship to other men. In a sense, therefore, theological truth, like all other truth, is general. It is not satisfied with describing the experience of the person who affirms it in his concrete situation, but claims also to assert something about God, of whom it is speaking. It seeks to communicate something which it hopes that the hearer will be given power, at a later moment, to verify from his own experience.

Indeed, the lack of clarity in Bultmann's thinking is shown by the fact that he does make a number of general statements *about* God, and also *about* man. God, he declares, is 'the One who determines our existence' (note, not my existence).[3] 'God is the wholly other'.[4] God is the 'Lord of reality'.[5] In affirming this last truth, Bultmann provides an excellent instance of just that kind of passage from the concrete *existentiell* situation to a general truth, for whose validity I am contending against him. 'Because God is my Lord', he affirms, 'there is meaning in my speaking of him as the Lord of reality'.

If what Bultmann was doing was merely to assert that thought about God could not be conducted in categories suited merely to thought about empirical objects, there would be no grounds for criticizing him. But what he has in fact done, is to confine our language about him in

[1] *G.u.V.*, I, p. 27.
[2] See also *G.u.V.*, I, p. 115.
[3] *G.u.V.*, I, p. 29.
[4] *G.u.V.*, I, p. 29.
[5] Ibid., p. 33.

such a fashion that discourse about him becomes logically impossible. And then, with the disarming inconsistency which is inevitable in a situation of this kind, he proceeds to make a number of general statements about God. If this essay is to be taken as typical of Bultmann's thought, then theology will be impossible.[1]

6. A contrast with Emil Brunner

How much sounder is the general position taken by, for example, Emil Brunner in his Dogmatics![2] I choose this theologian, for his thought has also been influenced, though not immoderately, by existentialism. Brunner asserts that in faith itself the moment of thought is also present; even in Peter's confession, 'Verily, Thou art the Christ, the Son of the living God!' there is present a thought which in the confession continues to be logically expressed. Prayer, thanksgiving, praise, all are acts of thought, the thought of the heart.

But in theology thought plays a much more important part than in faith itself. What is the difference between the thinking of faith and the thinking of theology? Here, Brunner suggests, we have a dimensional change, in the reflection which substitutes a 'thinking-about' for a 'thinking-in-confrontation'. There is a change from the second person to the third person, and the personal element, 'the heart', is for the moment excluded. One is now engaged in the matter as a thinker, not feeling or willing. The act of personal decision lies, as it were, behind one, and is taken for granted. Dogmatic reflection is carried out under the general abstraction of all those elements which do not contribute to the objective grasp of the subject of inquiry or attention. Faith says 'God is the Lord', or rather, 'Thou, Lord, art my God'; and theological reflection asks, 'What does that mean?' Not, 'What, Lord, do you say to me in my existence?' but 'What does that mean in general?'[3] 'What is the particular content of this concept, "God the Lord"?'

One must not be shocked, Brunner concludes, at this assertion, as if something terrible had happened. 'True, the Word of God is not given for this purpose, but if the teaching of the church about the word of God is to be correct, this abstracting operation of thought must be undertaken. . . .'

[1] Consequently a wag has made the untranslatable pun on the title of this essay, asking, 'Welchen Sinn hat es, mit Dr Bultmann zu reden?' ('What is the point of speaking with Dr Bultmann?').

[2] E. Brunner, *Dogmatik*, I, Zürich, 1946, pp. 86-7.

[3] Surely Brunner is right in saying that the discussion of such concepts is part of theology, though Bultmann (*G.u.V.*, I, p. 115), denies it.

7. *Bultmann's essay on the Christological Confession of the World Council of Churches*

As we have seen, Bultmann directs us to some of his own writings as examples of existential interpretation. Of these, perhaps the most illuminating is his essay on the Christological Confession of the World Council of Churches.[1] Only Churches subscribing to the faith that 'Christ is Saviour and God' are admitted to the Council. It is this definition of Christ as God which Bultmann, as a New Testament scholar, calls in question. He asks whether the statement 'Christ is God' is meant to designate his metaphysical nature, or his significance. Is the pronouncement soteriological, or cosmological, or both? This, he says, is not clear. He goes on to review the Christological titles in the New Testament, saying that only once is Christ roundly there stated to be God, in Thomas's confession in the Fourth gospel, 'My Lord and my God'.[2]

There follows a succinct summary of the titles given in the New Testament to Christ. Bultmann's general conclusion is that, on the basis of Palestinian and Hellenistic mythology, there developed conceptions of the cosmic significance, divine, or semi-divine nature, and pre-existence of Christ. But, he goes on to ask, is the real intention of the New Testament to describe Christ's metaphysical nature, or his significance for me?

Bultmann concludes that the New Testament pronouncements about Jesus' divinity are not in fact pronouncements about his metaphysical nature, but seek to give expression to his significance. 'So far, then, I would say, as such pronouncements digress into objectivizing propositions, they are to be interpreted critically.'

What they really mean is that in Jesus God acts towards us, and Bultmann goes on to cite in his support a number of the many passages where certain functions are ascribed alternately to Christ and to God in, as it were, a naïve and unreflecting manner. This evidence, it may be noted, is two-edged, for it is also confidently used by those who argue that this vacillation indicates that the writers are unconsciously speaking of Jesus as sharing in the divine nature, since what is predicated of God can so simply be predicated of him.

If Bultmann be right, the divinity of Christ means that in him, more precisely in the preaching about him, God meets us with saving

[1] *G.u.V.*, II, pp. 246-61 (Eng. tr.: *Essays—Philosophical and Theological*, pp. 273-90).
[2] John 20.28.

power. 'Christ cannot be objectively established as an eschatological event, so that one could then and there believe in him. Rather he is such, indeed—to put it more exactly, he becomes such—in the encounter, when the word which proclaims him meets with belief; and, indeed, when it does not meet with belief; for whoever does not believe is already judged.'[1]

Now we will agree that our knowledge of God is a personal knowledge, a knowledge of encounter, which we cannot supplement by a scientifically demonstrable knowledge. But Bultmann is here in danger of reducing or annihilating the truth-claim of the assertions of faith. Is it only when the word is being preached and believed or rejected, that Christ is the Son of God?

In this attempt to formulate Christianity in existential terms, there is a strong reaction against the concept of substance, and what Bultmann calls 'objectivizing propositions'. There is here too an attack on the schema 'subject-object', which has a validity in dealing with the world of things but, it is claimed, can never apply either to the sphere of the human-personal or our relations with God. It is indeed possible that these concepts should be unsuited to theology, yet there is a legitimate demand that the statements of theology should be true, and if objectivity be an unfortunate term to use in this context, then we must use trans-subjective validity or some other term. It is obvious that Bultmann's intentions are to satisfy this fundamental claim of theology. But good intentions are not enough, and it is equally clear that at least some of his statements in this essay are exceedingly vulnerable.

Earlier in this chapter we came to the conclusion that he was on dangerous ground in his essay, 'What is the meaning of discourse about God?' and here again he is in trouble of the same kind. He suggests that the words 'And we believe and are sure that thou art that Christ, the Son of the living God' on his interpretation would be, 'quite simply just a confession of significance for the "moment" in which they were uttered and not a dogmatic pronouncement'.[2]

But it was never intended that these words should be a dogmatic pronouncement. They were a confession of faith, and as such they claim to be true. Bultmann's suggestion, if it means anything, means

[1] John 3.18.

[2] *G.u.V.*, II, p. 252 (Eng. tr.: *Essays—Philosophical and Theological*, p. 280. I am aware that 'moment' has here the special Kierkegaardian sense of the word, but this does not seem to alter the sense of Bultmann's statement for the better.

that a few minutes later the disciples might have said with justification, 'At the "moment" we said that you were the Christ, because we felt that way. But now the "moment" has passed, and we are not so sure.' But if the statement has real significance, it is not just the expression of the feeling of a group of people at a certain time. It is not a statement about feeling at all. It is not even an expression of their conviction that a moment ago God spoke savingly to them through Christ. It is a statement about Jesus. It signifies that they believe him to be the Christ.

Bultmann goes on to say 'How far is a Christological pronouncement also a pronouncement about me? Does he help me because he is God's Son, or is he God's Son because he helps me?'[1] Let us consider this second sentence, 'Does he help me because he is God's Son, or is he God's Son because he helps me?' Hitherto theologians have said that both of these statements are true, and that they are not, as Dr Bultmann seems to assume, alternatives. In the order of knowing, the second is true. In the order of being, the first is true.

From the decisive way in which he helps me, I am driven to make a statement about him which claims trans-subjective validity. If I am a theologian I am aware that in making this statement 'He is God's Son', I am not using the word 'Son' in its usual, literal sense. But I am convinced that I am expressing, however inadequately, a relation of Christ to God which is more than just the fact that through him God speaks to me. If it means anything, 'Christ is God's Son' holds good beyond Christ's relationship to me. In his relationship to me, this 'plus', this 'Christ beyond me', is seen shining through that relationship, 'Christ for me'. The 'Christ for me' is of such a kind, that I am aware that it has cosmic implications. He helps me in such a way that I see that he is God's Son, a statement which has meaning, relating him not only to me, but to the world, to other men, and to God himself.

So much for the order of knowing. In the order of being, the other statement, 'He helps me because he is God's Son', is also true.

For Bultmann it would appear that the sentence 'He is God's Son because he helps me', must surely mean, 'His being God's Son means no more than that he helps me'—even if that help be interpreted, as Bultmann surely means it to be, in the most decisive way, that God through him reveals or revealed in the 'moment' his saving love and command to me. But has this the necessary claim to self-transcending validity? Is it more than 'just a confession of significance for the "moment" in which it was uttered'?

[1] Ibid.

8. Conclusions

What then are we to make of Bultmann's version of the demythologizing enterprise? In the chapter on 'Mythical Thinking and the Preacher', and in this chapter, we have seen that the claim to translate myth entirely into non-mythical language could not be carried through without draining the life-blood from the Christian faith. And in this chapter we have seen that Bultmann does not carry out his demythologizing project to the bitter end, while the examples which he gives of existential interpretation at work fail to emerge convincingly from the morass of subjectivism. Not only has he been unable to prove that mythical thinking is bankrupt, but he has given us a very vague and unreliable prospectus of the existential interpretation.

This does not mean, however, that the theologian, the preacher, and the evangelist can afford to disregard the project of demythologizing. Far from it. Some of the most urgent problems in theology today are connected with this project. The men of the Bible lived in a world of thought different in many respects from ours. They expressed their beliefs about God against a background of beliefs about the origins of the created world, about angels, spirits and demons different from those which come naturally to our contemporaries. How far are modern Christians bound to accept with their faith these ancient formulations, and, if they cannot be accepted wholly, how are we to disentangle what is essential to our faith from what is no longer possible for thinking men today. And is this severance possible? It is not enough simply to set the Hebrew way of thinking over against the Greek, and to opt for the former, assuming without question that truth always lies there. However powerfully the gospel may be preached today Bultmann is right in claiming that it would be intolerable to demand that, as a price of faith, believers should be asked to accept propositions that they know to be untrue.

So much may be said for the importance of a demythologizing project in theology and preaching today. But there is another merit in Bultmann's endeavour which must be appreciated and acknowledged. Demythologizing can sometimes show that there is not, as had been supposed, a conflict between our faith and what science has a right to tell us. The existential interpretation has a virtue of its own when it reminds us that the truth which encounters us in the Bible is not a truth that leaves our will and conscience unchallenged, but a truth that God speaks to us in our life situation today, a truth that meets us when we hear or read the word of God and know that God is calling us to obedience and faith. The fatal weakness of Bultmann's position is surely this, that contrary to his own intentions his project of existential interpretation emphasizes the existential moment of the word only at the cost of compromising its transcendent reference to God.

Since this is too early a stage in our argument to give our own detailed conclusions on the nature and limits of demythologizing, we promise the reader that at a later stage in the book we shall face the problem squarely, and offer our own conclusions. For the moment it will be enough to say that we differ from Bultmann as to the extent to which it is possible, and believe that in many fields we must continue to apply our mythical concepts, though with a constant sense of their inadequacy. Yet we must be grateful to him for the contribution which he has made to the task of preaching and evangelism, by raising the problem of mythology, and developing the project of existential interpretation. He has thrust the problem before the world, and made everyone think about it, though he has not, as he believes, in principle solved it.[1]

[1] It is true, I believe, that Bultmann thinks he has in principle solved the problem of demythologizing, though he is aware of its complexity and difficulty.

In his most recent volume, *Jesus Christ and Mythology* (Eng. tr. SCM Press, London, 1960), Bultmann has expounded afresh some of the points set forth in his essay, 'Zur Frage der Entmythologisierung' (On the Problem of Demythologizing') in *K.u.M.*, II, pp. 180-208, which I have discussed above. This small book has considerable value as a straightforward and clear handling of a number of themes dealt with in various scattered places in Dr Bultmann's earlier works. But it does not appear to record any fresh developments in his thought, and so I have not in this book taken it into special consideration.

VI

MYTH AND MIRACLE

1. Introduction

AFTER dealing with the various problems raised by an existentialist theology, we must now endeavour to fulfil a promise made in the chapter on 'Mythical Thinking'. There we saw two unexpected results for preaching of Bultmann's demythologizing enterprise. One of these was the historical scepticism which produced a gospel without the Gospels, a gospel whose Jesus was more a signpost on the crossroads of decision than a human figure. And we suggested that one of the main reasons for this scepticism was Bultmann's philosophical conviction that the miracles had not and could not have taken place.

In this chapter it will be our task to investigate his reasons for this belief, and to see whether it is well-grounded. This discussion is not merely a matter of theoretical importance. Should we decide that there is no philosophical veto in principle on miracle, we shall take in general a less sceptical view of the Gospels as affording us a picture of the man Jesus. And we shall be able more confidently to believe in the mighty acts of God, and to preach them with greater assurance. Our faith will have a more buoyant and hopeful character if we believe that some, at least, of the miracle stories are records of the mighty acts of God, and not mere 'pious fictions' (the phrase is Bultmann's) pointing out the existential importance of Jesus for us.

Twenty years ago it would have been agreed in theological circles that an educated Christian could, with a good intellectual conscience, believe in the possibility of miracle.

F. R. Tennant had shown that the philosophical arguments against this possibility were very insecure. Further, the work of Heim and Brunner on the continent, and of Farmer and D. S. Cairns and others in this country, had seemed to many to break open the doors of an intellectual prison. No longer was it necessary to believe that the hand of God was held back by the barrier of a rigid system of laws through which he either could not, or would not break, in order to deliver his children. Miracle had not been impossible in New Testament days, nor was it impossible today.

Rudolf Bultmann's theology seems, therefore, to many, to surrender without striking a blow a large tract of territory to the sceptic, a territory which was won, not without blood and tears, some thirty years ago. And, what is more exasperating, he seems to surrender it to an opponent no longer attacking in force. It may be objected that Bultmann does believe in the possibility of miracle. To this objection, however, we may make the rejoinder, that while this is so, the concept of miracle, like those of prophecy and incarnation, does not pass through the mill of his theology without becoming so changed as to be almost unrecognizable. He backs up his surrender of what has been commonly known as miracle, by the assertion that no miracle recorded from the past can have importance for faith today.[1] This is however an opinion which we shall oppose in the later part of this chapter. And it is founded upon a view of the relation of faith to history and a theory of knowledge which will be unacceptable to many, and which are discussed in other chapters of this book.

Bultmann's famous essay on 'New Testament and Mythology' was not translated into English until 1951, the year when Volume I of *Kerygma und Mythos* appeared in this country. To many this exposition of his views in that essay came like a sudden thunder-plump, and they wondered what the theological foundation of some of its statements might be.

As a matter of fact Bultmann's views have a logic of their own, and have altered very little in the last twenty-five years. And on the subject of miracle the authoritative source in his writings is still the essay in the untranslated first volume of *Glauben und Verstehen*, the essay entitled 'On the Question of Miracle'.[2]

Here we have already everything on the subject of miracle that we are accustomed to recognize in the later Bultmann, save the explicit use of the term 'myth'. And therefore, since the question of myth has become more central in his theology since 1931, it is necessary to give here, once more, from among his definitions of myth that one which seems especially designed to consign the notion of miracle, as ordinarily understood, to the lumber-room of mythology.

Myth treats, says Bultmann, of what does not belong to the world of spatio-temporal events, as if it did so belong. Hence, 'it speaks of transcendent powers in an inadequate manner, conceiving of them as

[1] *G.u.V.*, I, p. 227. [2] 'Zur Frage des Wunders', *G.u.V.*, I, pp. 224-8.

analogous to powers within this world, and only superior to these powers by reason of their unpredictable character and might. That is clear in the mythical concept of miracle.[1] For in this concept the working of the transcendent power (the action of God), is conceived of as an event which interrupts, and yet at the same time links together, the natural or psychological course of events.'[2] 'Mythological thinking objectifies the divine action, and projects it on to the plane of world-events.'[3]

Miracle, thus conceived (the figure is mine, not Bultmann's), is like the halo round a saint's head in a mediaeval picture. As a photographable ring of light, it was not there, but it is painted in, because it signifies something important, the holiness and significance of the saint. The true, though unconscious, intention of the New Testament miracle stories, is understood when they are existentially, not literally, interpreted. Their real purpose is to indicate the critical importance of Christ for all men. For this is the man to whom God has done the greatest honour. The gospel preached about him has been chosen by God as the sole means of salvation, and the supreme opportunity for decision for men. Are we to accept that this, and this alone, is the status and significance of the New Testament miracles? Before we can answer this question, we must examine the essay mentioned above, 'On the Question of Miracle'.

2. *Bultmann's essay 'On the Question of Miracle'*

Here Bultmann claims that two elements are contained in the conception of miracle. First, it is conceived of as an act of God in distinction from an event arising from natural causes, or human will, or action. Second, miracle is an event contrary to nature, nature being conceived of as the course of natural events happening according to orderly sequence. (Let us henceforward call this latter concept the concept of 'prodigy'. This is the concept which today Bultmann would describe as mythical.)

Either of these two conceptions, he claims, may be developed in a onesided manner, and in theological discussion this often happens.

[1] The word used is *Mirakel*, which we shall henceforward in this chapter translate as 'prodigy', to distinguish it from *Wunder*, which we shall translate as 'miracle'. 'Prodigy' is chosen by us, for Bultmann uses the word *Mirakel* when he wishes to emphasize the sense of contrariety to law, to the exclusion of other shades of meaning.

[2] *K.u.M.*, II, p. 183.

[3] *K.u.M.*, II, p. 196.

But both of them, each in strict relation to the other, constitute the (Biblical ?)[1] conception of miracle. (The line of argument taken subsequently by Bultmann is, in fact, to accept a notion of miracle not far different from the first one, while rejecting entirely the concept of miracle as prodigy.)

Bultmann proceeds to argue that the conception of miracle as prodigy is impossible for us today. For us conformity to law is not an empirical concept, but a presupposition of all our thinking about the world. For us it is impossible to conceive clearly an event within the context of nature which is contrary to nature. So the thought of prodigy has to be surrendered, and in any case it has no religious value. For such actions might be done by magicians or devils just as well as by God. Christian faith has therefore every reason to get rid of this concept, though the Bible records events which could only be described as prodigies.[2]

In comment at this point I shall say that I think we may safely let go the concept of prodigy, as defined by Bultmann. Thus here for reasons to be given we shall express a qualified agreement with him. But we must secure our position by making three points against him.

(1) The assertion that the notion of conformity to law is a presupposition of all our thinking about the world, in the form in which Bultmann states it, is an expression of a Kantianism which is today by no means so secure or authoritative as he believes it to be.[3]

(2) Bultmann here confuses two things, when he speaks about an event within the context of nature which is contrary to nature.

(*a*) An event which illustrates an 'infraction' of the laws of causation, an event which has no cause within the natural world, because God is its cause.

(*b*) An event which is contrary to the *usual* course of nature, an event strange and startling.

When he claims that the miracles of Christ have the character of prodigies, he assumes that they fall under heading (*a*), whereas at the most all that can be said is that they fall under heading (*b*). It may safely be said that the conception of prodigy as he defines it is not to be found in the Bible. The Biblical writers certainly believed in ordinances of nature, but they had not developed the thought of orderly causal sequences with the rigidity which later tempted men to think

[1] This word is not in Bultmann's text, but is inserted by me as a query.

[2] Bultmann claims later (p. 227), that especially the miracles of Jesus are depicted by the New Testament in this light.

[3] This point will be taken up later in this chapter.

of miracles as demonstrable infractions of natural law, and therefore, on that score, as proofs of God's existence.

The view of miracle criticized by Bultmann as 'prodigy' is found, rather uncertainly formulated, in the *Summa* of Aquinas,[1] but it became a staple of apologetic thought in the seventeenth and eighteenth centuries. Tennant has rightly said that this view is really useless for the purpose of apologetics, since it would never be possible to demonstrate that there was no natural secondary cause of an event.[2]

(3) While the conception of miracle as proof of God's existence because it is an infraction of the law of causation is absent from the Bible, there are certain passages in the Old Testament where miracle is looked upon as a demonstration of God's existence in a different manner. In some narratives God or his agents are reported as having done startling things with a view to authenticating a message or vindicating a person. There is the story of Moses' rod, which became a serpent, Gideon's miraculously dry and wet fleece, and there is the fire which destroyed the prophets of Baal. This conception of miracle is, however, contrary to the central insight of the New Testament. It is not found in the Fourth Gospel, whose teaching about 'signs' is much more subtle than a careless reading might lead one to suppose. But in this sense, it must be admitted that the conception of miracle as prodigy is to be found in the Old Testament, though not in the sense that Bultmann claims. And for the reason given by Tennant, not for Bultmann's reasons, we may be ready to drop the conception of prodigy as event contrary to law. It is neither Biblical, nor does it achieve what it sets out to do.

Bultmann's argument continues. There can be no doubt that faith is vitally interested in miracles, in so far as miracles signify 'acts of God in contrast to natural events'. Certainly the concept of prodigy safeguards this notion of contrast, but we have seen that it is impossible for modern thought. Must we then give up the notion of miracle altogether, though it is essential to faith, or can we retain the notion of miracle, while rejecting the notion of prodigy?

[1] *Summa*, I, 105, 6. 'I answer that the word "miracle" is derived from admiration, which arises when an effect is manifest, whereas its cause is hidden; as when a man sees an eclipse without knowing its cause. Now the cause of a manifest effect may be known to one, but unknown to others; as an eclipse is to a rustic, but not to an astronomer. Now a miracle is so called, as being full of wonder; as having a cause absolutely hidden from all, and this cause is God. Wherefore those things which God does outside those causes which we know, are called miracles.'

[2] F. R. Tennant, *Miracle*, p. 67.

There is one way out of this impasse, which turns out to be a cul-de-sac. That is the line taken by Schleiermacher, who gave up the notion of a divine action in contrast to natural events, expounding a view which led to the conclusion that all events are miraculous. This view Bultmann describes as 'the evacuated concept of miracle'. Thus the word 'miracle' would become nothing more than a religious term to describe 'event'.

No, says Bultmann, the concept of miracle as God's action is in absolute contradiction to the concept of nature, and it is also essential to Christian faith. Therefore, as soon as it is entertained, it demands nothing less than the cancellation (*Aufhebung*)[1] of the whole thought of nature as a system conformed to natural law. The contradiction between the thought of miracle and the thought of nature as a system conformable to law remains, but the contradiction is now not between the system and an event lying *within* it, but between the miracle-event and nature conceived as a system. The event and the system of nature, if one may so put it are the objects of mutually incompatible and temporally successive outlooks.

Faith in God, and faith in miracle, Bultmann continues, are identical. Only in the event of the miracle of God's revelation becoming actual *can* we believe, and no other grounds for belief can be given than the fact of the occurrence. Miracle is in no sense a verifiable event in the world, for to verify it would be to separate it from God, and God cannot be verified or perceived. The assertion that an event is a miracle is in flat contradiction to its verification as a world-event. Faith is the contrary of sight, and faith in miracle is the contrary of all that I see in the world. My inability to see world-events as miracles is the result of my godlessness. The thought of nature as a system conformed to law is in fact a sinful one. But I cannot give up this outlook by exerting an effort of will, and it is idle to pretend that I can.

Let us here interpose some critical remarks. First, with regard to the assertion that miracle is in no sense a verifiable event in the world, Dr Bultmann fails to draw a necessary distinction. He would surely concede that when faith sees a miracle, it sees that miracle in, or through, certain events in the world. For it is of such events that we have experience. And these events are in principle verifiable. But for the miracle to be seen *as a miracle*, there must be faith, which is enabled

[1] I am aware that in the thought of Hegel this term does not mean mere negation, but has in it the notion of synthesis, the affirmation of what was of value in the position negated. But the term in Bultmann's use of it seems not to bear any such positive meaning.

to interpret these events, as it were, in depth, as the action towards the believer of a personal God.

Thus the event which we see as miracle is in principle verifiable as event. It is only the fact that it is a miracle which is not in this sense verifiable. Take an instance. A man on a desert island is dying of thirst. He puts out an empty pail on the shore, and prays for rain. The rain comes. The coming of the rain is a verified event. But the fact that this event is a miracle, or an answer to prayer, is not verifiable. Now the fact that this event is miracle is not incompatible with its being also an ordinary perceptible occurrence, as Bultmann maintains. It is merely different from it!

It is owing to the fact that the events of a miracle *can* be separated from God, contrary again to Bultmann's assertion, that it is possible for miracle to be misinterpreted by unbelief. From this separability arises the possibility of failing to see these events as also divine action, as miracle, the possibility of seeing their constituent verifiable facts as strange natural events, and nothing more.

Let us further consider Bultmann's grounds for the position he takes up in these pages. He declares, 'The assertion that an event is a miracle is in flat contradiction to its verification as world event.'[1] What leads him to this conclusion? He is forced to it only if he believes that our knowledge of a world-event as such depends upon its being ranged among other events according to a certain pattern of causation. This pattern must be such that it permits no divine initiative within the world. If we accept this view, we arrive at his extremely gloomy conclusions that 'Faith is the contrary of sight,' and 'All faith in miracle is the contrary to all that I see in the world.' There can, if one holds these views, never be any evidence, however ambiguous, within the series of world events, which might count as favourable to faith. It should be noticed that on this view miracle has been so completely reduced to the world of interiority that any discourse about it is on a level with assertions about the immediacy of feeling.

Following Bultmann's line of reasoning we come, in the end, to his extraordinary assertion that the thought of nature as a system conformed to law is in fact a sinful one, from which we cannot escape except under the momentary compulsion of faith.[2] This would lead to the astounding conclusion that all the blessings of science were due to our lack of faith, a very remarkable deviation from the teaching of the

[1] *G.u.V.*, I, p. 220.
[2] *G.u.V.*, I, p. 225.

Bible, which claims that man's lordship over the created world is a gift from God his Father.

In the next section of his essay, entitled 'The Reality of Miracle',[1] Bultmann continues: there is, indeed, only one miracle, the miracle of God's grace to the godless; forgiveness, not as a general idea, but as an event. The Jews were legalists, they understood themselves in terms of their visible achievements, and they wanted to understand God in terms of his. Therefore they demanded a sign, a prodigy. But they did not feel the need of the real miracle of forgiveness; indeed it was an offence to them. For to receive forgiveness is to give up all attempt to rely upon one's past achievements. There is only one possibility of our becoming free of our past; that God should forgive us.

The outlook resulting from this is not a speculative theory, for it can only be received from moment to moment as we hear the voice of God telling us that we are forgiven men. The New Testament, admittedly, speaks of other miracles than this.[2] These have the character of prodigies. The stories of healings by Christ tell of acts which were events for men whom they concerned in the past. Even if they were established as trustworthy accounts, they do not concern us immediately. They are no works of Christ, in the sense that redemption is his work. 'Therefore in the discussion,' says Bultmann, 'we must surrender to the critics without reserve the "miracle of Jesus", in so far as they are events of the past, and we must insist with the utmost emphasis that Christian faith can have no interest in proving their possibility or actuality. Christ is only actual and present for us as the preached Christ, and so these miracles can only come in question for us as belonging to the preaching about him, as witness.' This means that they have the same ambiguity as the figure of Christ. They can be interpreted by faith or by unbelief. They cannot prove that Jesus was the Christ. The question is whether we are content to see Jesus as a merely relative historical figure in the past, or as God's miracle for our salvation in the present.

This material about the miracles of Jesus must be taken up again at a later stage of this chapter in relation to the question of preaching on miracle. For the moment we must confine our attention to the epistemological background of Bultmann's views on miracle. As we have seen, he sets in the sharpest opposition the spheres of knowledge and of faith. Theologically, we know that faith is opposed to works, and that works

[1] *G.u.V.*, I, pp. 221-6.
[2] *G.u.V.*, I, p. 227.

are sinful, if regarded as a means of justifying ourselves before God. Faith, on the other hand, holds on to God 'in spite of the evidence'. What is easier, more tempting and, superficially more edifying, than to say that the sphere of scientific knowledge is essentially godless and sinful, because it belongs to the sphere of works? We cannot lift ourselves by our efforts out of the sphere of works, we cannot lift ourselves out of the sphere of knowledge of nature where law-abiding processes operate. But in the moment, and for the moment when God speaks to us, and we receive forgiveness, we are enabled to live by faith, which is the contrary of works, and to see miracle.

This may be plausible, but it is surely one of the most illegitimate uses to which man has ever put the doctrine of justification by faith. For here Bultmann, as a philosopher of religion, is using that doctrine to escape from the disastrous results of his faulty epistemology. It was not to facilitate confusions of this kind that the doctrine of justification by faith was given to mankind.

Let us sum up Bultmann's arguments thus far. It is not, he believes, possible to regard miracle as an action of God breaking into, and yet linking, the series of natural events. Nor is it possible to think of all events as miraculous, on the ground that all come from God. The notion of miracle is necessary to faith, but contradicts the thought of a series of natural events in conformity to law, which is essential to science and knowledge of the world in general. The only way out, accordingly, is to acknowledge that in the act of knowing the world, and in the act of faith we have two contradictory activities, and that we alternate between the one and the other, not voluntarily. For we cancel out the idea of a system of nature only in so far as God empowers us to the act of faith.

What has led to this disastrous conclusion? It is Bultmann's view of scientific knowledge and its presuppositions, and to a criticism of this view we must proceed. His latest utterance on this theme is to be found in the second volume of *Kerygma und Mythos*, in his concluding essay there. Here he says that for mythical thinking the world and world-events are 'open', open, that is, for the intrusion of transcendent powers, and consequently not watertight. From the standpoint of scientific thought the world and world-events are 'closed', closed, that is, to the intrusion of powers not belonging to the world. The argument continues, 'It is not at all relevant for critics to point out that the world-picture of natural science today is no longer that of the nineteenth century, and it is naïve to seek to use the relativization of the causal law to refurbish the belief in miracle, as if by this relativization the door had been opened for the intrusion of transcendent powers. Does science today renounce experiment? So long as it does not, it stands in the tradition of thought that began in Greece with the question of the cause, and the demand that a reason be given for things.'[1]

Bultmann here assumes that the fact that science has not abandoned experiment proves that belief in a closed system of the kind he declares necessary for systematic knowledge of the world, has not been abandoned. In such a world there is no place for any divine action.

3. *An alternative view of miracle*

But there is a different outlook upon this matter which has many persuasive arguments on its side, and many weighty names behind it. If we can accept this view, the whole Bultmannian impasse is avoided, and freedom is left for the possibility of miracle. One form of this view is expounded by Emil Brunner, who says that whatever the outcome of the determinist-indeterminist controversy may be, we do not have to wait to see the end-result before we take our stand on the problem of miracle.[2] For pan-causalism was refuted long ago. All scientific inquiry is governed by two principles.

(1) The principle of economy (*Sparsamkeit*); (2) the principle of openness to reality. There can be no doubt that causality exists. Galileo's laws of movement are a witness to this. There is, accordingly, a perfectly natural tendency to explain all events in terms of this (mechanical) causality. But here the principle of openness to reality supervenes. Observation of organic processes was always a factor limiting the applicability of causal mechanism. The causal formula may continue to operate, but it is quite inadequate to explain organic events in their essential appearances, e.g., biology must explain the part in terms of the whole, and not merely in terms of elementary processes working the one upon the other in a causal manner.

Another startling novelty arises when intellect is at work. In each case the higher-level explanation, seen from the standpoint of the lower-level one, appears as a kind of 'miracle', and the possibility arises that there is a last level, the level of the freedom of God. This, if it exists, is miracle in the proper sense of the word. It breaks through the

[1] *K.u.M.*, II, p. 181.

[2] E. Brunner, *Offenbarung und Vernunft*, Zürich, 1941, pp. 290-305 (Eng. tr.: *Reason and Revelation*, SCM Press, London, 1947, ch. 19, 'Science and the Miracle of Revelation', pp. 294-309).

realm of intellectual freedom of man just as that breaks through the realms of the mechanical and the organic, though it does not annihilate these lower realms any more than each of them annihilates the realm lying directly below it. Thus far Brunner.

Now, according to Bultmann, the only possibility of our admitting a divine causality to be active in the phenomena known by 'objectifying thought' (*Objektivierendes Denken*), would be given if we could claim that God broke the causal nexus. Bultmann seems to think that 'Either God breaks in as one cause among others on the mechanical cause-level, or else there is a closed system of causes. If God breaks in in such a manner, then it is useless for science to go on experimenting. Science does go on experimenting, and this means that it rejects the notion of divine action as impossible.'

But if Brunner's argument holds good, the notion of God's action does not *replace* the other categories of interpretation. There are cases where faith holds that in order to understand what has happened, we must believe that God's action has *supplemented* the other causalities. If Brunner's view be right, as I believe it is, then the world of objectifying knowledge is not such a unity as to demand an *a priori* exclusion of higher categories at any point. We must not expect to find that there will be universal agreement as to what categories are adequate to interpret any given situation, but we must repudiate the claim, in the name of a supposed 'Science', to reject *a priori* the use of a 'higher' category which may seem to illumine the matter before us.

Further, if Brunner be right, the error of Bultmann is to regard all causality as of one type and, since God's agency in the world cannot be thought of in terms of this model, recourse is had to the thought of temporally successive and mutually cancelling world-outlooks, in order to preserve the reality of miracle, which is confessedly essential to faith.

At this point it is relevant to adduce certain evidence from a philosophical quarter, which may be thought to corroborate Brunner's point of view, though the context from which it is taken is not that of the discussion of miracle, but of human freedom. In his book, *The Concept of Mind*,[1] Professor Gilbert Ryle speaks of the bogy of mechanism, and says that the laws which the physicists have found may, in one sense, govern everything that happens, but do not ordain anything that happens, since the laws of nature are not *fiats*. He gives the brilliant illustration—it is confessedly no more than an illustration—of a scientifically trained spectator, unfamiliar with chess or any other

[1] Gilbert Ryle, *The Concept of Mind*, Hutchinson, London, 1949, pp. 76-9.

game, who is permitted to look at a chess-board in the intervals between the moves. He does not yet see the players making the moves. After much research he will have worked out the moves of chess, and then at last is allowed to see the players in action. He commiserates with them on their bondage, telling them that 'The whole course of what you tragically dub your "game" is remorselessly foreordained. Heartless necessity dictates the play, leaving in it no room for intelligence or purpose.'

This illustration, Ryle continues, is meant only to prove that there is no contradiction in saying that the same process, such as the move of a bishop, is in accordance with two principles of completely different types, and that neither of them is reducible to the other, though the one of them presupposes the other.

G. J. Warnock has similarly shown that certain phenomena are susceptible both of a mechanical and a teleological explanation, the latter supervening upon the former, rather than cancelling it out.[1]

We see a number of golf-balls flying through the air, and landing short of a row of bunkers. A mechanical explanation of this could be given in terms of speed of impact of club-face on the balls, conditions of atmosphere, weight of balls, and so on. But we feel that more light has been thrown on the matter, when we see the player walk up, and hear from him that he has been practising playing balls just short of a bunker, over which he knows that he cannot drive in one full shot from the tee, and that the whole series of events has been planned.

One last illustration may be given, which more closely illuminates the problem of miracle. A man is in a dark room, and hears a sound of tapping. At first he thinks in terms of a purely mechanical explanation of the sound. Perhaps the wind is coming in through an open french window in the next room, and swinging it to and fro. But suddenly the situation, as it were, develops for him a new dimension. He springs to the conclusion that someone in the next room is trying to communicate with him.

What happens to make him come to this conclusion? He does not go through the possible purely mechanical explanations of the sound one by one, decide that none of them will do, and argue with himself, 'Therefore a person is trying to get in touch with me.' No, he suddenly comes to the conclusion—and here there is no infallibility of judgement more than anywhere else—'There is something purposive in these

[1] G. J. Warnock, Essay VI in *Logic and Language*, O.U.P., London, 1953, p. 96. 'Every event has a cause.'

sounds; someone is trying to communicate with me.' The category of mechanical causation has not been rejected, not been proved to be broken. But it has proved *inadequate* for the interpretation of the situation. Here the factor of 'openness to reality' mentioned by Brunner has come into play. What the listener in the dark room does is not to infer from the noises to the existence of a person as the cause of them. He sees a new depth in the situation; he interprets a person seeking to communicate with him *in* these sounds.

In spite of the obvious imperfections of the analogy,[1] may we not use this experience as a model of what happens when faith sees certain events as miraculous? We are, on occasion, convinced that no mechanical explanation alone, and also no explanation in terms of human purpose alone, would ever be adequate to explain a situation, which speaks to us of a divine act of deliverance in response to our need, or, perhaps, even in answer to our prayers.

Looking back now on Bultmann's two definitions of miracle, if we affirm the general position enunciated by Brunner we can see that the second of Bultmann's definitions, the definition of miracle as prodigy, becomes quite unnecessary. If orderly sequence be understood as the course of events in mechanical causation, then it is not necessary for an event to interrupt this before we can hold it to be a free act of God. The first definition of Bultmann remains, however, in full power. 'Miracle is conceived of as an act of God in distinction from an event arising from natural causes, or human will, or action.' (It is surely not assumed in this definition that there are no natural causes, no human will, no human action in such events. Many of the Biblical miracle stories assume human agents to have been active. The divine agency is however supposed to have been there in addition to the other agencies, supervening upon them.) Unlike Bultmann, however, we do not have to accept the truly desperate device of the mutually cancelling, temporally successive world-outlooks in order to admit the possibility of miracle.

If the line of argument propounded here be sound, then this frankly untenable position which Bultmann has taken over from his teacher Herrmann,[2] can be evacuated. The reaction of one critic who listened to an exposition of this view may be given. He sat silent for a moment, and then said, 'Ah, I see. In the moment of faith, God by his grace

[1] Chief among these imperfections being, of course, the fact that God has not a physical body.

[2] Herrmann, *Offenbarung und Glaube*, pp. 34, 37.

enables me to believe what I know is not true.' This may be unsympathetic, but it has point.

4. An alternative line of argument

Thus far in this chapter, we have, in opposition to Bultmann, assumed the validity of different categories of interpretation at different levels, as Brunner does, none contradicting the others, and each higher category supplementing the lower ones where necessary. Now, for the sake of argument, let us accept the validity of Bultmann's assumption, that God's freedom cannot be accepted within the field of objectifying thought, if mechanical causation be accepted as a category constitutive for thinking within this field. It will now be our line of inquiry to ask whether, even on the presuppositions accepted by us for the purposes of argument a moment ago, the category of causal mechanism is by any means able to bear the weight which Dr Bultmann lays upon it. There are many philosophers today who would consider Bultmann's acceptance of causal mechanism as the unquestioned presupposition of all our thinking—in Kant's phrase, the transcendental precondition of our knowledge of objects in general—as itself, in these days, a mark of no inconsiderable philosophical naïveté. It is not only, as he seems to suppose, in relation to atomic processes,[1] that doubts have been raised, and questions asked. For many years philosophers of the first rank of eminence have been criticizing the concept of mechanical causation, and claiming that it is by no means the precision instrument in scientific research which Dr Bultmann assumes it to be.

It is generally agreed, and apparently also by Bultmann,[2] that particular causal laws can claim no absolute necessity. There is, however, more debate about the status of the universal law of causality, which Kant thought he had demonstrated to be a precondition of all knowledge of the phenomenal world. It appears that von Wright believes that while the universal causal law can never have logical necessity, yet, if the time-series is to continue, it will hold good.[3]

Warnock, on the other hand, treats the universal causal principle more cavalierly, suggesting that, far from being a universal precondition of all knowledge, it is 'vacuous and utterly uninformative'.[4]

[1] *K.u.M.*, II, p. 181. [2] Ibid.

[3] G. H. von Wright, *The Logical Problem of Induction*, p. 32.

[4] G. J. Warnock, *Essays on Logic and Language*, vol. II, ch. VI, 'Every event has a cause.'

Here Warnock argues that the universal causal law is not a necessary presupposition of all scientific investigation, fulfilling in the natural sciences the

Bertrand Russell has said that modern science hardly uses the concept of cause at all, but that it has been wished on the scientists by the philosophers. Its place has been taken by deterministic systems, which are empirically discovered, of finite extent, and for which no such high *a priori* claims are made as the Kantians have put forward on behalf of the general law of causality.

There are certain defects in the concept of causation to which Russell drew the attention of his readers as long ago as 1913.[1] What, in effect, he asks, is an event? It is obviously something which is expected to recur, and to recur frequently. If no event ever happened twice in the history of the universe, then the discovery of causality as a method of securing the prediction of events would obviously be impossible. As a matter of fact no happening does ever precisely and exactly occur twice. For there will always be some difference, however minute. The notion of an event therefore presupposes that certain details have been left out of the description of a happening, as irrelevant for the purposes of predicting the recurrence of another happening coming after it, which investigators are to regard as its effect.

But it may turn out that one of these details has not in fact been irrelevant, and that its influence has been sufficient to prevent the repetition of the expected sequence. In which case the investigator will go back and define the prior happening more precisely, in the hope that some unnoticed detail, which he suspects has proved of crucial importance, will not be neglected this time. But the more precise his definition becomes, the less is the likelihood that the recurrence will happen. So he is faced by two alternative choices. Either he may define the prior event somewhat roughly, so that there will be a high probability of its recurring, attended by a high probability that it will not be accompanied by the hoped-for sequence. Or else he may define the prior happening with a great deal of precision. In which case there will be a high degree of probability that *if* the first event does recur, it will be followed by the expected sequence. But there will be a correspondingly high degree of improbability that the first event will recur at all! Thus far Russell.

same role as is fulfilled by the laws of logic in the deductive disciplines. Nor is it, as is often supposed, a recommendation for heuristic procedures. It has not the necessity of tautologous analytic *a priori* statements, yet like them it cannot be falsified in experience. It seems to make statements about the real world, like synthetic *a posteriori* propositions, but it does not in fact do so. It is, in effect, vacuous and uninformative.

[1] Bertrand Russell, *Mysticism and Logic*, Allen & Unwin, London, 1918, ch. VIII, 'On the Notion of Cause'.

The reader of this book may feel inclined to ask what is the purpose of introducing this criticism of the category of causality in a chapter where obviously both space and the lack of specialized knowledge on the part of the writer forbid a detailed discussion of the theme.

In a recent article, Professor Gregor Smith has warned us against the desire to locate God in the gaps which have not yet been filled up by science. 'God,' he says truly, 'is not the answer to questions of that kind. . . . The modern form of resistance to the methods of rational investigation, which we find chiefly in popular works in defence of religion against science, is nothing more than a flight into illusion.'[1]

It is not with the purpose of flying into illusion that the criticism of the causal principle has been here undertaken, and it will be remembered that the main argument of this chapter has been along another line, urging that the causal series within the empirical field offers no veto in principle to miracle. But the criticism of the causal concept has been offered with the purpose of suggesting that in fact an unbroken series of causes and effects is not today universally postulated as necessary, and that a denial of the category of cause as a transcendental precondition of knowledge is philosophically respectable, and that there are certain essential characteristics in the concept which prevent its close-fitting application to experience. The result of these reflections is, I suggest, in general to indicate that mechanical causality, whatever its range and scope, is only one category among a number, and that while it does reveal certain aspects of truth, it yet has only a limited applicability and value.

5. Further epistemological and theological reflections in connexion with the problem of miracle

Warnock has admitted that his conclusion that 'Every event has a cause' is vacuous and uninformative, may well cause some dissatisfaction.[2] There is a natural feeling that it does say something, and, furthermore, something of the greatest importance. This feeling, however, he believes, arises from confusion between it and other, important, propositions. There are many people today who do seek for statements of law, and those who 'seek to formulate such statements meet with considerable, and, on the whole, with constantly increasing, success'. The implication here, he suggests, is that unless there were,

[1] *Kerygma und Mythos*, IV, Hamburg, Volksdorf, 1955, p. 79.
[2] G. J. Warnock, Ibid.

in fact, a very great reliability and a considerable measure of regularity of sequence in events, we would not be able to gain our concepts, or to formulate laws at all. To state this is, however, something very different from stating the universal law of causation.[1]

It seems to me that there is another consideration which influences us, when we question the credibility of a narrative, uncertain whether we are to accept it as a possibly correct account of what happened. Through our own experience we come to have a conviction that we approximately know what kind of things happen in the real world. To say this is not that we reject some stories as involving a breach in causality, for we accept many phenomena in our own experience of which we can give no causal explanation. But we read accounts of past events in the light of the analogy of our own experience. Men who have seen a ghost will, other things being equal, be more likely to believe their neighbour when he tells them that he has seen one! The same thing would be true, if any of us were to have had a vision of angels. We would not accept any and every story, throwing criticism to the winds, but our minds would be open, in a new way. Quite legitimately, we try to explain the unknown and provisionally inexplicable in terms of what we have experienced and understood. In dealing with the stories of Biblical miracles, all of us are rationalists up to a point. It is the degree that differs. The more unlike the recorded event is to the analogy of our own experience, the stronger the evidence necessary to convince us that things happened as they are recorded to have done. The confusion of these two valid, if not precise, arguments from the regularity of sequence in events, and from the analogy of our own past experience, with the seemingly rigorously precise scientific universal causal law, has given to them, when used critically against miracle, a prestige and apparent conclusiveness, which they do not in fact merit or possess.

To these epistemological considerations we must now add a critical reflection which is itself religious and theological and which has clearly much influenced the views of Bultmann. There lies behind his scepticism a justified fear that miracles, understood as manifest and unambiguous events in space and time, would constitute such a lifting of the divine incognito as would endanger the moral and spiritual character of faith, which is an entrusting of ourselves to the unseen God who meets us in forgiveness and grace. If miracle were too obviously startling an

[1] And the affirmation of this law, we may add, if Brunner be right, does not itself imply the negation of the possibility of miracle.

event, then, it may be said, there would no longer be room for faith, which would prematurely be swallowed up in sight.

The Fourth Gospel, if it were all taken as a literal account of what happened, would be open to this objection. Here the incognito of Christ appears retrospectively to be lifted, and his claims are made openly from the first. That John does preserve the notion of the judicial blinding of the enemies of Christ, is true, but the whole picture has a spiritual rather than a biographical verisimilitude.

It may be felt that even in the Gospel and recorded miracles of Mark, there is something of the same character. Written from the standpoint of men who had experienced the resurrection, even this gospel makes the figure and mighty deeds of Jesus stand out so obviously, that the blindness of the disciples, who for long did not recognize who he was, seems hard to understand. It is intelligible that readers may feel that in a Christ who not only healed the sick, but raised the dead, walked on the water, fed thousands from a few loaves and fishes, Mark has painted a picture in which there may be heightenings of fact. There lies here a real problem which must be honestly faced.

It is a true observation, which is sometimes made in this context, that Christ was not an ordinary man, and that therefore he must be expected to have done extraordinary deeds. Yet it is not wholly relevant in this context. For here the critical argument is not being made from the analogy of our experience and performance to his. In that case the difference between him and us would be wholly relevant. Here, however, the argument is being made from the nature of faith itself, which, if the works were too obvious and startling, might be endangered. And yet, on the other hand, we may be sure that one thing is central in the gospel tradition, that Jesus refused to give a sign,[1] and that both he and the gospel writers believed that the acts which he did were not calculated to batter down opposition, or to serve as supernatural attestations of revelation, but were regarded rather as indications to faith of the presence of the Kingdom.

6. *The implications of Bultmann's view for preaching and evangelism*

We must now return to the concluding pages of Bultmann's essay on miracle, in order to examine his views on the gospel miracle stories, and see what effect these views, if accepted, will have on theology,

[1] In the sense of a proof to his enemies of his authority.

preaching, and evangelism. In these pages,[1] Bultmann declares that the miracles recorded in the gospels have the character of prodigies. The stories of healings by Christ tell of acts which were events for men whom they concerned, in past days. Even if they were established as trustworthy accounts, they do not concern us immediately. They are no works of Christ in the sense that redemption is his work. 'Therefore . . . we must surrender to the critics without reserve the "miracles of Jesus", in so far as they are events of the past, and we must insist with the utmost emphasis that Christian faith can have no interest in proving their possibility or actuality . . .' Christ is actual and present for us only as the preached Christ, and so these miracles can come in question for us only as belonging to the preaching about him, as witness to him. This means that they have the same ambiguity as all preaching has, and as the figure of Christ himself has, they do not demonstrate his authority and short-circuit the need for faith. The question is whether we are content to see Christ as a merely relatively important figure in the past (which he is for the unbeliever), or as God's miracle in the present, there before us challenging our decision and offering us salvation.[2]

In discussing this passage let us ask what is the ground on which we are being invited to throw the miracles of Jesus 'in so far as they are events of the past' to the wolves of sceptical criticism? We seem to be faced by an Either-Or. Either the verifiable events of the past, as seen by unbelief, or God's miracle in the present, the word spoken in Christ for our forgiveness. Either history or preaching. Preaching then has nothing to do with history. History deals with the past, preaching with the present.[3]

Now all that here needs to be said about this whole way of looking at things is that it is utterly contrary to the outlook of the gospel writers. They included in their witness and preaching the assertion that certain empirical events had taken place, and that in these events they saw the action of God. The events themselves were public and verifiable. The action of God was hidden in them, and visible as such only to faith. Bultmann (and Gogarten whom he has misled on this issue) seem to assume that any reference to the historical factual character of any past event, means a dependence on verification which is destructive of the life of faith. This would only be the case if it

[1] *G.u.V.*, I, pp. 227-8.

[2] The passage is too long for reproduction verbatim, but this is the best summary of a tangled argument that is in my power.

[3] We shall be dealing with this view in the next chapter, 'The Flight from History'.

implied the belief that God had at some point in the past offered himself for public inspection, so that a reference to history, if well established, would amount to proof of revelation. The doctrine that the miracles were intended as proofs of Christ's divinity would be consonant with such a view, but neither did the New Testament men regard them in this light, nor does modern theology do so. It is only when one is moved by philosophical prejudices against the possibility of miracles, and when one's mind has been befogged by the belief in a divorce between preaching and past history that one can surrender them in the wholesale manner Bultmann does to the critics. And we must notice that on the grounds he here gives us, it is not as miracles that they are no immediate concern of ours, but because they are 'the works of a man in the past'. Thus all the historical actions of Christ would be declared of no significance for preaching, as historical actions. As stories told about him, without any question as to their facticity being raised, Bultmann believes that they still have the power to mediate God's challenge and salvation to men. Here again, surely the atmosphere is very different from that of the Bible, with its emphasis on the mighty acts of God.

In contrast with this passage, it will be of interest to cite a passage about the miracles from another writer, expressing a different outlook.

'These signs, therefore, are integral parts of the revelation, and not adjuncts to it. They are revelations of the ideal purpose of God for mankind, and therefore of his character. They must therefore necessarily influence our idea of God. Inasmuch, also, as they imply the coming into the order of nature of powers that cannot be explained in terms of mere nature, they must inevitably affect our whole conception of the world. And, finally, as they are works wrought through the Perfect Man, and are meant by him to be imitated by imperfect men, they must affect our conceptions of the possibilities of men, and the possibilities and range of prayer.'[1]

If this be so, then is it not important for faith and for preaching to know whether we can honestly believe that Christ's miracles were in principle possible? And may not the further question be asked, 'Why should not events in the past of other people have revelatory significance for me now? Can the living God not speak to me through what he did for a man in the past? Is it of no importance for my faith today, in my condition of physical weakness, that in his revelation of himself in Christ, he is seen (by faith) to be a God who cares for the deliverance

[1] D. S. Cairns, *The Faith that Rebels*, SCM Press, London, 1928, p. 93.

of his children from disease, and for the health of the body as well as that of the soul?' Thus for us, if we reject Bultmann's views, the preaching of the gospel from a miracle story, for example from that of the resurrection, is a quite different and a much more powerful thing. For example, our preaching of the resurrection will have more power and conviction if we can believe that in the resurrection we have one of the mighty acts of God, and not just an aspect of the significance of the cross. In the chapter 'Will this Preach?' we shall take up this point again, and deal with it in more detail.

There is another point which falls to be made here. The acceptance of miracle as in principle does not mean that we can accept every miracle story within or without the Gospels as an accurate account of what happened. There is the empirical question of the evidence for the occurrence of the strange event which is reported as a miracle. Historical criticism of the accounts is here wholly in place, and sifting of the sources.

But here again the acceptance of the tradition that Christ did actually do mighty works, gives the preacher who believes in it, an advantage over the preacher who does not believe in it. For the former may, without dishonesty, preach the saving gospel at times from a story as to whose historical accuracy he may be in doubt. But what are we to say of the honesty of a preacher, who does not believe that any of the recorded miracles took place? Here an illustration from another field may be suggestive.

If a bank has considerable assets in real property, then it can easily stand a few sudden demands for cash payment. But if it has no backing at all, and a great number of demands are made, then all is up. If we can believe that Jesus did in fact perform many wonderful works, it will be possible honestly to preach powerfully even about an incident as to whose historical facticity we may have uncertainty.[1] But supposing that we believe that there is no such backing in the solid currency of historical fact for the miracle stories, and all of them belong to the paper currency of existential significance, then the preaching about the miracles will have the same disastrous results as dishonest banking transactions always and inevitably bring in their train.

In concluding this chapter it is relevant to ask whether Bultmann's view on miracle has not profoundly influenced his whole conception of God and the gospel. If this can be shown, then the influence on his preaching cannot but be momentous.

[1] This surely does not apply to the resurrection!

We have seen how he feels himself able to thrust on one side the question of the historicity of the New Testament miracles. On occasion here he will say, 'What happened we do not know.' This agnosticism is however in strange contrast to the unspoken implication: 'We do know very well what did *not* happen; we know that the events did not happen as they are reported.'

We come now to our own experience. Here Bultmann does not deny the possibility of miracle. Indeed he positively asserts that there is such a thing. There is one miracle and one only for us, the miracle of God's grace and forgiveness, whereby we learn that we are at the same time sinners and justified men. In the moment in which God enables our faith to receive this miracle and revelation, we realize that he is here active, and the world-outlook of objectifying knowledge is momentarily in abeyance.

But, as we have seen, even in the moment of faith, there must be an experience of empirical events running on. And these are world-events, events seen in the world. And Bultmann has told us that all faith in miracle is the contrary of all that I see in the world. Therefore we must conclude that these events through which faith apprehends miracle can never, in Bultmann's opinion, offer *any* encouragement to the leap of faith, the intuition that here God is at work. There can never be, if we take Bultmann at his word, what, in this context Dr A. C. Craig has beautifully described as 'finely-pointed conjunctures of outward circumstance which look like the response of a person, and powerfully suggest nice contrivance by a co-operating will'.[1]

When we ask why, we are told that faith has nothing to do with demonstrability or evidence. But the real reason, we suspect, is that the whole world of fact has been surrendered, because it is believed that God could only be active within it by breaking a closed causal sequence, and such a concept must be rejected as mythical. It is true that here I am drawing out the conclusions of Bultmann's thinking rather than expounding what he has explicitly said, but if my extrapolation be legitimate, then we must conclude that in the unequal struggle with objectifying thinking, faith has lost the day, and is reduced to the status of a protester, who declares in spite of all the facts, 'Nevertheless, here I must see the will of God.'[2]

[1] A. C. Craig, *Preaching in a Scientific Age*, SCM Press, London, 1954, p. 67.

[2] Here we are reminded of the gentleman in the Chester-Belloc rhyme:
'When they asked him why,
He made no reply.'

It is, therefore, not surprising that in Bultmann's writings on this theme we have the same kind of depressed and depressing outlook that we are accustomed to find in the writings of modernists on the subject of miracle, and that his chosen example of miracle seems to be a situation where, in spite of everything, I declare that God is active, and where I must respond, 'even if my response be one of bearing what happens in silence'.[1]

It is true that in our life we all come across such situations, but surely we find in Bultmann less the atmosphere of joy and deliverance which breathes in the New Testament, than the atmosphere of the tragic sermon of F. W. Robertson on Unanswered Prayer,[2] a sermon whose gloom really comes, not so much from submission to God's will, as from enslavement to a false epistemology, an epistemology of the closed circle similar in this respect to Bultmann's.

At this point I must recall to the reader one of the conclusions of our chapter on the existential interpretation. There we saw that Bultmann's emphasis on the existential moment in faith was such that the truth claim of statements of faith, and consequently of theological statements, was dissipated.

In this chapter we have seen what appears to be a flat contradiction between Bultmann's two temporally successive and mutually contradictory outlooks, the outlook of faith on the one hand, and that of 'objectifying knowledge' on the other.

When, however, we take these two positions together, we see that something even more distressing from the viewpoint of the believer has happened. What Dr Hepburn has said in a slightly different context, is exactly applicable here: 'As Professor A. N. Prior has well put it, if the believer's hypothesis is meaningless, the choice between it and a meaningful alternative cannot be a fifty-fifty gamble, nor even a hundred to one, but "a hundred to nothing against belief".'[3]

In criticizing Dr Bultmann's general outlook on our life and fortunes under God's providence, it is hard to speak without an undue presumption. God sends varying experiences to each of his children, experiences of happiness and trial. It is to the lasting honour of the man whose theology we are examining that, under conditions of religious persecution and trial, he stood forth with steadfast courage,

[1] *K.u.M.*, II, p. 197.

[2] F. W. Robertson, *Sermons*, vol. IV, no. 3, pp. 23-33.

[3] R. W. Hepburn, *Christianity and Paradox*, Watts, London, 1958, p. 88, citing A. N. Prior, *New Essays in Philosophical Theology*, SCM Press, London, 1955, p. 8.

and in no way abated his Christian witness. But, leaving on one side all questions of personal experience and response to the divine call, for which each one must answer to his Master alone, we may yet ask the question whether the full note of Christian hope and joy is sounded in these writings, and in Bultmann's own preaching. And if it is not, what chance has it of sounding in the theology and the sermons of lesser men who accept his teaching, and have not his greatness of mind and spirit? What is the result of this kind of demythologizing likely to be on the preaching and evangelism of a generation? Is this the Christianity that first came upon the world like the rising of the sun?

VII

THE FLIGHT FROM HISTORY

1. Introductory

THOUGH in certain areas theology profits by the advance of historical and other scholarly disciplines as, for example, by the discovery of important new documents, it is not a discipline like those sciences which can advance all along the line by the verification or refutation of new hypotheses. As a result, its conclusions at any one time may be too much influenced by such things as a swing of opinion or a revulsion of mood. The result of this is that on occasion one theological generation may celebrate too easy a triumph over the tendencies of its predecessor. And such a triumph usually brings in its train a reaction, as a result of which it must be admitted that territories have been too quickly overrun, and pockets of resistance left behind, so that sometimes a painful retreat and rueful consolidation becomes necessary.

It is probably true to say that too easy a victory over liberalism was celebrated by the recent emphasis on Biblical Theology, useful and necessary as that was. An idea is not necessarily adequate for our faith today because it is Hebrew, or even because it is found in the Bible. Further it may also be true that moderate critical views have celebrated too easy a victory over the radical criticism of sceptical scholars. When we gave up the doctrine of verbal inspiration, as was necessary, we assumed that we could at once find quite solid ground for the preaching of the gospel. And on either side of us there were those who dissented from our views; on our left the more radical critics, who could not stop where we did, and who seemed to us to have surrendered what was vital to the faith; and on our right the verbalists, who feared that if they gave up anything, all would be lost. It may have been that the triumph we celebrated was a little premature, and that this is the reason why issues which we had more or less considered closed have been opened again. Is not the great and almost painful contemporary interest in the question of the relation of history to revelation a sign that we realize that all is not wholly well?

An illustration of the somewhat confused state of the battlefield today may be chosen here. One of the central concepts of the Bible is that of the covenants. It may well be questioned whether without the notion of the covenants the Christian religion could continue its separate existence. Let us consider the Old Testament Covenant in particular. Without going into details as did the federal theology, we may recall that the Old Testament tells us that God made a covenant with Abraham, reaffirming his promises both to him, and to Isaac and Jacob and Moses. But now, as a result of historical criticism, the figures of the patriarchs become increasingly dim in the mist of antiquity. At times the figure of Abraham seems almost dissolved into a migration and then again scholars affirm their conviction that he was a historical figure. And in the midst of vivid personal stories about Jacob and Joseph, there comes the strange story of Dinah, Hamor and Shechem,[1] where it seems so clear that not individual men and women, but racial groups are the subject of the story.

If the personal individuality of the patriarchs be questioned, what becomes of the wonderful preaching themes from the story of their lives? Are these to be thought of merely as 'stories told in ancient Israel', embodying the beliefs of the Hebrews about God's ways with men? But if so, what is there here of more importance than the beliefs of other peoples about the ways of the gods with men? Even more important, what becomes of the covenant if the men with whom it was made disappear? Can it still be affirmed, as a covenant which God made, not with individual men, but with a people?

It may be considerations like these which have caused scholars to say that the deliverance of Israel from Egypt must be regarded as the birthday of the Hebrew people, and to base all on the covenant made at that time. The people of Israel, through their long history, looked back on these great events as the beginning of their history, and so, it is argued, we can be confident that here at least we have a core of historical events which could safely be regarded as the vehicles for a divine covenant with the people of Israel. Relying on this, it is urged, we can look back on the more shadowy preceding events, and say 'Here too we may see at least traces of the preceding grace and promise of the God who bound himself still more firmly to his people at the time of the Exodus.' And yet even the Exodus stories, in the narrative of the plagues and the Sinaitic Covenant, bear unmistakable traces of the

[1] Gen. 34.

mythical.[1] Where are we to stop? Are we to be reduced to the minimum of saying that all through its history, the Hebrew people considered itself to have been a partner in a special covenant with God? Here at last we have reached a fact which not even the most sceptical of historians would dare to challenge, just as in the New Testament story it cannot be doubted that the first Christians believed that Jesus had risen from the dead.

Here too, in relation to this central event of the New Testament, there is no longer the same kind of certainty as there was in former days. For example it is no longer possible, since the collapse of verbal inspirationism, to say, as was naïvely said in former days, that the resurrection of Christ is the best attested fact of history.

Yet personally I would be prepared to say that it was not enough to agree that Israel was convinced that God had entered into special covenant relations with her. What faith would be needed for this affirmation? It is necessary for faith to affirm that God really did enter into this covenant relationship, however many elements of folk-tale may have gathered round the stories of the initiation and the reaffirmation of that Covenant.

And further, it is not enough to affirm that the earliest Christians believed that Jesus had risen, for what faith is needed to make this statement? It is necessary to believe that Jesus really did rise from the dead, however frankly we have to acknowledge that the accounts of his appearances are not fully coherent with each other, and however frankly we must acknowledge that here we are moving in a sphere of mystery and cannot define 'resurrection' sharply and adequately by means of our human concepts.

Here, however, an issue has been raised, not to receive a definitive answer, but merely to illustrate a problem which is more then ever a live one today, the relation of the historical to revelation. And this problem has been one of the main concerns of Rudolf Bultmann's theology. So, as we are about to offer a trenchant criticism of his answer to this problem, yet once more we must salute him as one who, whatever we may think of his solution, has placed his finger firmly on a life and death problem for our faith.

[1] The word here is used in its most general sense, where the mythical is set against the historical.

2. *The problem stated*

In his book *The Mediator* Emil Brunner has said, 'Faith is indeed compatible with criticism of the Biblical tradition about the life of Christ, and perhaps compatible with an extremely radical criticism. But it is not compatible with every kind of criticism. . . . Faith is compatible with any kind of historical criticism which does not so alter the historical picture of the existence of Jesus, that faith cannot recognize in him the Christ to whom the apostles bore witness.'[1]

Can faith recognize in the historical picture of Jesus as Bultmann portrays it the Christ to whom the apostles bore witness? A critical student with pencil in hand might note down the following outline, drawn from Bultmann's own writings: Jesus called on men to decide for God now, because God was about to bring in the new age (*New Testament Theology*, E.T., I, p. 21). In this latter conviction he was wrong, for the new age did not appear (ibid., p. 22). He did not believe that God's reign was present in his own person and in the followers gathered about him (p. 22). He did not believe himself to be the Messiah (p. 26), nor the eschatological Son of Man (ibid.), nor did he believe that he himself was the Messiah to be (ibid.), whose coming he expected in the immediate future (p. 9). In this expectation which he had about the coming of the Messiah, he was again wrong. The early Church believed him to be both Messiah and Son of man (p. 26); here they were also, on both points, wrong. The early Church thought that he had risen from the dead, an erroneous belief.[2] But the truth behind it was that through the preaching about his death, God offers men salvation, and a new future, in faith. But what kind of man he was is unimportant for Paul[3] and, the hostile critics may dare to say, not of the first importance for Bultmann, since 'Only the historian can answer such questions, and faith, being personal decision, cannot be dependent on the historian's labour'.[4]

A critical reader might well at this point pause, and ask whether 'the historical picture of Jesus' has not here been so changed that 'faith can no longer recognize the Christ to whom the apostles bore witness'. If this were the case, then the results of Bultmann's views on the relation

[1] E. Brunner, *Der Mittler*, Tübingen, 1927, p. 143 (Eng. tr.: *The Mediator*, Lutterworth Press, London, 1934, p. 168).

[2] *K.u.M.*, I, p. 49.

[3] *Theology of the New Testament*, I, pp. 293-4.

[4] Ibid., p. 26. This is actually said of the question whether Jesus was conscious of being the Messiah or the Son of man.

of faith to history could be set down here and now as disastrous, and this chapter brought to an end.

But the question before us is complex. It is clear what Brunner meant in the passage quoted from *The Mediator*, and his meaning is illustrated by the examples he cites. 'Faith,' he says, 'is not compatible with a criticism which could deny the existence of Jesus, or depict him as a psychopath, or a proletarian revolutionary.'[1] But the words 'the historical picture of Jesus' are not so clear as they at first seem. It might be said that the disputants in the later discussion have here disclosed—or perhaps imported—a whole nest of ambiguities. So that a fuller discussion of Bultmann's position cannot be avoided, in which we shall remember our particular interest in the matter of theology and preaching.

Bultmann's flight from the historical must be distinguished from his historical scepticism. The latter may have various causes, some of which I have indicated, but whether it is justified or no, this scepticism is for him something given, he has to accept it, and to take it into account in the formation of his theology. His flight from the historical is something quite different. It consists in his declaration that this historical scepticism does not matter; faith does not need to be alarmed by it. Our attention will be directed to the reasons given for this flight from the historical, and the arguments adduced in its favour will be tested one by one. And we shall have to ask whether the scepticism and the flight from history do not in fact deeply influence Bultmann's understanding and presentation of the gospel. And finally, we shall ask whether they ought not to influence his gospel more than in fact he allows them to do!

3. The flight from history: its nature and attempted justifications

Many writers have pointed out one striking characteristic of Bultmann's theology. In it he seems to traverse the old and familiar boundaries of the theological schools. In the past those theologians who have ascribed a decisive position to the work and person of Christ, have on the whole been those who held a more or less conservative position with regard to the New Testament documents. In relation to the Gospels in particular, they were prepared to acknowledge that here the picture given of Christ's figure and his claims was substantially correct. But in the work of Bultmann we have something startling and new—a very radical historical scepticism about the sources combined

[1] E. Brunner, *Der Mittler*, p. 143 (Eng. tr.: *The Mediator*, p. 168).

with a high estimate of the central and decisive place of Christ. This it has been which has astonished—and attracted—students. They have been led to ask whether perhaps the Christian faith was less exposed to the risks of historical contingence than they had thought. When they read Bultmann's sermons, and appreciated their deep reverence and piety, they were further puzzled—and reassured. And the more thoughtful among them may have gone on to ask, how was this result achieved? Was it a real achievement? Would it bear close examination, and stand the test of time?

There can be little question as to the manner in which Dr Bultmann has come to his results. He has done so by a radical pulling apart of faith from the historical. This severance can be more or less forcibly expressed, according to the needs of Bultmann's system at the particular moment, but sometimes it can be put as violently as in a sentence noticed by us above, which is worth while reproducing in this context as an illustration of the tendency we are describing as 'The Flight from History'. The sentence occurs in the treatment of the theme of the Messianic consciousness of Jesus.[1] In discussing this question, Bultmann says, 'it is important to bear in mind that if the fact should be established that Jesus was conscious of being the Messiah or the Son of Man, that would only establish a historical fact, not prove an article of faith. Rather, the acknowledgement of Jesus as the one in whom God's word decisively encounters man . . . is a pure act of faith independent of the historical question whether or not Jesus considered himself to be the Messiah. Only the historian can answer this question —so far as it can be answered at all—and faith, being personal decision, cannot be dependent on a historian's labour.'

It is not the earlier part of this statement to which I wish to draw the reader's attention, but the general principle on which Bultmann rejects the question of Christ's messianic consciousness as irrelevant for faith. There is only one word to describe this general assertion, that pure acts of faith are independent of historical questions and that is 'brash'; and one suspects that Bultmann makes it rather impishly, with a desire to shock us. But let us take him at his word, and ask, 'What then is the relation between faith and history?' On the strength of this passage he would be compelled to answer, 'None at all', a reply which it would be hardly fair to claim as the total result of his writings. For it would imply that faith in Christ was compatible with Jesus never having lived at all.

[1] R. Bultmann, *Theology of the New Testament*, E.T., I, p. 26.

This passage will have served to provide us with an extreme example of Bultmann's flight from history, and we can now also see what has led him to take refuge in it. It is the result of an innate and possibly also reasoned extreme historical scepticism, combined with a deep evangelical faith. This is the only way in which to combine these two characteristics, one of which is, so to speak, Dr Bultmann's intellectual fate, and the other is his religious need. By this attenuation, or even severance, of the cord linking faith to the historical, faith can be, at least partially, and in appearance, isolated from the relativities and uncertainties of all events in the past. And what Paul Althaus has well described as 'the retrospective historical question' (*die historische Rückfrage*) can be discouraged, or even vetoed. Thus a recurring pattern in Bultmann's reasoning can be traced as follows—'What actually happened' (e.g. in the events underlying the narratives of the miracles, the passion story, the resurrection story), we cannot know now. But it is not of any importance for us to know, for those events were perhaps experienced by the men who wrote of them, but they cannot be a matter of experience for us today, and therefore have no relevance for our faith.[1]

Now we come to the various arguments and justifications with which Dr Bultmann seeks to support his divorce of faith from the historical. The first of these has been hinted at a moment ago, when it was said that past events cannot be a matter of present experience.

(*a*) We can put this argument more clearly by saying that a fact of the past is something about which, at the best, I can know on the authority of others. But faith is not a knowledge-about, on the authority of others. It is the result of an I-Thou encounter now with the living God; it concerns not the past, but the present. And God meets us in the word of preaching.

I shall quote again a passage from the essay on 'The Question of Miracle', this time drawing attention to what one might call the 'dimensional difference' (Bultmann does not use these terms) between knowledge about past historical fact and the present existential knowledge of faith. Bultmann says,[2] 'In the New Testament miracles are reported which have the character of prodigies—especially miracles of Jesus. In so far as acts of Jesus are there reported (healings of the sick, and so on), they are acts which were events in the experience of the people concerned at the time. Even if they were all historically verified

[1] In relation to the cross, see *K.u.M.*, I, p. 43; the miracles, *G.u.V.*, I, p. 227; the resurrection, *K.u.M.*, I, p. 47.

[2] *G.u.V.*, I, p. 227.

(and in so far as they *are* verified), yet it remains that as works done by a man of the past they are no immediate concern of ours. Thus regarded they are not works of Christ, in the way that we understand by the work of Christ the work of redemption. Therefore in the discussion we must surrender to the critics without reserve the 'miracles of Jesus' in so far as they are events of the past, and we must insist with the utmost emphasis that Christian faith can have no interest in proving their possibility or actuality, as events of the past; that on the contrary this would be a sheer mistake.

'If Christ is only our contemporary as the preached Christ, then the miracles of Jesus can only come in question in so far as they belong to the preaching about Christ—as witness . . .' (These two last words do not mean for Bultmann what they mean for other people, witness to the fact that certain things did actually happen, in which the narrators saw the hand of God. They mean rather that such things as the miracle stories are indications of the crucial significance of Christ for me, of what God wishes to say to me through him, the question of the historicity of the events being irrelevant, since it belongs to the past, and not to the existential confrontation now which occurs when preaching meets with faith.)

In criticism of this argument brought forward in support of Bultmann's flight from history, it will be enough to point the reader to the last chapter of this book in which we shall outline a very different theory of personal encounter and knowledge about persons from that which Bultmann holds; a theory which, with the necessary modifications, we may apply to our encounter with and knowledge of God. If Bultmann's view here expounded be right, then it is extremely difficult to see how the personal encounter with God can ever be more than a blank immediacy. For no knowledge about him can ever be transmitted from one person to another, since such knowledge always belongs to the past. Further, though Bultmann does not seem to see this, his veto on knowledge about God from the past ought to apply to our own past encounters with God also, for they have the essential disqualification that they also belong to the past, though they certainly in no way make us dependent on the reports of others. But why should not my knowledge of God in personal encounter today be enriched by knowledge of what he has done in the past? If I can believe that Jesus, the revelation of God, did certain mighty acts, then I have certainly in no way escaped the necessity for an encounter of faith today, but my whole approach to that encounter of faith may be influenced, and that encounter itself enriched, by the knowledge of what he has done in the past. Thus the legitimacy of the 'retrospective historical question' is again vindicated, and the question as to whether Christ really did these things is declared legitimate. And this in no way sidesteps the need for faith today, or seeks to place reliance on verified fact rather than on God himself.

(*b*) This reflection leads us to consider Bultmann's second argument in defence of his 'Flight from History'. In a word this argument is, that any consideration of the retrospective historical question implies an attempt to rely on verifiable fact which means the death of faith. This point need not be discussed at length here, since it has already been fully dealt with in the chapter on 'Myth and Miracle'. What was there said of events which are claimed to be miraculous, may here be repeated of all historical events which faith claims to be revelatory. These events have a verifiable aspect, as events, but the fact that here God acted in miracle, or that here God acted in revelation is not verifiable in any sense which could remotely endanger the nature of faith. It is true that miracle conceived as the bell rung by the 'Heavenly Bellman' to attest his divinity, would be miracle in the sense rightly objected to by Bultmann, a proof to the eyes of those who saw it that God was revealed, a proof which would endanger or destroy the nature of faith itself. But we must remember (as Bultmann himself rightly points out) that miracle had always the same ambiguous character as the figure of Christ; it did not compel faith, men could ascribe it to the powers of evil, or merely regard it as strange, or offer other interpretations than that of faith. And the same can be said of all the historical events which are claimed to be the vehicle of revelation. Further, men can accept as historical the miracles of Christ, and in word at least accept the fact that in him God was revealed, and still not make the existential decision of faith. So whether we accept the New Testament miracles or not, and whether we take an interest in the historicity of the facts recorded about Christ or not, the need for the leap of faith remains. But the man who can accept the miracles may find that he can make the leap of faith to better advantage, for he is at liberty to believe (he has not proved, in any objectionable sense of the word) that God is a God who does mighty works. And—if he believes that the gospels give a real picture of the Jesus who lived and died and rose again—he is at liberty to believe as the disciple of Bultmann is not, that God is a God who really does mighty works. But the freedom to ask the retrospective historical question is by no means an infringement of faith, especially when the New Testament so eagerly asks it, and encourages us to ask it ourselves. Dr Althaus is certainly right when he distinguishes the word of God as uttered through the prophets from the word of God borne witness to by the Gospel writers in the life of Christ.[1] He is criticizing Bultmann and Gogarten for their assertion that when the word of God meets us, it is already a sign of unbelief to ask any questions; it is our duty to obey. This is true, Althaus grants, of the word spoken by the prophets, 'Thus saith the Lord'. Such a word bears its authentication in itself. And this is true also of the saving significance of the apostolic message. 'If preaching says to me, "The death and resurrection of Christ concern you in your existence, he died for your sins and was raised for your justification, acknowledge that, and let yourself be reconciled in Christ to God," then in fact here I can only say "yes" or "no".' 'But', Althaus continues, 'to say "yes" or "no" to this question is already to presuppose consciously or unconsciously that the event of which the message speaks is a real, and consequently also, a historical event.' Far, then, from faith here demanding the suppression of the retrospective historical question, it actually presupposes that that question has been asked, and answered in the affirmative! It would accordingly appear that Bultmann's second argument in defence of the flight from history is as ill-conceived as the first.

(*c*) There is, however, a third, and extremely important difficulty and problem to which Bultmann's flight from history is an attempted answer.

It is a problem raised by Lessing; and Kierkegaard, Herrmann, and Kähler have all struggled with it, without conclusive success. The problem is 'How can the certainty of faith be reconciled with the permanent uncertainty attaching to all historical events?'—or, as Kähler in effect puts it, 'How can the Reformation principle of the immediate access of the believer to God in Christ be subjected to a papacy of the Professors (*Gelehrtenpapat*)?'[2] Would this not mean a surrender of a vitally important truth recovered by Luther?

Kähler has his own answer to this problem, and it is clear that just as elsewhere Bultmann is dependent on Herrmann, so here he is facing the problem set by Kähler and if confirmation of this point is required, it will be found in the fact that Bultmann uses Kähler's own termin-

[1] Paul Althaus, *Das so-genannte Kerygma und der historische Jesus*, ch. 2, p. 20 (Eng. tr. *The so-called Kerygma and the Historical Jesus*, Oliver and Boyd, Edinburgh and London, 1959, henceforward cited as *The so-called Kerygma*, pp. 32-33.

[2] Kähler, *Der so-genannte historische Jesus und der geschichtliche biblische Christus*, 2nd ed., Munich, 1956.

ology, in his use of the two terms *historisch* and *geschichtlich*. It will be our task now to discuss this problem set by Kähler, and also to indicate his solution of it—and the apparently similar but really profoundly different answer given by Bultmann in his flight from history.

Towards the end of the nineteenth century Martin Kähler wrote a small and difficult but important book called *Der so-genannte historische Jesus und der geschichtliche biblische Christus* ('The so-called historical Jesus and the historic Biblical Christ').[1] Bultmann uses these terms also, and his use of them is nowhere systematically defined in the *Kerygma und Mythos* volumes, and readers of his Gifford Lectures on 'History and Eschatology' will not find enlightenment there.[2]

It is worth our while to give a thumbnail sketch of an important part of Kähler's argument, in order that the reader may see how like, and yet how unlike, his views are to Bultmann's, and also may appreciate the likeness and difference between the meaning of the concepts 'historical' and 'historic' in the work of Kähler and Bultmann respectively.

Kähler's book consists of four parts, of which the first and the second will concern us chiefly. In the first he deals with the problem that we have been discussing. If we give up the doctrine of verbal inspiration, how are we to avoid a complete relativism? Will the certainty of faith not be terribly impaired by its dependence on the continually fluctuating results of historical scholarship? The solution Kähler offers will appear later.

The second essay is a sustained polemic against the nineteenth century 'Lives of Jesus', Beyschlag's Life being here and in the third essay specially singled out for criticism. Here, says Kähler, we have an illegitimate attempt to go behind the only sources that we possess. Beyschlag and the other writers go against the evidence, and where there is none, they let their imagination run riot, as, for example, in describing the psychological development of our Lord. This is bogus history, not only for these reasons, but because the assumption is made that Christ's sinless being can be interpreted by analogy from our sinful nature. A systematic *life* of Christ is impossible; we simply

[1] Here and elsewhere in this book *historisch* will be rendered 'historical' and *geschichtlich*, 'historic'.

[2] In his Gifford Lectures Bultmann expresses a lively admiration for the work of R. G. Collingwood, quotes much from him, and has evidently been influenced by him, especially by his *The Idea of History*. If we are, however, to judge by the content of Bultmann's use of the concept *historisch*, and the understanding of the work of the historian we find in his first Essay in *Kerygma und Mythos*, we cannot be altogether confident that the author of *The Idea of History* would have expressed himself in such cordial terms about his admirer.

do not have the materials. Hence the historical Jesus of the 'Lives' is 'the *so-called* historical Jesus'. He is a phantom; he never existed.

But we do have sources, the Gospels and the Acts and the Epistles, though they were not set down to give an unimpassioned account of the life of Jesus. They were testimony written by believers, written from faith to faith. From them the Church can get a real and vivid picture of the work of Jesus, his character, his teaching, his resurrection. This is the real Christ, who lived on earth, and still represents us before the Father, though we do not know, and do not need to know, the story of his psychological development, or the exact order of the events in his ministry. From this generally trustworthy picture, presented by faith, and preached with conviction, the believer can receive an assurance that does not depend on the detailed work of the historian. And the knowledge gained from this picture enriches the believer's communion with the living Christ who also lived in Jerusalem and Galilee.

There are points in this exposition which one might be inclined to inquire about, or even to question, but our present task is to determine what Kähler means by 'historic' and 'historical'. It will be quite clear that for him there is but the one Christ, the historic Christ, the Christ of the Bible and of faith, about whom the Church can know a good deal, all that is necessary for salvation. The words 'the historical Jesus' refer in Kähler to a phantom projected into the past by rank bad historical method.

In Bultmann we find a very strange shifting of the meaning of these terms. What do the terms 'historical' and 'historic' mean for him? Kähler did indeed deal with the problem of the highest common factor of knowledge agreed upon by both sceptical and believing historians in relation to Jesus of Nazareth, but he never used the phrase 'the historical Jesus' to describe this agreed minimum. For Bultmann, on the other hand, the phrase, 'the historical Jesus' has precisely this significance which Kähler steadfastly refused to give it. In his first essay, Bultmann declares that there can be no doubt that the New Testament conceives of the Christ event as a mythical event. But the singular thing is this, that its central figure is not merely a mythical figure, not only God's Son, a pre-existent divine being, but also a historical man, with a human destiny, which ended in the crucifixion.[1]

Now, what does this mean, 'a historical man'? It looks as if it meant a man who actually lived and died, as opposed to a figure in one of the Hellenistic cult-myths. It might seem that we have here the ordinary

[1] *K.u.M.*, I, p. 141.

everyday use of the word 'historical', meaning 'someone who actually lived'. But while this is intended, we must note that for Bultmann nothing may be included in this picture of the historical Jesus save such traits as can be included in 'the verifiable account of the historian'.[1] The word 'historical', therefore, still means 'the actual Jesus', but nothing may be asserted to have happened to him, or to have been done by him, except things for which evidence may be brought forward such as would convince a sceptical historian.[2]

For Bultmann, then, the historical Jesus is the actual Jesus, the Jesus who really lived. For Kähler the historical Jesus is a phantom, who never lived. For Kähler the historic Jesus is the Jesus who really lived, for Bultmann the historic Jesus is 'what God wishes to say to me through the historical Jesus'.

Bultmann would indeed reject the psychological studies of Jesus by scholars like Beyschlag, just as Kähler did, and for the same reason, that they are bad history. But the fact remains that the words 'historical' and 'historic' have suffered a remarkable change in passing from the hands of Kähler to those of Bultmann.

It may thus be concluded that while we have in Bultmann concerns which we also find in Kähler, for example, the question as to how the certainty of faith can be related to historical[3] material, yet the younger man here turns the work of the older upside down as thoroughly as Marx turned upside down the work of Hegel, which he claimed to have stood upon its head.

And so we find that Kähler's answer to the question, 'How can faith become independent of the never-conclusive results of the historian?' is to say that faith has its own access in the Gospels to the historic Christ, to whom the Gospels bear witness. This is the Jesus who lived in Galilee, and also the Jesus of faith. Here, we may see, there is no flight from history, only the rejection of a phantom, the so-called historical Jesus. Bultmann's answer, on the other hand, is to fly from history—excepting in so far as it provides the merest springboard in fact for the leap into existential significance of 'what God wishes to say to me'. If there were not this residuum left in 'the historical Jesus', there would be nothing left to distinguish the gospel from mythology pure and simple.

[1] *K.u.M.*, I, p. 141.

[2] *K.u.M.*, II, p. 118. This article is by Hartlich and Sachs, but it has Bultmann's imprimatur.

[3] Here the word 'historical' is used in its common sense, indicating the story of past events.

There are various forms of answer to the question 'How, and how far, can faith be independent of the never-conclusive results of historical research?' Herrmann thought that the impression gained by faith of the figure of Jesus was in itself sufficient to guarantee its historicity in general; such a figure could not have been invented.[1] Althaus believes that even without faith a perceptive intelligence can gain an intuitive authentic general impression, which the labours of historians may correct in detail, but can never controvert in its main outlines, while faith has its own deeper historical understanding.[2] The question is still under discussion, but our provisional conclusion in this chapter must be that none of the justifications urged by Bultmann in support of his flight from history carries conviction. The whole enterprise resembles too much the remedy of decapitation as a cure for headache.

4. The flight from history in John Macquarrie

If we turn to Dr John Macquarrie's *An Existentialist Theology* we shall find a very different answer given in general to this problem of the relation of faith to history. He very justly takes Bultmann to task for neglecting the questions which the historian must ask concerning the man Jesus Christ. But there is one passage where he seems to be inconsistent with this general trend of his own book, and where he commits himself to a statement almost as objectionable as that of Bultmann quoted above. Here[3] he describes the radical criticism of the French theologian Guignebert, who has indeed 'pretty well dealt the death-blow to all theories which regard the figure of Jesus as a purely mythical construction, and has proved beyond all reasonable doubt his objective-historical[4] reality. Beyond that, however, the positive results of his investigations are meagre in the extreme.'

'But,' continues Macquarrie, 'let us suppose . . . that the results of his investigation had been different. . . . Suppose he had . . . substantially verified the New Testament record as a whole, and shown that it gives an account of events which actually took place at a given time in world-history. Would that really make much difference for religious faith or for theology? It would not, and frankly, it would be

[1] Herrmann, *Begriff der Offenbarung*, pp. 18-23.

[2] Althaus, *Das so-genannte Kerygma und der historische Jesus*, Gütersloh, 1958, p. 40.

[3] J. Macquarrie, *An Existentialist Theology*, p. 169.

[4] Macquarrie translates *historisch* as 'objective-historical' and *geschichtlich* as 'existential-historical'.

intolerable if it did. For then, not only the theologian, but the ordinary Christian believer would be at the mercy of the historian. Faith would be founded on historical research, on the probability of certain events having taken place at a certain period in world-history. That certainly seems to be the unenviable position in which those theologians find themselves who stake their case on the objective-historical . . .'

Let us reflect on this passage. It is indeed true that theologians and believers in general would not be profoundly excited had Guignebert's results been more conservative than they are. But that does not show that faith is not vitally interested in what happened. It merely shows that most believers have never even heard of Guignebert, that theologians do not, on the whole, take his results very seriously, and that, in general, New Testament scholars are satisfied that enough is known about the events concerning Jesus from the records of the first witnesses, to give faith something fairly substantial to start from.

This seems, indeed, to be the position of Macquarrie himself in general, but here, perhaps in deference to Bultmann, he seems for the moment to have lapsed from it. Suppose that now we take Macquarrie's argument at this point, and state it in the negative form. 'Suppose that Guignebert had proved that Christ had never existed, would that make much difference for faith or for theology? It would not, and frankly it would be intolerable if it did.' Clearly something here is not in order. What is it?

It is this. Macquarrie has expressed the dependence of faith upon history in much too vague a manner. In fact Christian faith depends on the witness of the first Christians who declare to us that certain things happened in which God revealed to them his nature and will. Faith does not therefore rest upon the researches of Guignebert and his fellows, and would not be much elated if these turned out to be unexpectedly conservative. But suppose that Guignebert or any other historian were able to prove, or make it extremely likely, that Jesus had never existed, or had been an evil man, then faith would be profoundly disturbed to say the least.

Thus faith is not positively dependent on the results of historical research, but it *is* vulnerable to the possibly negative conclusions of historical research. The sources on which it depends are not the minimum of facts on whose authenticity sceptical historians and believing theologians are agreed. These sources are constituted by the testimony given to the Church by the first witnesses, who spoke from faith to faith about certain past historical events, in which they testified that God had acted and spoken. The believer today is not compelled to believe that everything happened just as recorded, but if he were told, on the other hand, that none of the things recorded as past events had in fact happened, then he would be upset, and surely not without cause. Christian faith is indeed vitally interested in the actual occurrence of 'certain events at a certain period in world-history'. Those who deny this are in the 'unenviable position' of declaring Christian faith to be independent of the historical fact of Christ.

The reader will see that the logic of the argument against Dr Macquarrie has brought us to state a position not unlike that of Martin Kähler, and it is most probably along these lines that a solution of the problem is to be found. The significance for preaching seems to be that while the mighty acts of God are not simply identifiable with historical events, yet without such a vehicle or substratum of historical events, these mighty acts could not be done, and there would be nothing to preach about save human ideas or fantasies.[1]

5. Defence of our title: 'The Flight From History'

One word must be said at this point in defence of the title of this chapter, 'The Flight from History'. Bultmann's critics have urged that he is guilty of such a flight. His supporters rejoin that his critics are ignorant of the recent important work done by philosophy on the concept of history, and that when this has been digested and assimilated, it will be seen that the Bultmann school and not their critics are the thinkers who do justice to history. And that the precision of Bultmann's thought can be seen by his distinction between the historical and the historic. For him an event has historical character in as far as it happened at one point of time, is over and done with, and is accessible to the verifying methods of the historian. An event is historic, because it not merely happened at one point in the past time-series, but because it also transcends that time-series and is the vehicle whereby I can arrive at a new self-understanding of my own possibilities, or the vehicle whereby God is ready to speak a decisive word to me.

Now we must admit that history is not merely a matter of past occurrence but of present significance, but we must also refuse to allow any display of new concepts to become an excuse for vetoing the legitimacy and the necessity of the retrospective historical question, 'Did this actually happen?' Both Bultmann and Gogarten show a quite inadequate sense of the importance of this question, and yet, when it

[1] See Appendix A.

comes to the point, they do not quite dare to sidestep the question of historical occurrence.[1] The point against their school of thought could not be more forcibly put than by Dr Ronald Hepburn,[2] 'Questions of objective history thus cannot be smuggled out of the way by extolling the importance of the "significance for life" of the doctrines concerned. The appeal to significance cannot properly displace the anxiety and risks attending historical research into New Testament origins. . . . Events of history have to be realized existentially, if they are to be more to us than brute facts about the past. But to be realized existentially, they must first be facts. Prayer to a living Jesus today is a possibility only if Jesus did rise in the first century A.D.'

The reader's attention will be drawn to this point again in the next chapter, where its importance for preaching will be considered. There we shall ask with what right Herr Hans Werner Bartsch can speak of the 'cry of victory; "Christ is risen!" ' in a sermon on the resurrection, when he does not, as a matter of fact, believe that the resurrection took place.

6. The vulnerability of this type of apologetic

Before passing on to the next section of this chapter, it will be necessary to point out how extremely vulnerable the 'flight from history' is as a method of Christian apologetic and evangelism. It is unfortunate that such a scepticism and irrationalism as are here embodied should have become fashionable today. For, if generally accepted, these views would lay open the flank of the Christian position to a most damaging cross-fire from the linguistic philosophy. The more extreme exponents of this philosophy used to suggest that statements of religious faith were merely expressions of emotion or of intention, and had no objective reference or validity.

It would, indeed, be no wise defence of the Christian faith to try to assimilate its knowledge to the knowledge of empirical fact, or to claim that it could submit to verificatory procedures like those suited to the exact sciences.

But today, when these topics are under discussion it is certainly not the time for Christian apologists light-heartedly to cut our faith adrift from connexions with historical events which the Bible clearly asserts

[1] For an admirable discussion, see Althaus, *Das so-genannte Kerygma und der historische Jesus*, ch. 3, 'Der Begriff der Geschichte und des Geschichtlichen'.

[2] Ronald W. Hepburn, *Christianity and Paradox*, pp. 102, 104.

to exist, and which the Church has always maintained to be necessary for its own life.

In considering Bultmann's position, we must also keep in mind the fact that at least one Christian philosopher, under the pressure of linguistic criticism, has offered an account of the meaning of statements of faith, which makes Bultmann's theology look cautious and conservative. Professor Braithwaite has, in effect, defined such statements as declarations of the speaker's intention to pursue a certain policy of action, coupled with the use of certain stories as paradigms for attitude and action, which stories are not necessarily thought of as being true.[1]

In the thought of the linguistic philosophers a very important part has been played by the test of verifiability. This test is not easy to formulate, but, roughly, it affirms that our statements can claim meaning only when we can point to some empirical consequences which might go some way towards confirming them or 'falsifying' them. Now, if my statement of religious faith means no more than 'I intend to pursue such and such an ethical policy', then it is true if, in the event, I pursue the policy and false, if I do not, since everyone can see whether I do pursue it or not. Hence my statement of faith will, on Braithwaite's theory, satisfy the verification test. But too high a price has been paid, for this clearly was not the main thing that men have always meant when they made statements of religious faith.

If Braithwaite's view were to gain currency, then what men have always believed to be the central content of statements of faith would have been surrendered and, with it, all claim to dependence on a historical revelation about God, man and the world. Such a position as this would surely never have been adopted, unless under the pressure, real or supposed, of a philosophical difficulty.

While this kind of thing looms beyond Dr Bultmann on the theological left, there are a number of acute philosophers with a linguistic training, who will be eager to submit his arguments to the same kind of criticism as Hepburn has recently applied to his views, along with Niebuhr's and Gogarten's, on the resurrection and other kindred matters.[2] The upshot of Hepburn's analyses has been to show that these views are philosophically much more vulnerable than a somewhat more conservative position. In apologetics, truth is naturally the

[1] R. B. Braithwaite, *An Empiricist's View of the Nature of Religious Belief*, C.U.P., 1955.

[2] See Ronald Hepburn, *Christianity and Paradox*, ch. 6; also see *New Essays in Philosophical Theology*, XII, 'Demythologizing and the Problem of Validity' by R. W. Hepburn.

supreme consideration, but when we are being told so much about what the modern man can accept, and what he cannot, it is perhaps permissible to remark that the timing of the existential theology, at least in the British and American situation, against a background of linguistic philosophy, is unfortunate.

7. *Bultmann on the life and death of Christ*

In the next chapter we shall have to examine Bultmann's own preaching, and accordingly, in preparation for this, we must now examine what he teaches as a theologian about those events which are the foundation of the gospel, and how he believes they are to be interpreted. Our examination will also serve to illustrate his whole attitude to the historical.

We have already noticed a singular indecision in his treatment of the historical element in the gospels.[1] Whenever he wishes to establish the difference of Jesus from purely mythological figures, he makes use of the historical as a springboard, from which he may leap to the safety of the historic. For this function, the historical plays a quite indispensable part in his theology, but it is the bare fact of its historicity on which he relies, the *content* of it does not interest him. 'As saving event,' he writes, 'the cross of Christ is no mythical event, but a historic happening which takes its origin in the historical event of the crucifixion of Jesus of Nazareth. This death is in its historic significance a judgement upon the world, and an acquittal of man.'[2] Granted that it is only the historic understanding of faith that grasps the significance of the historical event, it is yet the historical event ('this death'), that has the significance. Hence, we may conclude, that it is important that the historical death had just the empirical characteristics that it happened to have. Yet, as we shall see, it is only for the moment that the logic of the argument has wrung this concession from Dr Bultmann.

Let us leave him for a moment, and ask ourselves how we can express this significance, do justice to its trans-subjective reality. The church has from the very earliest days found two ways of doing so. In John 13, verse 3, we read, 'Jesus, knowing that the Father had given all things into his hands, and that he was come from God, and went to God; he riseth from supper, and laid aside his garments, and took a towel, and girded himself. After that he poureth water into a bason, and began to wash the disciples' feet.'

[1] *K.u.M.*, I, p. 43. [2] Ibid., p. 16.

Here the Evangelist draws our attention first to the mystery of the Person of Christ, his divine origin and destiny. And secondly, our attention is drawn to the character of his historical actions. In this double way the New Testament bears witness to the significance of Christ and his work. But, as we shall see, both these methods of displaying to faith the transcendent significance of Christ are vetoed by Dr Bultmann.

We are forbidden by him to use the dogmatic concepts of divine sonship, pre-existence, and we are forbidden to use any of the concepts of Atonement hinted at by the New Testament. All these, we are told, are mythological. Contrary to Bultmann's belief, all these concepts have always been understood by the Church to be inadequate, and yet Christian thought has always claimed for them a real validity, and applied them without hesitation to the man Jesus, whom we come to know in the gospels as one who lived in Palestine.

And here comes the strange, and contradictory element in Bultmann's teaching. When it was important for him to lay weight on the historical element in the Christ event, in order to distinguish it from the mythological stories of Hellenistic religion, he was willing to speak of the significance of Christ's death as a historical event. But now he forbids us all recourse to the Jesus who lived and died. Thus the historical life of Jesus, and the historical event of his death (not to speak of his resurrection, which is denied any independent event-status), are so evacuated of any content that it becomes very hard to see why God should have chosen Jesus rather than any other man, through whom to speak a decisive word of salvation to mankind. When we look for some content of a historical kind, we are told, 'The facts which historical criticism can verify cannot exhaust, indeed they cannot adequately indicate all that Jesus means to me. His story, his cross, is not to be investigated as a matter of historical interest; the significance of his story comes from what God wishes to say to me through it.'

Surely, one may comment in passing, what God intends to say to me through the cross should not be thrown thus into opposition to the historical grounds of the cross. Had Jesus been justly crucified as a zealot rebel, then neither Bultmann nor any other preacher would be happy proclaiming God's salvation through the cross!

We are left here with the irresistible impression that Bultmann has checkmated himself by his dichotomy of the historical and the historic, as he has defined the terms. No understanding of the New Testament can ever be gained by trying to fit its contents into the framework of

(1) what can be verified by historical criticism; and (2) what God intends to say to me through these data.[1] Is not the answer, as we suggested above, to be found in Kähler's alternative solution, that the Gospels do not indeed give us a life of Jesus, but spoken from faith to faith, they give us a trustworthy picture of the man Jesus Christ, who was also more than man, and of his work?

The conclusion would appear to be that for Bultmann in the end, the historical has one function and one only, to serve as a springboard from which he may leap and escape from the mythological. The content of the historical would appear to say nothing to him. To such a pass has his historical scepticism brought him. And what an irrational concept of faith this implies! If this picture be accurate, it would not be right to picture the Christian preacher before his congregation as one pleading with them and displaying to them the love of God in the life and death of Christ. Rather he should be depicted as a circus trainer holding out a hoop to a troop of performing dogs, cracking his whip, and crying in menacing tones, 'Jump!'

It is true that there is no sign of this arrogance in Bultmann's preaching, though the cloven hoof does appear at points in his theology. But what is likely to be the result when lesser men imbibe his ideas, and then climb into our pulpits?

As we have seen, Bultmann rejects as mythology the traditional doctrines whereby the Church, following lines indicated by the New Testament itself, has sought to interpret the cross. What has he to set in their place? Christ as the sacrifice whose blood atones for our sin, the sufferer who bears vicariously the sin of the world, and by incurring the penalty of sin frees us from death; these, he claims, are all mythological interpretations which do not succeed in saying what the New Testament means to say, even if our modern age could understand and accept them. For these figures cannot do more than express the fact that penalty is remitted. But the truth is that the believer has been freed by the cross of Christ from the dominating power of sin.[2]

The New Testament, he continues, exalts the event of the cross to cosmic dimensions, and by the use of this strange (still mythical?) cosmic language it is trying to express truths of an existential significance. When it speaks of the cross as the judgement of 'the world' and says that by it the rulers of this world are brought to nothing, its

[1] Still less can the New Testament be understood if the question whether it be history or fiction be entirely suppressed!

[2] In this and the next paragraph I have given a free rendering of the argument of *K.u.M.*, I, p. 42, as I understand it. But it is exceedingly obscure.

real (existential) purpose is to say that by the cross God passes judgement upon us ourselves, as men who have become enslaved to the powers of this world.

'By allowing Christ to be crucified, God set up the cross for us. To believe in the cross of Christ is not to look on at a mythical happening which has taken place outside of us and our world, an objective visible event which God reckons as having taken place for our benefit. No, to believe in the cross of Christ is to make the cross of Christ our own, to let ourselves be crucified with Him.'[1]

How are we to interpret this important passage? There seem to be two main ways of taking it. One of them would be to regard the cross of Christ as, in Bultmann's opinion, no more than a supreme illustration of the kind of life that God requires of us. Here was a man who refused to seek for security, but surrendered himself utterly to what he believed to be the Father's will. And by allowing this to happen, God has judged us who, unlike Jesus, seek continually our own will and our own security, and are afraid to surrender our future wholly into God's hand. Here is authentic living, and here we see that such living is possible, for such a life has been lived, and such a death has been died. And consequently here we see our guilt in failing to live like Jesus. Or, alternatively, here we see our sin, in that we put to death the one man who dared to trust God and obey him unconditionally.

This is the interpretation of Bultmann adopted, for example, by Regin Prenter, who writes,[2] 'According to Bultmann the fact that the crucifixion is saving history (*Heilsgeschichte*) means that it has a historic significance which transcends that of a mere event in the past. But in what manner does this significance enter into my existence? It faces me with the question whether I am ready to make it my own, whether I am ready to be crucified with Christ. But that means that the historic event of the crucifixion has only the significance of an example. (Bultmann rejects all satisfaction and sacrificial theories as mythological.) The crucifixion represents the authentic existence of man, and faces me with the question whether I am ready to lay hold on this existence. Faith in the Crucified is understood, as the mediaeval expression puts it, as an *imitatio Christi*.

Thus Prenter criticizes Bultmann as holding a view which does not bring us any further forward than that of Schleiermacher. But we must note that if this is all that Bultmann succeeds in saying, it is certainly less than he intends to say. If anything is clear in his first essay it is this,

[1] *K.u.M.*, I, p. 42. [2] *K.u.M.*, II, p. 78.

that he wishes to regard the Christ event as more than a symbol of authentic existence and a model for our imitation. This was the point of his criticism of the idealists and the men of the history-of-religions school, that they did not, in the end, regard Christ as a decisive saving act of God, but only as a symbol of authentic humanity. However, the best of intentions are not enough, and Bultmann's results are sometimes less satisfactory than his intentions. But these reflections are sufficient at the least to make us suspicious of Prenter's interpretation, and keen to look for another, if another and more satisfactory one is to be found.

We now come to the second interpretation of Bultmann's teaching on the cross, which is that offered by Malevez. Bultmann has twice described the cross as God's judgement upon us. In the first instance[1] it is clearly a judgement of condemnation on us who have fallen under the sway of 'the world'. In the second[2] it is a judgement of liberation and acquittal. Here I cannot do better than cite Father Malevez[3]: 'But in what sense are we told that this judgement is effected in the cross? This, we think, is what Bultmann means by the phrase . . . It certainly does not mean that Christ has by his death merited our salvation and acquittal.' (This would be the reintroduction of mythology.) 'But it means that the judgement of God upon us is an act of God which, considered on the side of its divine principle, is in some sense transcendent of time, and the cross accomplished it in the sense that it gives it its temporal expression. In the cross of Christ God manifests the condemnation which he makes to fall upon all men. It is there that he reveals to us our personal condition as sinners, condemned and crucified men. In fine, the cross of Christ is less an achievement than a notification.'

The cross thus understood is understood only by faith. Naturally no trace of its revelatory character can be seen by the unbelieving historian. But how can this empirical event manifest even to faith God's condemnation and acquittal, if no reference to the historical character of what was done by the man 'who hung and suffered there' is permitted? We are simply told that if we have faith we shall see the cross as God's double act of judgement and acquittal. If we do not see it as such, we have no faith. But how is the cross a saving event? We shall see in a few minutes that to this question Bultmann has no other answer to offer than the astonishing one, 'Because it is preached as such'.[4]

[1] *K.u.M.*, I, p. 42. [2] *K.u.M.*, I, p. 43.

[3] L. Malevez, *Le Message Chrétien et le Mythe*, Brussels, 1954, p. 71 (Eng. tr.: *The Christian Message and Myth*, SCM Press, London, 1958, pp. 74-5).

[4] *K.u.M.*, I, p. 46.

When the man in the street says to Bultmann, 'How is Christ's death of saving power for me?' he is refused an answer, and simply told, 'It is so, don't ask questions!' There is surely poor hope for an army of evangelists who set forth to preach a gospel intelligible for men today with a motto of this kind inscribed on their banners. This is not theology. It is the death of thought.

We shall, however, concede that Bultmann manages to conserve the decisive act of God in Christ by taking this step; whatever else may be lost, we are thus carried beyond the realm of mere symbol. But where are we carried? Into a limbo where no answers are forthcoming to our eager and anxious questions.

8. Bultmann on the resurrection

Bultmann is right in saying that the cross cannot be rightly understood apart from the resurrection. In order to deal with his arguments in detail we have had to speak of the cross separately. Now he proceeds to deal with the resurrection. Here I must be satisfied with a summary of the three main heads of his argument, which will each be criticized in turn.

(1) The resurrection is not a historical event, which might enable us to understand the significance of the cross. It is not 'a verifiable miracle whose demonstrable certainty might prove to the questioner that the cross really has the cosmic significance attached to it by the Church.'[1]

Now the New Testament most certainly declares that the resurrection was a historical event, a datable event which either happened or did not happen. 'The third day he rose again.' The New Testament affirms that he did rise. If, however, the word 'historical' be defined in the quite singular sense that an event cannot be declared historical unless it was public to all, and demonstrable even to the sceptic, then the resurrection was not historical. But who is Dr Bultmann to demand that language be used in this manner? Had the resurrection been historical in this sense, then its occurrence *would* have endangered the nature of faith. Faith *would* have been imperilled had the risen Christ appeared in a blaze of glory to the Sanhedrin and asked them what they proposed to do now.

'The resurrection,' Bultmann avers, 'is not a verifiable miracle whose

[1] *K.u.M.*, I, p. 44. It will be remembered that Bultmann can allow historical character only to events for which the evidence is convincing enough to silence the doubts of a sceptical historian.

demonstrable certainty might prove to the questioner that the cross really has the significance attached to it by the Church.' Here, as often, by the term he uses, Bultmann tries to prejudice the argument in his favour, so that the opposing view is, so to speak, shouted down before it can gain a hearing. 'Verifiable', 'demonstrable certainty', 'prove' are all terms which caricature the case which Bultmann is opposing.

However, if anything is certain about the events under consideration it is this: had the first disciples not been utterly convinced that the resurrection had happened, there would have been no church, and therefore no ascription of cosmic, or any other, significance to the cross. What the men did, who believed themselves to be witnesses of the resurrection, was to bear witness to what they were convinced had happened in their own experience. Their hearers did not need to believe them, and so talk of proof is quite out of place. Cut down to the barest, Bultmann's argument would seem to be, 'If the resurrection happened, then faith is impossible; there is no room for it.' This is the precise contrary of what St Paul says, 'If Christ be not raised, then is your faith vain.' But Bultmann is a brave man; he is not afraid of calling St Paul's arguments 'fatal'[1] when they do not fit the measurements of the Bultmann theology.

(2) The New Testament however, Bultmann avers, ascribes to the resurrection in many places precisely this character which he repudiates.[2]

To this we must rejoin that the New Testament does not in fact hold the view which Bultmann feels obliged to ascribe to it, 'in many places', that the proofs of the resurrection are sufficient to bludgeon the unbeliever. Bultmann's own outlook on this matter seems opposed both to the outlook of Jesus and that of the Gospel writers, though it may be that complete agreement between the Synoptic and Johannine views on this subject is not to be assumed. The view of Wrede, which Bultmann adopts,[3] that the Messianic secret was an invention of St Mark's, is quite unconvincing. If we can accept the view that Christ did assert his claims in a veiled manner, we may fairly assume that at least part of his motive in so doing was the anxiety that no violence should be done to the freedom of men spiritually unready to acknowledge him. And it may be suggested that it was for the same reasons that the resurrection appearances were withheld from all save those who had loved him. One only of all the passages cited by Dr Bultmann to show that the New Testament regards the resurrection as a publicly demon-

[1] *K.u.M.*, I, p. 45. [2] *K.u.M.*, I, p. 44.
[3] *Theology of the N.T.*, E.T., vol. I, p. 32.

strable miracle is even susceptible of this interpretation, and it is clear that this verse should be interpreted in the light of others whose teaching is unmistakable and explicit, rather than that in its ambiguity it should be made the touchstone for the others.[1]

There are, in fact, only two places in the New Testament from which evidence might be cited to indicate that the risen Christ appeared to his enemies. The first is the passage about the keepers of the tomb in Matthew 28, v. 3, which Dr Bultmann would probably approve of my condemning as highly suspect on other grounds. And the second is the passage, or group of passages, which relate the appearing of the risen Christ to Saul on the Damascus road (Gal. 1.16; Acts 9.3ff, etc.). In this second instance it will, I think, be agreed that there are qualifying factors present, though this does not mean that the whole event is to be taken as the projection of a subjective uprush from the subconscious. Here certainly it does seem as if Christ had, by his appearing, subdued the unbelief of an enemy. But we must in this whole context take into account the words of St Peter recorded in Acts 10.40-41, 'Him God raised up the third day, and shewed him openly; not to all the people, but unto witnesses chosen before of God, even to us, who did eat and drink with him after he rose from the dead.'

(3) 'Faith,' says Bultmann, 'in the resurrection is nothing else than faith in the cross as saving event. The two must be taken together. "The Easter event", so far as it can be spoken of as a historical event alongside of the cross, is nothing other than the rise of faith in the risen Christ, in which the preaching about Christ originated.'[2]

This is one of those points where the New Testament and Bultmann are in at least verbal agreement in relation to the saving work of Christ. Both believe that the cross and the resurrection must be seen together if they are to be rightly understood. But how different the New Testament teaching about both cross and resurrection is from Bultmann's. We have already dealt with the difference on the theme of the cross. We must now point out the difference as to the resurrection.

Here again we have Bultmann's dichotomy between history and faith. The (sceptical) historian finds his unquestionable datum in the Easter faith of the disciples.[3] He can up to a point explain this in terms

[1] The passages cited by Bultmann are Acts 17.31; Luke 24.39-43; and I Cor. 15.3-8. Only the first passage might be interpreted as a demonstration to a sceptical world, the second is an experience granted to men who love Christ, and the third is a witness to such an experience, repeated to strengthen the faith of faltering believers.

[2] *K.u.M.*, I, pp. 46-7.

[3] Ibid., p. 47.

of their previous attachment to him, and he confines his attention to their 'visionary experiences'. Christian faith, on the other hand, is not interested in the historical question. It interprets the Easter faith as 'the self-authentication of the Risen One', the act of God in which the saving act of the cross is completed.

Here we must note, that to use no stronger language, the use of the words 'The Risen One' is inappropriate. Their use is only justified if something datable happened above and beyond the faith of the disciples, if Christ datably rose again. But these words cannot bear this sense for Bultmann, since he has declared that Christian faith is not interested in the historical question. It is true, as Bultmann says, that the risen Christ meets us in the word of preaching, when faith is created in us. But it is not right to reduce the resurrection and the resurrection appearances to such an encounter and nothing more, as he seems to do. Only because the resurrection was more than this can we have this encounter today.

Further, we must note the criticisms brought by Dr Hepburn against this school of interpretation from the philosophical side. Here the Bultmannian case may take two forms. The records of the resurrection appearances are declared incredible, and it is averred that the real miracle is the rise of faith in the disciples. Or else it is suggested, as by Bartsch, that 'the man who cannot believe the story of the resurrection, must believe that "God awakened this faith in the disciples in some other way",[1] that God, the living God declared himself in the midst of death to be on the side of his Son'. Here the witness of the disciples is rejected, and what they solemnly declare to have happened is replaced by an unknown quantity. Here Hepburn asks, what is the nature of the 'must'?[2] Is there not a more plausible alternative, the rejection both of the apostolic narratives (now shown to be untrustworthy) and of the apostolic interpretation? As Hepburn puts it, 'If you are confronted with form, human facial expressions, gestures, a voice responsive in conversation (and the detailed resurrection narrative provide all these with respect to the risen Christ), then the possibilities of illusion . . . are enormously diminished.' But if we are given merely the faith of the disciples that in some way God had vindicated Jesus, surely the alternative hypothesis of hallucination, uprushes from the subconscious, wish-fulfilment and so on, become enormously more probable.

[1] H. W. Bartsch, *Die Anrede Gottes*, p. 22.
[2] Ronald Hepburn, *Christianity and Paradox*, p. 101.

Now we come to Bultmann's conclusion. He has shown to his own satisfaction that an inquiry into the historical Jesus cannot throw light upon the significance of his cross, nor can we be helped by the various doctrines of his atonement, pre-existence, divine sonship, and so on. The resurrection too has been looked at, and he has shown that it does not play the part of a proof to all and sundry that 'God was behind Christ'. So again he faces the question, 'How do we see from the cross, that it is Christ's cross, that it is the eschatological event? How do we come to believe in the cross as saving event?'[1]

Here, he replies, there is only one answer that we can give. We believe in it as saving event because it is preached as such. Christ the crucified and Risen One meets us in the word of proclamation, nowhere else.

The second part of the sentence is nearly true, in so far as it is only faith that can see Christ and his cross as saving events. And it is true that in history the preaching of Christ and his cross has been the occasion of salvation. But the preaching of what a different gospel from that which Bultmann as theologian allows himself! How much richer this gospel is than Bultmann's!

But it is not because it is preached, that it is the cause of salvation. It is the other way round. So that Bultmann's answer here could not be more false than it is. But it is the only answer his theology permits him to give.

In the next chapter I shall be dealing with the question, 'Can this theology be preached?' I would not like to feel, as I went into church to preach, that I had no better warrant that what I had to preach was God's word, than the fact that I was about to preach it, or even that others had done so before me. Here, surely, we are faced with the final proof of the bankruptcy of Bultmann's historical scepticism and his flight from history. And here too, I would suggest, we have at least a warning that Bultmann's combination of historical scepticism and evangelical faith will not bear close examination, and will not stand the test of time.

[1] *K.u.M.*, I, p. 46.

VIII

WILL THIS PREACH?

1. Material considered: Bultmann's and Bartsch's sermons

THERE are two final tests to be applied to any theology. The first of these is, 'Is this true to the Biblical revelation?' and the second, 'Will this preach?' A large part of this book has been devoted to the first of these questions, though from time to time we have indicated the consequences which Bultmann's theology ought to have on preaching. It is fitting that this last chapter should be given to an examination of Bultmann's sermons with a view to answering the second question. I have judged it sufficient to include in the material considered only the twenty-one sermons contained in his volume *Marburger Predigten.*

These sermons cover a period of twenty-five years, and were preached to very different types of congregations. Three of them were addressed to divinity students at Marburg at the end of their academic Semester; one was delivered on the Sunday morning when news arrived that Hitler had invaded Russia, and one a few days after the final collapse of Germany, on the 17th June, 1945. These sermons belong to a time when great and terrible events were happening in the earth, and men were in need of all the resources of the Christian faith. Among the sermons some are brief and simple, others are much more elaborate. There is, for example, one on the very difficult passage, John 16, vv. 5-15, where the theme is that of the Spirit convicting the world of sin, righteousness and judgement. There is also one sermon on the Miraculous Draught of Fishes, which, as an example of a sermon on a miracle story (the only one), is of importance for our consideration.

In addition to Dr Bultmann's own sermons I have considered some by Hans Werner Bartsch, one of his disciples, and the man who has put us in his debt by publishing the five volumes of *Kerygma und Mythos*, and also by producing works of his own on the demythologizing controversy. In studying the effect of a new theology it is advisable not only to take into consideration the work of its leading exponent, but also that of those who follow him. For it is the latter, perhaps, who show the tendency, or the ultimate tendency, of the movement most clearly. Herr Bartsch has certainly courage, for his first sermon is on the text I Corinthians 15, v. 12, 'Now if Christ be preached that he rose from the dead, how say some among you that there is no resurrection of the dead?'[1]

2. *A general appreciation*

No one can read and re-read this volume of Bultmann's sermons without being impressed by their spiritual distinction. They bear witness to a profound religious experience, and they are written in simple and moving language. There is to be found here nothing of that obscurity and ambiguity which occasionally irritate the readers of Dr Bultmann's theological writings. Nor yet is there at any point the impression that the preacher is out to shock or startle his hearers by his scepticism.

It is difficult to say what needs to be said at this point without conveying an impression of patronage which is very far from the impression intended. The study of the sermons themselves will indeed show how out of place such an attitude on the part of the critic would be.

There is one characteristic of these Marburg Sermons which is worth noting. In not a few of them the teaching of Jesus is the theme, but in only one is there any reference to his historical personality, to the kind of man he showed himself to be in his life among men. This sermon is the one which deals with the Miraculous Draught of Fishes, an incident which Bultmann tells us he considers to be a pious invention. It is worthy of note that Bartsch's sermons convey a much richer picture of Jesus himself, and many of his sermons are on miracle incidents, though it is probable that his scepticism about miracle is as profound as his master's.

It is an interesting point that in Bultmann's preaching there should be what one can only call a vague and shadowy impression of Christ himself; so different from that given in the gospels. It may be that this is due to his conviction that the New Testament is not interested in Christ's personality—a conviction which we shall have cause later to dispute, urging that it is only one type of personality-interest that is foreign to the gospels. Or it may be due to Bultmann's historical scepticism; and, indeed, if you cut out as pious fictions all, or nearly all, of the miracle incidents, you will be left with but a small residue

[1] See Appendix C: pp. 224-7.

of factual information about Jesus. But we must point out that if faith is so comparatively little interested in history as Bultmann assumes, and so exclusively interested in what God existentially may say to me now, then there is no reason for this reserve. God can speak to me quite as well through a miracle story which is a pious fiction, or through an unreliable narrative about Christ's doings, as he can through the record of Christ's teaching, which can only with equal uncertainty be traced back to him. Here Bartsch, with his more vivid picture of Jesus, would appear to be more logical than Bultmann. Whatever the cause of Bultmann's lack of interest in Jesus as a man among men may be—and we must use no less stringent a phrase than this—its undoubted result will appear at a later stage in this chapter. Then we shall have to ask, if the figure of Christ is really so shadowy an outline as the one he draws in his sermons, what right Bultmann has to his belief in the love of God, a theme which he powerfully preaches.

There are naturally certain themes and texts preached on in this volume, which will especially stimulate the curiosity of the theological reader, since he will be eager to see what a thinker of Bultmann's known views can make of them. But before studying these in closer detail, I cannot refrain from drawing attention to two sermons which have perhaps less direct relevance to the theme of our criticism. For these sermons enable us better to appreciate the calibre of the thinker whom we are studying.

The first is a truly noble meditation on the subject of God in nature, preached on the text, 'While the earth remaineth, seedtime and harvest, and cold and heat, and summer and winter, and day and night shall not cease.'[1]

Here, after quoting Eichendorff's song of praise to God in nature, 'Wem Gott will rechte Gunst erweisen', and Goethe's Spring Song 'Ganymed', Bultmann says, 'Who can deny that in such songs, and in others like them there is something religious—an awareness of God? And, as Christians, shall we deny that such songs are really meant to praise the God whom we know through Jesus Christ as our Father? If we do so we shall come under the same condemnation as the priests in Jerusalem in Malachi's day, whom the prophet asked whether they thought that their sacrifices alone were pleasing to God.'[2]

The sermon goes on to suggest that in man's relationship to nature there is an analogy to his relationship to the God of grace. For, how-

[1] Gen. 8.22.
[2] *Marburger Predigten*, p. 30. The Biblical reference is to Mal. 1.10-11.

ever much man may seek to control the powers of nature, there is here a power and a glory which he cannot master, and so here he feels himself liberated and carried, as it were, in a greater hand. So man is right when he speaks of the God who meets him in nature; he is more right than he himself knows. And yet, because of this ignorance, he is also wrong.

For the world of nature is not eternal. All true honour to nature is honour to God; yet, if it is given only to nature, and not to the God who created nature, it is idolatrous, for the glory of nature is only a hint of his glory. So easily man can think that nature is divine, and then, because he shares in nature, he comes to believe that he shares also in divinity. And then, how easily he will turn to the worship of blood and soil! Nature is an ambiguous entity, and nature worship can easily turn to horror. Only the man who knows God as the God of grace and forgiveness can truly recognize his lineaments as the God of nature. And is our very flight to nature not a sign that we do not meet God as we should in our daily life? So Christian faith understands nature-religion as a flight to God that does not truly comprehend itself. 'The Christian believer rejoices in the presence of God in nature; the Word, that called him to faith, gives him the assurance of God's presence in nature also, and makes him receive all the gifts of nature as gifts of God.'[1]

Such a schematic summary can naturally do but scant justice to this tender and beautiful utterance. Whose heart would not warm to the man who can show such a sensitive appreciation for these things and the poetry that celebrates them—an openness of mind and heart so unlike the somewhat scolding denunciations of nature-worship which we are accustomed, from time to time, to hear from Christian pulpits?

The second sermon to which attention must be drawn here is one that uses the insights of modern psychology to illumine the parable of the Pharisee and Publican, and to present in a guise intelligible to modern man the Pauline antithesis between works and grace. The Pharisee, says Bultmann, is really a pious and diligent man, his only mistake is to think that he can face God on the strength of his righteous works—i.e., that God must give him recognition for what he has achieved. His deepest instinct is thus not the love of God, but the need for recognition. Bultmann goes on at this point to speak about the universal human need for recognition. How many of man's actions, he says, are shown by psychology to be motivated by this need, man's

[1] Ibid., p. 39.

greatest achievements as well as his greatest crimes! And, in truth, this need is universal, and not in itself sinful.

As we ourselves need recognition, so we should give it to others. But we must not make it our aim in life; we must not try to exact it from others. It can come to us only as a gift, by a kind of grace. When it is so given, then one's whole nature is liberated. For until this happens, all our work is done, not so much for its own sake, as for the recognition that it may bring. This false aim in life always takes its revenge; men think more of the impression they are making, than of the solidity of their work. Men hungry for recognition never make others love them, for love cannot be compelled; at the most they may compel respect. Such men are envious and, contemptuous of others, they try to live up to a false picture of themselves. Unable to love, they can only demand.

The need for recognition is fundamentally a need for recognition by God. Every man who is hungry for recognition feels that he must be sure of his own worth; he must be able to stand before his own tribunal. And, whether he knows it or not, that tribunal is God. The only way to escape from this bondage is to flee, not from God, as the Pharisee does, for all his praying; but to flee to God, by making a simple frank confession. In so doing, one must not compare oneself with others, for that is still to claim recognition as being better than they are. Nor is it any good to try to make a complete confession, for that is again to make a claim that one has done something that should receive God's recognition. This simple and open confession is what the Publican made.

There is something very suggestive and stimulating about this sermon, with its hinted parallel between the relation of man to his human neighbour, and the relation of man to God, and the need of some gift, in both relations, which we cannot ourselves supply. This sermon does not go on to deal in detail with the theme of the divine grace in Christ, which, by forgiving us, and showing us love, liberates us from the hopeless quest for recognition. It does not go on to deal with this theme, for it is not germane to the text. But this is a favourite turning-point in most of the sermons, and we shall have to deal with it later.

3. The demythologizing theology and the preaching of miracle

(*a*) *BULTMANN*

Of the twenty-one sermons in Bultmann's volumes, only one is on the theme of a miracle story; the story of the 'Miraculous Draught of Fishes'. Some time ago Dr A. C. Craig wrote that he never heard a preacher announce a text from a miracle story without wondering whether he would have 'anything to say which properly touches the miraculous aspect of the story. . . . Or will he quickly sidle and shuffle off into the well-trodden paths of exhortation and the moralities? If he grapples with the miraculous aspect of the story, will what he says be vertebrate, displaying the bony structure of thought-out theory, or will he be slippery as an eel?'[1]

Whatever his views may be, the preacher dealing with a miracle story is in a difficult position. He knows that among his hearers, some will believe all the miracle stories, while others will find it hard to believe any. He knows that his main aim is so to preach from the story that the faith of his hearers will be quickened, and that disquisitions on the philosophical possibility or otherwise of miracle are not directly contributory to this purpose. In any case a sermon is hardly the place for a full-length discussion of this theme, and few preachers would feel competent to give one, even in a lecture-room, while few of their church hearers would be able to follow! On the other hand he may feel some difficulty in preaching on a miracle story which he does not think has a solid basis in past event. Such are the difficulties which today face men proposing to preach on miracle stories, whatever their own theological or philosophical positions may be.

In this sermon Dr Bultmann bravely grasps the nettle with both hands, saying that for his part he believes the story to be a pious invention (*eine fromme Dichtung*). He makes the distinction between the acceptance of a story as true, and Christian faith. It is not faith to accept such a story as true, and God will never demand that we sacrifice our intellect, or believe what we know is not true. The main aim of the story is to show the power that Jesus had over a human life (Peter's), so that God may be given a chance to exercise a like influence on us. Jesus is reported to have told Peter to launch out into the deep; that is, where a catch of fish was unlikeliest. So it is with us that, when our powers are at an end, God's power gets a chance with us. We must be

[1] A. C. Craig, *Preaching in a Scientific Age*, p. 55.

ready to see miracle, to see God in events. But we do not do so, because we are so set on mastering our world, that we let the outlook we use for this purpose dominate all our thinking and our relationship to the world. The world can indeed be understood in terms of scientific law, but when thus understood, is it seen in its full reality? The temptation does indeed continually return, to think that this world is only our workaday world, and not also the place where the Creator is revealed. But it is both, though there still remains the question, insoluble by our reason, how the world can be both at the same time. The Christian must surrender his thinking to God, not by giving up the use of his intellect in those fields where it is competent to investigate, but by giving up the attempt to plan his own path and attain his own security in life.

There is here a great deal with which the reader will remember we have ourselves agreed. It is true that we have here the same weaknesses as were pointed out in the chapter on 'Myth and Miracle', in particular the weakness of the doctrine of the mutually cancelling outlooks.[1] But here the antithesis is less harshly and crudely expressed than it was in the earlier Essay on Miracle.[2] Taking the sermon as a whole, it may be said that Bultmann manages to preach a Christian message from a narrative which he believes to be a pious fiction.

One more point in connexion with this sermon may be made. What is epistemologically a weakness, the doctrine of mutually incompatible and temporally successive outlooks, is actually from a religious point of view a strength! For it enables Bultmann to speak of the Christian experiencing, and even doing, miracles.[3] Thus, though at the price of logic, a freedom for God in events is left. Our own view is that another viewpoint on miracle is possible, a viewpoint which is both religiously and epistemologically strong.

On the other hand, while conceding that Bultmann has succeeded in preaching effectively from one miracle which he does not believe to have happened, we may note that he has not ventured forth as bravely on such themes as Herr Bartsch. We cannot help feeling that if he did so, he would be as unconvincing in his preaching on this theme as he has been in the part of his essay on 'Neues Testament und Mythologie'

[1] See ch. VI, pp. 117, 124, 134. [2] *G.u.V.*, I, pp. 214-28.

[3] Bultmann here expresses himself more optimistically than in the above mentioned essay. The belief that the Christian will not only experience, but also do, miracles is to be found in W. Herrmann, *Offenbarung und Wunder*, ch. II, 'Der Christ und das Wunder', an essay marked by the same epistemological weaknesses as Bultmann's. A study of this book will reveal how very dependent here Bultmann is on his old teacher.

which treats of the resurrection.[1] And he might have carried as little conviction as does Herr Bartsch in some of his sermons on miracle incidents.

(b) *BARTSCH*

Among Hans Werner Bartsch's published sermons,[2] thirteen in number, nine are on miracle stories, ten are on texts from the Gospels, one is on the resurrection, one on the ascension, and one on pentecost. We shall consider the last three first. The resurrection sermon is preached on the famous passage on that theme taken from I Corinthians 15.[3] Here the preacher asserts that the centre of the sermon is not the reality of Christ's resurrection. The men to whom Paul was writing, he claims, did believe that Christ was risen; but they were not applying the truth of the gospel in their own lives. They were looking forward with joy to Christ's triumphant return, but their anxiety was that, if death found them before it happened, they would perish. There was thus one fear for the future from which the resurrection of Christ did not deliver them. But to have any such reservation in one's faith is not to believe in Christ's victory at all. So sure is Paul's faith in our solidarity with him in death and resurrection.

The most dreadful thing about suffering is its power to separate us from God. The passion story puts Jesus at men's side. He has suffered all that we can ever suffer, and more. The meaning of the story is not that a man should rise from the dead, and that we should gaze open-mouthed at this wonder. The Corinthians believed all that, and yet Paul declares their faith vain. On the other hand, he who cannot accept the recorded story of the resurrection, should not think that he has rejected the Christian faith, and that God has nothing more to say to him.

The important thing is that we should hear what God has to say to us in this story. The disciples thought that it was all up with Jesus. But now, of a sudden, it became clear to them that God had declared himself for this crucified Jesus. The man who cannot accept the story of the resurrection must believe that God in some other way awakened in the disciples this faith; that in the midst of death he had declared

[1] *K.u.M.*, I, pp. 15-48. For example let us consider what in fact happens in Bultmann's preaching about the resurrection (see below, pp. 187-9). There is no reason to suppose that he would fare better if he preached about lesser miracles.

[2] H. W. Bartsch, *Die Anrede Gottes*.

[3] See below, pp. 224-7.

himself for his Son. So the story means that God is on the side of those who are cast down and despised. 'Christ is risen' is the cry with which the supremacy of God over all his enemies is declared. To believe that nothing can take us out of God's hand is to be risen with Christ.

Here, surely, we cannot but feel that a piece of legerdemain has been played upon us. The story of the resurrection has been snatched out of our hands, and a question-mark left in its place. Easter is thus very near to becoming the occasion for the rise of a faith without grounds or basis. The primitive church is like a series of concentric rings spreading on the surface of a lake into which no stone has been thrown. When this unknown quantity behind the rise of the easter faith has been left in our hands, it is hard to feel that Bartsch is justified at the end of his sermon in speaking of 'The revelation of the power and goodness of God'. What revelation?

I need not deal in such detail with the metamorphosis undergone in Herr Bartsch's hands by the stories of pentecost and the ascension. Admittedly preaching about either incident is far from easy, but it is sometimes easier to know that something has gone wrong than to know how to do what is right. For Bartsch the story of pentecost is reduced to this, that the word was preached then by Peter, and that it had, beyond all expectation, power to convert. And the story of the ascension becomes the miracle of the survival of the faith of the punch-drunk church after the terrible blow struck by the cessation of the (illusory?) resurrection appearances.[1] Surely here imagination is at work as illegitimately and misleadingly on the sources as in the most baroque of the nineteenth century 'Lives of Jesus', so rightly castigated by Martin Kähler. What right has a modern preacher to construct so gloomy a picture from the so joyful pages of the beginning of Acts?

In dealing with miracle stories in general, Herr Bartsch's method is to preach quite simply from the episodes, with an eye to the challenge, warning, and comfort of the application. In dealing with the stories of the leper healed and the centurion of great faith, he says that the evangelist does not lay great stress on the miracles, but passes on at once to emphasize the faith of these two men. We understand the evangelist only when we let the faith of the leper and the centurion say to us that we too, today, may have a faith like theirs.[2]

Nearly all these stories are told by Herr Bartsch without any question

[1] Thus it would appear that the purpose of the ascension was merely to repeat the sombre message of the resurrection.

[2] *Die Anrede Gottes*, p. 42.

being raised as to whether the events as narrated occurred or not. Indeed, we might well believe that the preacher's own theological position was rather conservative. For example, in the story of the healing of the paralytic man borne by four, Herr Bartsch talks of Jesus, in the word of forgiveness uttered, as speaking with the authority of God, and of his standing for a moment, in that house in Capernaum, in the light of the redemption which he brought to the world; as if, in Kierkegaard's phrase, for a moment the divine incognito had been partially lifted.[1] Here we might assume a theology in the background like that of Dodd's realized eschatology. We have not the opportunity of knowing what Herr Bartsch thinks about the historical Jesus. Does he share the views of Dr Bultmann that Jesus did not believe himself to be the Messiah, or the coming Messiah, or the Son of man, but looked on himself rather as an eschatological preacher preparing men for a supernatural Son of man? To judge by this sermon, it would certainly appear that he does not hold Bultmann's views on these matters, but we are reminded that elsewhere Herr Bartsch has written that the Scripture passages on which the sermons are preached are not history, but preaching and witness themselves. So it may be that Bartsch preaches as if he believed that the Kingdom had already been present, though hidden, in the presence of Jesus, and that Christ had actually in that room in Capernaum raised the corner of the cloak of the divine incognito; while all the time the preacher does not himself hold that Christ made any such claims for himself, believing himself to be nothing more than a forerunner. And it may be that Bartsch is able to preach in this way, believing that in Bultmann's phrase, it is not his task to speak of what happened so much as to point out what God wishes to say to us today through what happened. And our difficulty will then be, why there should be such an abyss between what God wishes to say to me through what happened, and what he actually said in the language of past event. Why then should not the link with the historical be severed entirely, and why should not Christian preachers be free to invent edifying new incidents in the life of Christ and new miracles from which they may be able to preach what they believe to be the Christian gospel?[2] These are some of the difficulties and questions which arise in our minds when we read these spiritual and in some cases distinguished sermons of Herr Bartsch.

[1] The same impression is given in Bartsch's *Christus ohne Mythos*, p. 58.

[2] R. Hepburn has also asked this question, *Christianity and Paradox*, p. 105. It would be interesting to know what answer the Bultmann school of theology could give to it.

4. Bultmann's sermons: inauthentic existence

The reader of Bultmann's sermons cannot but be impressed by a contrast that runs through them all, which I have described above by a word in vogue among the existentialists—the contrast between authenticity and inauthenticity. Sometimes this appears as the contrast between the invisible and the visible, the invisible being the transcendent spiritual world, and the visible being the world of outward show and appearance. Sometimes the visible is spoken of in Johannine terms as 'the world', and again we are sometimes reminded of the Pauline use of the term 'the flesh'. It is also clear from the start that the contrast here indicated has some kinship with the Pauline contrast between faith and works.

It is the preacher's central aim in these sermons to bring his hearers to realize the hopelessness and futility of the inauthentic existence, and to decide for the authentic life—a decision which must continually be renewed, and can never be sealed in a single conversion experience, and safely committed to the past.

It will be our task in this paragraph and the next, to give some account of these two alternative ways of life as they are depicted in the sermons. Our aim will be twofold: first, to see how far Bultmann's existentialist studies have helped him to put the substance of the Christian gospel in a manner understandable to a modern congregation, and second, to see how far he is here dependent on Heidegger.

Bultmann has described the inauthentic manner of life in a number of different ways, and it will be worth our while to examine four of these, with illustrations from the sermons.

(*a*) *Inauthenticity as distraction*

Here we quote from a sermon on the use of Sunday.

'. . . But work does not only make a man's body tired and chafe him externally. It can also waste away his inner substance. A man engaged in a work which makes wholesale claims upon him with its projects and prospects, is in continual danger of forgetting his better self through his work. More and more seldom does he take thought for his own life, examining himself in the sight of God, and recalling that it is not his own power and care that blesses his work. We say well that such a man is wholly absorbed in his work, and often do not realize what a damning verdict we have passed on him.'[1]

[1] *Marburger Predigten*, p. 73.

Or again, from a sermon on 'Behold I stand at the door and knock.' '. . . But how do we come to ourselves? How do we become ourselves? If we listen to the voice of Eternity, "Behold I stand at the door and knock." Eternity stands at the door and knocks. It asks us if we are a self, or if we have lost ourselves to time and that which time brings.'[1]

The reader will recognize here very clearly the kinship with Heidegger's concept of inauthenticity, with its projects, and hustle, and shallow gossip.

(*b*) *Inauthenticity as the search for security*

Here we can group together both the search for recognition, and the wilful pursuit of our own aims. For behind both of these activities there is the urge for security, the acknowledgement of our claims by others and by God, and the achievement of such success as will once and for all lift us above any threat which the future may bring.

I have already dealt rather fully with the search for recognition as it is pictured in Bultmann's sermon on the Pharisee and the Publican. Here it is necessary to do no more than to point out the kinship with the biblical conception of justification by works. The search for recognition is always in the last resort a desire to have one's status recognized by God, and one's claims acknowledged by him.

In the wilful pursuit of our own aims we find another expression of the search for security.

'All life,' says Bultmann, 'that reaches out after a goal, is a provisional, unfulfilled, inauthentic life. What the man really wants to be, lies always ahead of him. His life is in a way a race, in which he tries to catch up with himself, his authentic existence.'[2]

'What they (men) hope for from the future, is always just what they want to hold fast to, if only they can get it, in order to possess it, to secure themselves against the future. From such striving of men, from such grasping and desiring to possess, comes also the curse which lies over all human history, the struggle of all against all, since each one wills to assert himself against the others, claims his rights, seeks to ensure his future. And, instead of living from the future, men in reality are living in bondage to the past, which prescribes to them their goals, dictates the motives and standards of their action; and so human history, like nature, presents the picture of a humanity which is not as it could be, or should be, but is distorted and deformed.'[3]

[1] Ibid., p. 122. [2] Ibid., p. 15. [3] Ibid., p. 65.

(*c*) *Inauthenticity as a flight from God*

'In truth, then, men seek recognition from God, and yet at the same time, they are in flight from God, inasmuch as they think they can extort from him the recognition for which they strive, by their efforts and achievement. How then shall they find that recognition? . . . How find the free security of life, the consciousness that they are not valueless, but that they have a genuine life? In one way only, by fleeing from themselves, and fleeing to God.'[1]

(*d*) *The inauthentic life a subjection to demonic forces*

Bultmann believes that the New Testament uses mythological language about the demons, but that under this guise it deals with an important reality. The inauthentic life is in truth a slavery, though the form of this slavery varies, according as the object varies under whose domination man falls. When the New Testament speaks about the prince of this world, or the demons from whom Christ came to deliver us, it is expressing much the same truth as has often been expressed in the words that man is either a servant of the living God, or else the slave of idols. Such idols can be of very different kinds. 'But the message that God is the judge reminds us of the fact that all the phenomena of the world are ambiguous, and therefore a source of temptation. That we can use them for good, and that we can lose ourselves in bondage to them. But we become enslaved to them when we forget this ambiguity, and when we no longer see the temptations in them. We must render an account of our use of them. This is above all true in relation to ourselves, our powers and instincts, our gifts and passions. They are not unambiguous, and not all that comes from the call of the blood, is good.'[2]

This is true also of the powers of external nature, as we saw in our study of the sermon on God in nature. Nature worship is, like nature itself, ambiguous. It can become idolatry, if this ambiguity is forgotten, and nature is worshipped in itself and not seen as a gift from God, in which his transcendent glory reflects itself.

And, above all, modern man is in danger of falling under the harsh sway of the most modern idol, that of technology. How easily we can be lured by technology to try to escape from our radical anxiety, from God and our true selves, and how easily, as a consequence, we can fall into a fresh servitude! 'In our technical domination of the world and

[1] *Marburger Predigten*, p. 115. [2] Ibid., p. 9.

its powers, the temptation continually meets us to regard our life as secured, and the world as a field for our exploitation, and to forget the fundamental insecurity and questionable character of our life.'[1] Accordingly, 'Technology, which ought to serve to tame and to place at man's disposal the powers of nature which once encountered him as demonic powers, has itself become a demonic power which compels him to serve it, so that he loses himself.'[2]

And so, in a sermon on John 16.5-15, Bultmann is able to speak of 'the prince of this world' as 'the strange power which this world of possibilities of gifts and tasks can win over man. He who submits to it (this world) experiences this strange power which seeks to master him, and claims him in his work as in his pleasure and his pain, so that his outlook, his thinking, and his willing are enslaved to it, and can no longer rise above it.'[3]

5. *Bultmann's sermons: authentic existence*

We may now treat of authentic existence as portrayed in this volume of sermons, dealing with the various points rather more briefly than we did with their counterparts under the heading of inauthenticity.

(*a*) Inauthenticity was described as distraction, as self-forgetfulness. Therefore authenticity will be a 'coming to oneself'. True knowledge of self, for Bultmann as for Calvin, is always the counterpart of true knowledge of God; each one of these conditioning the other.

Before a man can come to himself he must recognize that he is one of those that 'labour and are heavy laden'. And man cannot simply let himself be carried by the life-powers of the universe, or by the racial and vital urges of his people. No; man stands before God in his solitariness. He has to choose his way in responsibility and decision.[4] 'For this is what God requires of man, that man should not use God as a means of increasing his own human glory, but that man should subject himself to God, and give him the honour. . . . He who would approach God must take the path that leads through the darkness of self-surrender. Only out of the darkness of death, in which man's own will dies, does the life shine forth, which God gives.' In this self-surrender man comes to a true understanding of his own nature.

(*b*) Inauthenticity was also described as the search for recognition, the desire to extract by force an acknowledgement of our deserts by men and by God, and an acknowledgement of our rights over against

[1] Ibid., p. 6. [2] Ibid., p. 8. [3] Ibid., p. 51. [4] Ibid., p. 12.

them. Authenticity is given to the man who confesses that he has no rights over against God, and no claims upon him, and that he has nothing which he has not received. He must be ready to receive God's forgiveness, and to live in the continual receipt of it, knowing that God has given to him freely that gift which he previously strove to extort as his due. This false search for recognition and security is further on described as the wilful and stubborn pursuit of our own aims. Authentic existence is true living in the power of the future, not a wish-fulfilment future, but any future that God chooses to give us. 'A real life in the power of the future (*aus der Zukunft*) would mean the victory over fear of the future in the certainty that everything that it brings cannot but serve the best.'[1]

(*c*) inauthenticity was described as a flight from God; authenticity is given to our life when we flee to him.[2]

(*d*) Inauthenticity was described as a slavery to the demonic. Authentic life belongs to the man who no longer makes idols of outward things, or of human instincts or human goals, but has reached a certain detachment from them. Not that he should have nothing to do with them. Bultmann does not wish us to turn our backs on technology as did Gandhi with his proposed return to the spinning-wheel. Only we must no longer be worshippers and slaves of nature, or instinct, or wealth. The man who has surrendered his will to God's will is 'poor in spirit'. 'To be poor in spirit is not to conceal the poverty of our humanity by means of the apparent riches that man may win. It may be riches in visible property—then what Luther says is applicable, "To be poor in spirit means a heart that does not bind itself to property and riches, even though it possesses them. Yet it is all one to him as though he had it not." '[3]

Before we pass from this subject to the next, we must take up the two questions asked at an earlier point in this chapter. The first of these was, How far have Bultmann's existentialist studies helped him to put the substance of the Christian gospel in a manner understandable to a Christian congregation? Our answer must be that by describing the old contrast of works and faith in the four ways outlined above, he

[1] Ibid., p. 67. Cf. Newman's *Lead, kindly Light*:

'I was not ever thus, nor prayed that Thou
Shouldst lead me on;
I loved to choose and see my path, but now
Lead Thou me on;
I loved the garish day, and, spite of fears,
Pride ruled my will: remember not past years.'

[2] Ibid., p. 115. [3] Ibid., p. 181.

has in a remarkable manner made intelligible and concrete for our day an important part of the gospel. Modern man does flee from God by seeking distraction in the world. He does search vainly for security in the things of this earth. His claim for recognition and his wilful pursuit of his own ends can never bring him that peace which he inwardly desires. And the man who is not a servant of the true God inevitably, sooner of later, falls under the demonic sway of created forces of one kind or another. Of all these themes Bultmann's sermons make a telling use.[1] They are, indeed, as old as St Augustine, if not older, but the studies of the existentialists, from Pascal and Kierkegaard downwards, have drawn our attention to them once more, and here Bultmann's preaching may well have been enriched by his contact with Heidegger. There does not seem, however, in the sermons, to be any very powerful and important line of preaching which can be traced to Heidegger in particular. It will be remembered that from the start we have admitted that a general relationship to Heidegger might be of value to preaching and to theology, and that a careful and eclectic use of the type of concepts which he uses, might be of value in scriptural interpretation, if in each case the concepts were tried out, to see whether they actually illuminated the true meaning of the passage.

Our second question was, How far is Bultmann here dependent on Heidegger in the manner that Heidegger demands every theologian of the future should be? Is the theology of Bultmann's sermons an ontic discipline dependent on Heidegger's work already done in the ontological field? The answer is the same as that given in our chapter, 'Heidegger with the new Look?' which dealt with the relation to Heidegger of Bultmann's theological work. Bultmann's thought which underlies his preaching is certainly akin to Heidegger's. For example, Heidegger's view of the future as helping to constitute the authentic present has certainly left an impressive mark on Bultmann's preaching, but the latter is most certainly not the ontic child of a Heideggerian ontological parent!

6. Salvation through Christ in the sermons of Bultmann

At this point we must draw attention to a difficulty which may well have already been felt by the reader. The order of our study in the last two paragraphs has followed that in Bultmann's first essay in *Kerygma*

[1] Though it may well be that there is more in the demonic than he is prepared to allow.

and Myth, where he has produced a demythologized account of man's being in unbelief and in faith. There was, even in that essay, a certain artificiality of treatment, which arose from this division of the field. Bultmann could not at that stage speak of the Christ event, and so had to speak of inauthentic and authentic being without reference to that one event without which he certainly believes that authenticity cannot be received by man. He was compelled to be silent about Christ, because the most difficult task of all for his theology was the demythologizing of the Christ event, and this had to be reserved for the final pages of the essay.

The difficulty of provisionally leaving out all account of Christ has been even greater in our treatment of the subject, since we are dealing with sermons, and in preaching the preacher must in each sermon not only deal with inauthenticity and authenticity, but in some way must deal with the salvation whose bearer Christ is. The fact that authenticity and inauthenticity have been described, and thus far without reference to Christ, must inevitably have made the description of both inadequate, especially the description of authenticity. And it must clearly be said that nothing is more certain about Bultmann's theology than its assertion that authenticity cannot be achieved without the gospel of Christ. It must frankly be said that in nearly every sermon in this book there are some crucial sentences about Christ, about God's love shown in him, about his death and resurrection, and our dying and rising again with him; and that such sentences are the very foundation upon which the power of this preaching rests, and the fulcrum on which the whole system turns. And our question will each time be, whether the contents which Bultmann's theology in fact gives to each of these concepts really justifies the evangelical warmth of the language used. It is my opinion that in fact it is very far from doing so, though I would be the last to accuse Bultmann of insincerity because of this inconsistency. It happens frequently that men's faith is better and deeper than their theology, and this would appear to be a case in point.

The plan to be adopted here will be first to consider each of three themes dealt with in the crucial passages of these sermons, giving fairly long excerpts from them, which the reader will understand are necessary for the comprehension of the matter. And then we shall ask what the rest of Bultmann's theological writings lead us to understand him to teach on each of these themes. The themes are three in number; firstly, the love of God shown to us in Christ; secondly, the cross and resurrection of Christ; and thirdly, our dying and rising again with him. The use of this method will involve further abstraction, for clearly the love of God in Christ cannot be understood without an understanding of Christ's death and resurrection. And further, Christ's death and resurrection are intimately bound up with our dying and rising again with him. Indeed, in the theology of Bultmann, we would maintain that what happened to him and what happens to us are so closely linked, that there is danger of their being confused! Such are the drawbacks of the method proposed, but only by dividing up our material into these three blocks can we deal with what would otherwise be wholly unmanageable.

(*a*) *God's love for us in Christ*

The concluding paragraphs of the first sermon in the book, on Acts 17.22-32, contain the following sentences:

'The man who wishes to approach God must take the road which leads through the darkness of self-surrender. It is only out of the darkness of death, in which a man's own will dies, that the life which God gives shines forth.'

And what shall give us the confidence to make this venture, to enter into this darkness? What shall give us the confidence to let ourselves sink into this darkness, trusting that God's strong and gracious hand will enfold and hold us? This, and this alone, that the unknown God gives us knowledge of himself in his word. Because we have his word, that tells us to believe; his word that proclaims to us Jesus crucified and risen; his word, that makes promise to us; the resurrection from the dead.[1] His word, that shows its truth only to him who believes, but really does show it to such a one.[2]

The other sermon which I have chosen to illustrate Bultmann's handling of the theme of the love of God revealed to us in Christ, was preached on the passage Romans 8.18-27. Here Bultmann says: 'Thus love gives us a future, and thus love at the same time gives us confidence in the future. But our love is only a weak reflection of the love of God "that moves the sun in heaven and all the stars". How weak and broken is our power to give and to awaken love! But this is the Christmas message, that God's love has appeared in Jesus Christ. Here it comes out of concealment, and is proclaimed in word and deed to all who in anxiety and suffering long for freedom: God's love, which

[1] The punctuation makes it clear that in this sentence 'His word' is equated with the resurrection from the dead.

[2] Ibid., p. 12.

takes us not as we have made ourselves, but as we are not, as we wish to be, as we shall be. And by doing so, the divine love makes all that we are a mere appearance, and in exchange for that it gives us what we are not, our genuine, real, being. God's love is not a goal which we struggle to attain—who could ever attain to it? It is the power that always from the beginning embraces us, to which our eyes must be opened. And we must direct our gaze to him, in whom it appeared and became real in the world, Jesus Christ. To know oneself carried by this love is to be free from the past, free from oneself, free for the future that God will give, for the glory that shall be revealed in us.'[1]

Such is Bultmann's preaching on the love of God revealed to us in Christ. These are fine, even splendid passages of Christian preaching. But does Bultmann's theology give us any solid grounds for believing that they are true? Were the events of Christ's life and death, as reported to us by Bultmann, such as to justify such a conclusion? The question is one which cannot be by-passed. Before we attempt to answer it, let us refresh our memory of Bultmann's picture of the historical Christ event, and of the growth and formulation of the gospel in the primitive church. And here we shall have to be guided by the principle that there *is* a relevance of these historical questions to the preaching content of the gospel.

We must remember that in Bultmann's opinion, the Synoptic Gospels are very far from giving an accurate account of what actually happened. We must go behind them, and force them against their will, so to speak, to disclose to us the events which actually took place, if we wish to know these events. And Bultmann has an interest in this question, in spite of his disavowals, for he does reconstruct for us such a historical outline.

According to his *Theology of the New Testament*,[2] Jesus came before the public of his day as a preacher of the impending irruption of the reign of God, a miraculous event which would occur without the help of man. He did not believe himself to be the Messiah, nor the Suffering Servant, nor the future Messiah, nor the Son of man. He believed that the Son of man was a supernatural figure other than himself, who would come on the clouds of heaven, judging the world, and thereafter taking the faithful to Paradise. Christ's recorded predictions of his death are prophecies after the event. There is a curious haze over the

[1] Ibid., pp. 68-9.
[2] *Theology of the New Testament*, E.T., vol. I, pp. 3 ff.

Bultmannian account of the events which led up to Christ's death, but it would appear to have come upon him unexpectedly at the hands of his Jewish enemies and Roman executioners.

What of Jesus' message? The content of his message was not new, but new was his confident proclamation, 'Now the time is come; God's reign is breaking in!' The nearness of God's reign was, he thought, indicated by his healings. He believed that God's reign was not here actually, but only dawning. Christ did not summon men to believe in himself; his own person signified rather the radical demand for decision, decision for God.

His message was a demand for a whole-hearted and interior obedience to God's will. His expectation of the immediate coming of the Kingdom was a mistake, a mythological self-misunderstanding. Its true existential significance was the urgency of the call for decision, so that the ethic and the apocalyptic preaching were at heart one.

Bultmann contemptuously rejects the whole doctrine that with the coming of Jesus the Kingdom was already in essence here on earth[1]; that it was, accordingly, a gift of God's initiative and grace already present, to which the response of faith was a grateful reply. Hence for him, it would appear, there is but little apparent difference between Jesus' gospel and John the Baptist's. True, for Jesus, God meets the man who responds to his demands, with generous forgiveness, and is a loving Father to him, but this would seem to be, on Bultmann's interpretation, a secondary emphasis in Jesus' gospel. Would it be fair to say that, on Bultmann's presuppositions, Jesus' gospel ought to be depicted as primarily demand, and not gift?[2]

Thus for Bultmann the earthly ministry of Jesus can be by no means so powerful a revelation of God's grace and love as it is for those whose theology is more conservative, and who are ready to believe that Jesus was in fact what the gospel witnesses believe him to have been.

We pass now to Bultmann's interpretation of the preaching of the primitive church. Though Jesus did not in fact rise from the dead, the primitive church believed him to have done so. They were convinced that he would come to judge the world as the Son of man and as Messiah. During his life-time the disciples had accepted his challenge,

[1] *Theology of the N.T.*, E.T., vol. I, p. 22.

[2] Paul Althaus has shown how Bultmann's abstraction of the demand-to-believe, from the picture of Jesus and his life portrayed in the gospels, leads to a new legalism. Althaus, *Das so-genannte Kerygma und der historische Jesus*, p. 27, E.T., *The So-called Kerygma*, p. 46.

and followed him, preaching his gospel of demand for decision, and reception of the divine forgiveness. The cross, as a fearful disaster that befell Jesus, raised for them once more the question, 'Was he really the messenger bearing a decisive challenge to men from God, calling them to repentance?' 'The church had to surmount the scandal of the cross, and did it in the Easter faith.'[1] This we may perhaps interpret by saying, that although Jesus did not in fact rise from the dead, did not return to the disciples, yet somehow (we do not know how, and it is unimportant to know how[2]) they found the courage to preach his gospel and present his challenge even after his death.

The real, existential, meaning of what they were saying in their mythological assertion that he had risen, and would come to judge the world as Messiah, was that in his earthly appearance, he had already been God's eschatological messenger. Of this they were only dimly aware, but the fact that they regarded themselves as the eschatological community committed to preaching the gospel, shows that some inkling of the truth was already stirring in them.[2] Here we may point out in comment that all this means little more than a claim by Bultmann that God had *backed* Jesus' demand for repentance, and promised forgiveness to those who accepted his challenge. This is certainly much, but it is no less certainly very far short of the Christian gospel.

We pass now to Bultmann's account of St Paul. In his hands this gospel was considerably enriched, or at least it appears as if this were the case. Bultmann tells us that the personality of Jesus has no importance for Paul's preaching, nor indeed has it any importance for the writer of the Fourth Gospel, or for the New Testament in general. For Paul the deed of divine grace consists in the fact that God gave up Christ to die upon the cross, but the salvation-event also includes the resurrection. And, strictly speaking, this event also includes the incarnation, for he who gave himself up to die is none other than the pre-existent Son of God.

However, it appears that Paul's use of the resurrection, Christ's pre-existence, and the various concepts of atonement, sacrifice and vicarious suffering, are all mythological ways of expressing the same fact that somehow, through Christ's preaching and earthly career, God promises forgiveness to the repentant believer. So that the appearance of enrichment of the gospel in St Paul's hands is, we must conclude, illusory.

When we ask how the Christ event can be recognized and experienced

[1] *Theology of the N.T.*, E.T., vol. I, p. 45. [2] Ibid.

by men as the deed of grace, we are told: not because of Christ's character as revealed by his actions and life among men, for the New Testament has no interest in these things. Nor may we use the concepts which Paul used, for these are mythological. The fact remains, apparently, that through the Christ event God challenges men and offers them forgiveness. But when we persist, and ask still 'How?' and 'Why?' we are curtly told that the salvation event is recognized as such only when and because it is preached as such.

This stone which is offered us in place of the bread of the New Testament gospel will give our faith little nourishment. It is surely clear that the faith of the two fine passages quoted above from Bultmann's sermons was nourished on something better than this. And that remains true, even if for the moment we choose to disregard the final burst of Bultmann's irrationality, which declares that the saving power of the Christ event depends, not upon its content, but upon its being preached. For what nourishes the faith underlying this preaching is surely a sense of God's prevenient grace, in the person and kingdom of Christ as primarily a gift, and only secondarily as the embodiment of a demand; a Christ who is both human and divine, and not merely a blank cross-roads of decision.

But the startling irrationality of Bultmann's final answer is very significant. It looks as if we were to conclude that there is no significance in the events, not even a significance visible to faith. It looks as if only the *preaching* of these events had significance and saving power. One can hardly believe that this is what Bultmann really means, though he undoubtedly says it. If it were his real view, then the implication would be that faith as he understands it is wholly irrational, and utterly unable to give any account of itself. But whether this position be really more extreme than Bultmann is in general ready to maintain, the fact that it is even possible for him is highly significant. Underneath this extraordinary answer to the question, How and why is the Christ event recognized and experienced by men as God's supreme act of grace? is concealed the unbridgeable chasm betweeen Bultmann's historical scepticism and his evangelical gospel.

Is it merely a lack of faith when we ask for some better assurance about God than Bultmann's theology here seems to afford? If we are 'to sink into the darkness, trusting that God's strong and gracious hand will enfold and hold us', surely something more than this is required to rest upon. The New Testament would appear to agree with this criticism, for it gives us a great deal more than Dr Bultmann.

(*b*) *The Cross of Christ*

Here, adhering to our chosen pattern, we shall start with some quotations from Bultmann's preaching. The first comes from a sermon on II Corinthians 4.6-11. Here it will be necessary to include material, not only about Christ's death, but also about our dying with him.

' "We carry about with us the dying of the Lord Jesus in our body." That means that he (Paul) understands all our sufferings in the light of the cross. The cross of Christ is for Paul not only a historical event in the past but a happening which, taking its origin in that historical event, permeates the whole history of mankind; that event in which God judged the whole of this world, with its pride and splendour as with its care and distress, and declared it valueless.[1] Everywhere this dying of Christ happens, where a man understands that his sufferings must serve to bring to his consciousness the final worthlessness of this earthly world.'

According to this passage, God judged the world in the death of Christ. The same suggestion is made in a very difficult passage in the Essay on 'New Testament and Mythology', in which he says, 'For when the cross is called the judgement pronounced upon the world, through which the rulers of this world are brought to nothing (I Cor. 2.6 ff.) what is implied thereby is that in the cross judgement is pronounced upon ourselves, the men who have fallen under the sway of the powers of "the world".'[2]

We may judge that here Bultmann is demythologizing a New Testament utterance, and reinterpreting it existentially. But if so, we must ask him, 'How is the cross a judgement upon us?' Must we not in order to answer this question have recourse, in spite of his veto, to the historical character of the cross? This is certainly what the passage from the sermon would suggest. Surely we must turn to the Gospels and read the passion story about the way in which Christ came to his death. We must read about the man on whom his enemies inflicted that death. In short, must we not understand that here was a man who, unlike us, was willing to die to all human efforts to win recognition for himself, was willing to 'commit himself to him that judgeth righteously',[3] and to say in Gethsemane, 'Not my will, but thine'? Does the cross judge us and our world, because we are unwilling to act like

[1] *Marburger Predigten*, p. 191. This seems to be perhaps the only place where Bultmann lets extremely obscure theological conceptions find their way into a sermon!

[2] *K.u.M.*, I, p. 42. [3] I Peter 2.23.

this, and because it was our world in which this thing inevitably happened, as it would happen again today?

If we are to take Bultmann at his word, all such suggestions are struck out of our hand, for to do this is to have recourse to history. And, as we have so often seen, all attempts to understand the cross in terms of the self-humbling of the love of the divine Son are rejected equally firmly. It is mythology to say that the death of Jesus was the completion of the act of service by which Jesus became man, and 'knowing that he came from God, and went to God, girt himself with a towel, and washed the disciples' feet'.

So we are left with a pure unknown! But if so, why should the cross be a divine judgement upon us, any more than the signing of Magna Carta? The cross, avers Bultmann, has significance for us because it is preached, along with the resurrection, as an event of judgement and salvation! But, as we have seen, the resurrection is nothing more than the significance of the cross as saving event. So we are back in the old impasse. No other significance is to be found in the cross as saving and judging event, except that it happens to be preached as such. But if the cross as a historical event has so little significance, what can dying with Christ mean?

When, on the other hand, we look at Bultmann's preaching, it becomes quite clear that he does have recourse to the historical significance of the cross. For, as a matter of fact, his teaching about dying with Christ is a teaching full of content and is, indeed, the most moving and impressive part of all his preaching. Here again, it would seem that the gospel Bultmann preaches is much richer than the theology he teaches.

(*c*) *The resurrection of Christ*

In a sermon on the use of Sunday Bultmann asks, 'Does Sunday here too give us a new beginning? We remember that the Lord's day is the day of the resurrection, the day on which the new world of life broke victoriously into the old world of death, and made a new beginning, a new beginning for all who honour the risen One as their Lord. "If any man be in Christ, he is a new creature; old things are passed away; behold, all things are become new. And all things are of God, who has reconciled himself to us by Jesus Christ . . ." '[1]

Again, in a sermon preached to students of divinity in Marburg at the end of semester, he says, 'May the gift of the semester for us be,

[1] Ibid., p. 77.

that as weak men we let his power be mighty in us, that we know him in the power of his resurrection, and in the fellowship of his sufferings.'[1]

Now let us turn once more to Bultmann's theological writings. According to these, what is the resurrection? 'But the resurrection of Christ, is it not a mythical event, pure and simple? . . . Does the New Testament, in asserting that Jesus is risen from the dead, mean that his death is not just an ordinary human death, but the judgement and salvation of the world, depriving death of its power? Does it not express this truth in the affirmation that the Crucified was not holden of death, but rose from the dead?'[2]

So the resurrection for Bultmann is a mythological way of saying the same thing that the cross says, namely, that Jesus' death is the judgement and salvation of the world. It may be that the positive, saving, aspect of the cross, is what the mythical narratives of the resurrection emphasize, while the story of the cross itself emphasizes the death as implying God's judgement upon men. If we ask, how it is so, what makes the resurrection powerful to save men?—we are told, because it is preached as being such. But here there is not, as in the case of the cross, a separate historical event, unless we take into account the event of the rise of faith in the disciples after Easter morning. And why it arose in them we do not know, nor is it important to know. One thing, however, we do know apparently—though this is on the whole implied rather than said openly—we do know quite certainly, and that is, that Jesus did not rise again in any sense like that which the disciples and St Paul gave to the word 'resurrection' when they used it of him.

On reading again the two passages from the sermons, particularly the latter one, preached at the end of semester, we may therefore feel some small surprise. Were there not present on this occasion some students who, remembering Dr Bultmann's lectures and books, began to ask themselves with what right he spoke to them about the power of Christ's resurrection, when he did not believe that it had ever taken place? There are certainly a variety of views about the resurrection, which may be described as a belief in it. I have heard the word defined by a linguistic philosopher, with a conscious brutality, as meaning that a dead body got up and walked away. While we will be agreed that the resurrection implies a tremendous revelation of the divine power and love such as the mere notion of a revivified body cannot by itself suggest, this does not imply, as Bultmann and his school seem to assume, that there can have been no datable event, or no physical

[1] Ibid., p. 46. [2] *K.u.M.*, I, p. 44.

concomitants of the resurrection such as the stories of the empty tomb suggest.

But whatever our views on this may be, in brief, it seems that if we cannot believe that Jesus came back to his friends, after being dead, in a true personal confrontation, then we have no right to use the word 'resurrection' at all. To do so, and to hold what Bultmann believes, is uncomfortably like uttering false coinage.

It is, of course, exceedingly difficult to know what Bultmann exactly believes on this point. Probably Malevez is right when he says, 'In short, as has been said, he believes that nothing is to be said about the risen Christ, about his life after death, about the attestation which he brought to his friends of his triumph, of his meeting with them, before they were called by God to be the bearers of the message. . . .'[1]

If I understand him rightly, Bultmann regards any belief that the Christian can have a personal relation with the living Christ as a mythological expression of the fact that 'he calls upon God as someone led to God specifically by Jesus.'[2]

So it would appear that his right to speak of the resurrection and the day of the resurrection as 'the day on which the new life broke victoriously into the old world of death' is at least very questionable. It is more than likely that these words, preached to a congregation of lay people, meant to the preacher's hearers something quite different from what they meant to himself. Again we ask ourselves, 'Will *this* preach?' It is true that Bultmann's preaching is powerful and evangelical, but is it Bultmann's theology which is being preached?

(*d*) *Our dying and rising again with Christ*

On this theme I shall choose from a number of impressive passages two paragraphs from the same sermon, on John 16, which deals especially with the twenty-third verse, 'And in that day ye shall ask me nothing.' Here Bultmann says, Let us reflect further. 'That day' of freedom is, according to Jesus' word, also the day of Easter, the day of the resurrection, which follows the day of the crucifixion. 'Ye now therefore have sorrow'—it is the sorrow of the passion, of the cross, by which all wishes and hopes are annihilated. 'But I will see you again, and your heart shall rejoice.' It is to the man who mourns at the cross

[1] L. Malevez, *Le Message Chrétien et le Myth*, Brussels, 1954, p. 79 (Eng. tr.: *The Christian Message and Myth*, SCM Press, London, 1958, p. 83).

[2] R. Bultmann, *G.u.V.*, II (Eng. tr.: *Essays—Philosophical and Theological*, SCM Press, London, 1955, p. 285). See also Bultmann's answer to Schniewind, *K.u.M.*, I, p. 127.

that the certainty of the resurrection is given. And only he who is ready to enter with Jesus on the cross into the hour of dereliction by God, will also share in the life of the risen One. But this is sharing in the cross of Jesus, that we should surrender all our wishes and plans to the will of God, that we should place all that concerns us and our hopes as well as our work, under the cross, that is, that we should enter into the last solitude before God, that, as Paul says, we should let the condemnation of death be delivered on us, so that we may set our confidence not in ourselves, but in God, who raiseth the dead (II Cor. 1.9).[1]

Here especially, but also in the other passages to be quoted, we must note how deeply (contrary to his own protestations) Bultmann draws on the historical content of the passion of Christ, to which our own life, our dying and rising again with him, is to be assimilated.

From the same sermon I choose the following passage, dealing with the words 'I have overcome the world'. 'This is no word of easy consolation, as if Jesus' way through death had spared us all death and despair. It is rather consolation and warning at the same time—a warning that must become a consolation, our only consolation. That we take our suffering and despair upon us, and place them under the cross, take them into solitude in the presence of God, and so share in his victory over the world.'[2] And here is a last quotation, taken from a sermon already quoted on the subject of the cross of Christ. 'Everywhere this dying of Christ happens, where a man understands that his suffering must serve to bring to his consciousness the provisional character and the worthlessness of this earthly world when judged by ultimate standards. And everywhere the risen life of Christ becomes a reality where a man takes on himself the cross of Christ, i.e. does not hold fast to this earthly world, but lets it go, in order that God may give him the life of the transcendent world. All suffering should lead us to detach ourselves inwardly from the earthly and visible, in order to leave ourselves wholly to the grace of God.'[3]

In all these passages the pattern of Christ's death is the pattern for the life of the believer, and thus the retrospective historical question to which the Gospels give an answer, is *in fact* conceded a central importance. But is this for Bultmann the total relation of our dying with Christ to Christ's death for us? In how far does he allow Christ's death a priority, not just a priority in time, but an ontological priority to our dying with him?

[1] Ibid., p. 175. [2] Ibid., p. 177. [3] Ibid., p. 191.

This question we must raise again, but meanwhile let us note how important in fact this imitation of Christ is in the life of the believer. This was surely at least one component of St Paul's experience when he wrote, 'But what things were gain to me, those I counted loss for Christ . . . that I may know him, and the power of his resurrection, and the power of his sufferings, being made conformable unto his death.'[1]

This is the theme, too, of many a Christian hymn, such as George Matheson's *O Love that wilt not let me go*, written in a poignant moment of the failure of earthly hopes; and it is the theme of Richard Baxter's verse:

Christ leads me through no darker rooms
Than he went through before,
He that into God's kingdom comes,
Must enter by this door.

In all ages Christians have received courage to follow the pattern of their Master's fortunes, knowing that if they are really his, they must expect to repeat the pattern of his dying, trusting, like him, in God who raises the dead.

But, we must ask, is this the only relation of his dying and rising to ours? Is his to be nothing more than the pattern of ours. Or, again, is his dying to be so approximated to ours, or even assimilated to ours, that it loses its priority.

If Christ's death is only the pattern of ours, then how are we in any way advanced beyond the views of Yorck von Wartenburg, cited in Bultmann's first essay in *Kerygma und Mythos*?[2] Yorck seems to have insisted that the doctrine of Christ's vicarious death was only an illustration of the truth that holds for all mankind, that 'The child gains through the sacrifice of the mother; it works for his benefit. Without this virtual accrediting and transference of power there can be no history at all. (Note that the converse is true, all history is such transference of power, and not only Christianity.)' It would thus appear that, in the opinion of Yorck, what was mythically portrayed by Christian faith as a special act of God in Christ, is seen to be nothing more than a truth about humanity in general. Is Christ's death then nothing more than an example of how to live, a paradigm for our life?

Such, it would almost seem, is Dr John Macquarrie's rendering of Bultmann's view, of which he gives the following demythologized account. 'The decision of faith, which is at once renunciation of the

[1] Phil. 3.7-10. [2] *K.u.M.*, I, pp. 32-3.

world and surrender to God, abolishes worldly concern, and so puts an end to the tyranny of things over men, (and thus) brings men into a new life oriented to the eternal realities of God.'[1] But here we must ask the question, How is the teaching here given to be distinguished from the doctrine of non-attachment propounded by Aldous Huxley in *Ends and Means*. For non-attachment, in Huxley's sense of the word, is clearly one of the possibilities of human behaviour, without any need for a divine act of salvation in Christ. This viewpoint is then very far short of what Dr Macquarrie believes it to be, a 'powerful comeback of the Christus Victor doctrine of Christ's work'.

Bultmann, on the other hand, has emphatically rejected the suggestion that dying with Christ is simply an *imitatio Christi*. He says, 'To believe in Christ, therefore, does not mean . . . following him in the sense of letting oneself be drawn into his faith and his way of life. Paul never thinks of Jesus as a believer. What Paul means by faith came into existence only with the death and resurrection of Christ. It is indeed discipleship, as taking up his cross, not, indeed, in the sense of an *imitatio*, but as the laying hold of the forgiveness and possibilities of life disclosed by the cross. Faith for Paul is submitting to what God has done in Christ.'[2]

Here Bultmann maintains that in Christ new possibilities have been opened up for men, and forgiveness granted which we could not have won for ourselves. Christ is thus more than an example of the true way to face life, by dying to live. In him God does for man what man cannot do for himself. But when we ask, How does he do it? we are told, You must ask no questions, attempt no explanations. If you die with Christ, you will see that he does. Doubt here means a disobedient will! Thus the uniqueness of Christ and God's act of redemption in him have been preserved, but only at the expense of rationality.

In this paragraph the concluding point to be made is accordingly this, as we have seen before in this chapter, that by Bultmann 'dying with Christ' can be and is preached with great power, but when we come to the inevitable question why Christ's death should have the power to free us from our own past, and assure us of God's forgiveness, we are met with no answer. I would suggest again that ideas which drew their power from an older theology which Bultmann has discarded, are still at work to make effective his preaching. These ideas,

[1] *Expository Times*, November 1956, p. 63. As we saw above this seems to be in effect the view of which Prenter accuses Bultmann.

[2] See Appendix B.

as we have seen, are of two kinds. There are doctrines of Christ's Person and work which Bultmann regards as mythological. And there are rich elements of historical knowledge of the man Jesus Christ, the love shown in his dealings with men, and the conception of the gift of God's kingdom present in him, and the strange power of the detailed story of his death and resurrection.

7. Conclusions

Thus we cannot resist the conclusion that Bultmann's Christological substitute for the doctrine of the incarnation and work of Christ, together with his historical scepticism, has severely impoverished his theology, though it has had rather less effect on his preaching. Bultmann believes that God acted savingly in the historical life and death of Christ, and acts again for our salvation in the event of preaching and belief. But when the Fourth Gospel says, 'The Word was made flesh, and we beheld his glory, the glory as of the only begotten Son of the Father, full of grace and truth'[1] and when we read the words 'That which was from the beginning, which we have heard, which we have seen with our eyes, which we have looked upon, and our hands have handled, of the Word of life . . . that which we have seen and heard declare we unto you, that ye also may have fellowship with us, and truly our fellowship is with the Father and his Son Jesus Christ',[2]—we must surely perceive that we are facing something immeasurably richer than Bultmann's 'function-Christology'[3]. Here we have God, not just acting, however decisively, through the man Christ, but God dwelling with us in the mystery of the Person of Jesus Christ. Only if we believe in the mystery of Christ's Person and in his incarnation, can we say with the hymn-writer,

> Quaerens me, sedisti lassus,
> Redemisti, crucem passus,
> Tantus labor non sit cassus!

Only then can we say with the Fourth Evangelist, 'Jesus, knowing that he was come from God, and went to God, he riseth from supper, and laid aside his garments, and took a towel and girded himself . . .'

Secondly, if we believe in the incarnation in the full sense of the

[1] John 1.14. [2] I John 1.1-3.

[3] I do not reject all function-Christology. In a sense my own Christology is functional, since I do not believe that we can make a final separation between what a historical person is, and what he does.

word, we shall no longer be ready easily to accept the suggestion that the New Testament has no interest in the historical personality of Jesus.

Is it not true that there are at least two different kinds of interest in personality? The first is the kind of interest which has an aesthetic approach to its subject. This type of interest in a personality is in place in the author of a biography, who attempts to portray the man's gestures, the originality and perhaps the many-sidedness of his mind, and the feel of his personality. Such an approach is made, for example, in Boswell's *Life of Samuel Johnson*.

Of such an interest in personality there is no trace in the New Testament; and that is why the nineteenth century writers of Lives of Jesus were trying to make bricks without straw. Bultmann criticizes Johannes Weiss, not only because his interest in Jesus was of this type, but also because it was coupled with a Schleiermacherian type of Christology, which turned faith into a kind of imaginative empathy with Christ in his relationship to the Father.[1]

Reacting from this, may it not be that Bultmann, a little too quickly, has assumed that this type of interest in the personality of Jesus must be the only one, and will inevitably lead to the elaboration of this type of Christology?

But is there not a very different type of interest in personality, such as is hinted at in Karl Barth's splendid passage on Jesus, as 'The man for other men'?[2] This is an interest in Jesus, as the prolongation, within the visible world of human relations, of that descending line of divine grace which St Paul describes in the first verses of the second chapter of Philippians. Barth writes, 'It is . . . understandable that the New Testament has no place for the representation, or even the outlining, of a private life of the man Jesus. Not that it denies that he had such a life; it speaks clearly enough about his birth, his hunger, and thirst, his relations to his family, his temptations, his prayers, his sufferings and death. But it makes this private life of his visible only in order that it may show how it is in a manner caught up in his service to men, which is the concrete form of his service to God. Thus Jesus' private life can never become an independent theme in the New Testament.'

Surely it is the great theme of the Gospels to describe both of these stages in the movement of God towards man; the transcendent love which humbled itself in the incarnation and then incarnate, found its

[1] *G.u.V.*, I, pp. 249-50.
[2] Karl Barth, *Kirchliche Dogmatik*, III, 2, esp. pp. 249-50.

expression in the love of sinners, humbling itself at last to the death of the cross. If the New Testament has no interest in the personality of Jesus, why then does it deal in such detail with the story of the passion?

I believe that what lies behind Bultmann's preaching, and gives to it its undoubted power, is a theology of this richer and deeper kind. But whether such preaching can continue for long, if a theology like Dr Bultmann's is to continue in fashion, is more than doubtful.

IX

CONCLUSIONS

1. The continuing problem of the mythical

It is now time to attempt to fulfil our promise made earlier in this book.[1] There we undertook not to shirk the problem of which radical demythologizing describes an alleged solution. Though we may disagree with Bultmann's particular attempt at solving the difficulty, it remains nonetheless one of the most important problems in the whole field of theology. It is true that the men of the Bible lived in a different world from ours, and had to express their faith in Christ against a background of beliefs and in concepts largely different from ours today. If faith is to maintain its vigour in the world today, what is there in the language and belief of the Bible that demands reformulation? And what is there that is eternal, that has not lost, and never can lose, its ancient power? If Bultmann's project does not satisfy us, what alternative can we offer?

The situation is not made easier for us by the fact that Bultmann has spread his demythologizing net so wide, attempting, as we believe, to catch in it fish of very different kinds. There is, for example, the problem of doctrinal statements about God and the transcendent world. Are these mythical, and can they be translated without remainder into non-mythical terms? Then there is the problem posed to us by miracle. Here at least we seem to find the claim that certain things happened on this earth, in our time-series, whatever their transcendent significance may have been. Then again, we have the stories relating to Creation and the prophecies of the Last Things, which at least on the face of them seem to refer to events in the time-series. Then, further, we have the problem relating to the pre-existence of Christ; and the problem relating to the existence of powers in the universe which are less than God, but more powerful than men, the principalities and powers, the angels and demons of the New Testament. Bultmann does not exaggerate when he says that the clarification of these and

[1] Ch. 5, p. 111.

kindred problems will take the time and all the powers of a theological generation.[1] Here all that can be offered is a contribution to that discussion.

2. *Bultmann's substitution of the existential for the mythological*

We have seen how Bultmann's demythologizing project started from the realization that certain usages of theological language could not be taken literally. This led him to switch over to an existentialist interpretation which was confidently offered as a complete and satisfactory substitute. I would suggest that both the completeness of the rejection and the confidence of the reinterpretation are too emphatic.

Bultmann points out that many theological concepts cannot really mean what at first sight they seem to mean. We have only to think of the concept of 'Creation', to see that this claim is well-founded. I shall not linger on this point, as I shall be developing it later. Bultmann concludes that, accordingly, these concepts 'are not to be examined with a view to discovering their objectifying content, but with a view to discovering the outlook on life which expresses itself in these ideas'.[2] He believes that not only the mythological character of the concepts, but the need for a radically existential reinterpretation of them is shown by the fact that many of them, when taken literally, are mutually contradictory. When, however, we begin to consider the 'contradictory' concepts, as Bultmann displays them in his first essay,[3] we feel that he ought either to have offered a more serious study of this matter than he has done, or omitted it altogether. For it may very well be questioned whether a number of these 'contradictions' are contradictions at all. For example, it is impossible to see how the fact that Christ's death was in one place described as a sacrifice, could contradict its elsewhere being regarded as a cosmic event. And is there any more contradiction in his being at once spoken of as the Messiah and as the Last Adam, than, say, when the President of the United States is at the same time called the head of the armed forces of that country? Further, with regard to the 'contradiction' between the virgin birth and the doctrine of the pre-existence of Christ, we may concede that it is possible to regard these as alternative ways of trying to do justice to the discontinuity between him and the rest of mankind which is felt to be a vital part of the Christian faith. Yet it does not appear that there is any necessary contradiction between the two doctrines, though it must be

[1] *K.u.M.*, I, p. 26. [2] Ibid. [3] *K.u.M.*, I, p. 23.

admitted that where the one is found, there are no unmistakable traces of the other.

At least one of these 'contradictions' cited by Bultmann has direct reference to Christ's historical life. It is claimed that Paul's doctrine of the *kenosis* of the pre-existent Christ is in contradiction with the account of his miracles by means of which he proves himself to be the Messiah. Probably the reference here is to the Johannine account of Christ's miracles. Let us concede the doubtful point as to whether John really regards the miracles in this light. If that be allowed, then we may draw attention to the fact that in the synoptic account a wholly different place is ascribed to the miracles, and all that is logically necessary is to say that one of these accounts, that of John, is not historical in the picture it gives of Jesus' outlook upon his miracles.

Here, where two differing accounts of past occurrence are given, it is clear that one of them must be inaccurate, so long as the assumption continues that a record of past events is intended. It is, however, different where an attempt is being made to express by human concepts the nature of the transcendent. If we once grasp what must be the character of all human statements about the transcendent, then we will not claim that a human concept can be applied to it in just the same way as it can to an object within the field of our ordinary experience. So here, in the field of the transcendent, there should not be talk of contradiction, because the concepts are being used with at least a latent awareness of their inadequacy,[1] and in fact are being brought forward rather to point in converging directions, and to supplement each other, than sharply to define. Hence the 'contradictions' in mythological statements dealing with this field should not be urged as grounds for its wholesale abandonment, since only if the concepts were being literally used, would the contradiction really arise.

An example of the awareness of the Biblical writers of the inadequacy of each of their figures of speech, and the mutual support required by these figures, may be given here, by citing a number of figures which Bultmann does not cite in this context. Paul can sometimes speak of the relation of Christ to the church as that of the relation of the body to its parts. But since this might lead to the belief that he was identical with it, or dependent on it as it is on him, the modification of this figure is introduced, which speaks of him as Head of the Church, or Shepherd

[1] Surely this is the case with reference to the 'three-decker universe', which one might say never has been a serious theological difficulty, and which accordingly I have not discussed in this chapter.

of the flock, or king of his people. It may further be said that while Christ is not known without these figures, yet it is not the case that we are left with nothing but their totality from which to build up on our own initiative a picture of him and his relationship to his people. We have the narrative of his life on earth, and of his impress upon his followers through all the Christian ages.[1]

What is, however, most important for our argument at this point is the fact that these 'contradictions' are being used as an argument against the mythical, and in favour of a total switch-over to the existential. I am convinced that this is wrong, for in terms which are confessedly inadequate the mythical judgements still express a necessary truth about the transcendent, which can only be given in such terms. And until Bultmann has given us a great deal more confidence in the seaworthiness of his existential judgements than he has hitherto done, that is, in their ability to reach the shores of trans-subjective validity, we would be unwise, to say the least, in abandoning the ship of mythological judgements for the somewhat unseaworthy lifeboat of existential interpretation.

Advocates of Bultmann's views may interject here: You object to what Bultmann is here saying, but he is really saying exactly the same thing as yourself. I would reply: No: we are agreed that there is no knowledge of God without existential relevance for me. But Bultmann is using the apparently mutually contradictory relation of statements about the transcendent in order to throw the major, if not the total emphasis of such statements on to the subject who makes the statement. They are at least primarily, for Bultmann, statements about how I understand myself in my world. My interpretation, on the other hand, claims that the statements are still, as they claim to be, primarily not statements of how I understand myself in the world, but statements about the transcendent.

Having thus, as he believes, disposed of myth, Bultmann turns to its existential reinterpretation. As we have seen, his rather cavalier treatment of the claims of myth to tell us about God is due, not so much to the discovery of contradictions within it, as to his confidence that in the personal existentials of the existential analysis we have a

[1] In this context the reader may like to consult a suggestive passage in Professor Ian Ramsey's *Religious Language*, (p. 139). Here he says that Jesus chose the title 'Son of man' as a concept with few empirical connexions, but filled out its meaning 'in use'. In like manner the concept of 'God' has been filled out 'in use' in the experience of the men of the Bible and, subject to this norm, in the experience of Christians of later days.

completely adequate means of expressing the truths of our religious faith, since Heidegger has shown us in what terms we must speak of human personal realities, and our faith can be adequately expressed by these vehicles.

It is true that personal categories are the most adequate for the expression of our faith, and we have the authority of the Bible for using them, but Bultmann seems here for the moment to forget that even personal categories cannot be applied to God with exactly the same sense that they possess in dealing with human personal relations. Here too, then, there must be a certain element of inadequacy, and when we have seen that this is so, we may be ready to treat a little less cavalierly terms whose inadequate character is more immediately obvious to us. We may be ready to believe that they also can help us on the way to knowledge of the transcendent realities of our faith.

3. Mythical and existential—an alternative suggestion

Bultmann has thus drawn a sharp antithesis between the mythical and the existential. We must now go on to inquire whether this antithesis is not a false one? Perhaps we should not say, '*Either* mythological *or* existential'. Perhaps we may have to regard every statement made by faith as possessing a mythical moment, a moment of confessed inadequacy, as it tries to touch the transcendent by means of its human concepts. And, on the other hand, it will have an existential moment as it attempts to 'cash' the value, or some part of it, of this judgement, for the life of the believer. It is possible to reinterpret a theological statement, or a statement of faith, so as to emphasize one's realization that it *is* mythological, that is, inadequate to describe the reality to which it refers, and at the same time to 'cash' a part of its existential value for my life. This we may describe as a partial retreat from the mythological, a retreat involving an emphasis on the existential moment in the judgement.

An example may help to show what is meant by the above sentence. The statement 'God created the world' is in fact inadequate to describe the reality at which, so to speak, the words are aimed. 'Why so?' Because all the other creation that we know involves material already present, which is transformed by the act of creating. But God's act of creating is absolute creation. It is true that where a musician creates a symphony, there was in a sense nothing there before. But such human creation always involves a world in whose context the symphony was created, and in which there lay the possibility of its existence. But God's creative act is the act of creating the universe itself. And yet even here we are aware that we are forced to use concepts that we know to be inadequate. For here we speak of God's creative act, and we can only conceive of an act as occurring in time. But without an already existing universe by which to measure time, how can we conceive of time? But this act of God is the act by which the universe itself was created, as the theologians have said 'out of nothing'.

Clearly, we are here talking in a parable, in a myth, for our words fail adequately to penetrate the reality at which they are aimed. To talk of continual creation does not remove the mythical element, for that term is just as much bound up with the notion of time as the other. So at this point we must confess a mystery which prevents us pressing further in this direction of the transcendent.

There comes thus a moment when we realize that we cannot apply literally our notion of creation to God's act of creation. Indeed, we may come to realize that, unknown to ourselves, we have not been applying it literally, though we were hardly aware of this before. We realize that we do not clearly know what we mean when we speak of God's creative act, though we are sure, that when we speak of it, we are not talking nonsense. We are sure of this because when we ask ourselves whether we more nearly approximate to the truth when we describe this act as past, than when we speak of it as yet to come, we realize that the first alternative is nearer to the truth than the second. Yet we must admit that this 'past' is unlike our ordinary past!

So by our inability to grasp fully the notion of divine creation, we are driven from the mythical pole of our judgement towards the other, the existential pole of it. We are driven towards a formulation which emphasizes what we can more completely grasp, whose values for our self-understanding and our life is more easily elicited. We say accordingly that, whatever else it may mean, the doctrine of divine creation means that we must regard the world as fundamentally good, not evil; that we must believe that it is finally dependent on God as its Lord, that we do not believe that God is directly responsible for evil, that in the end of the day his victory will be sure, and so on.

But we cannot completely 'cash' the notion of creation. If we could wholly 'cash' it, that would mean that we could get rid of the notion of a creative act itself as applied to God in his relation to the universe, except in so far as it might be a convenient way of gathering together the above-mentioned elements of our interpretation.

We must however note that the existential judgements we have cited in connexion with the divine act of creation are still judgements directly about God, or else judgements which imply judgements about him. But there is here a more clear and direct relevance to our self-understanding than when we simply say, 'God created the world'. That is to say, the existential moment has been thrust into evidence.

Further, even here, in so far as there remains a reference to the transcendent God, there remains also an element of the mythical, or inadequate, which it would not be hard to disclose. Any attempt to get wholly rid of this mythical element would leave us with no God, but with the blank possibility of a new self-understanding on our part. It is to this that Bultmann has reduced the Holy Spirit, and it is hard to see why in his theology the same treatment should not be accorded to the First and Second Persons of the Trinity.

But surely even a possibility implies an actuality which is its ground, an actuality which, if the judgement were made concrete, would inevitably have referred to it concepts that were in some degree inadequate or mythological.

If this general line of reasoning be accurate, then the contrast will not lie between mythical thinking on the one hand and an existential reinterpretation thereof on the other hand, but, on the one hand, between various mythical representations, in some of which the mythical and objective element is more prominent and the existential less so, and, on the other hand, representations in which the existential element is more prominent than the transcendent and necessarily partially mythical reference.

There appears to be here a parallel, though not perhaps a very close one, to another field of human thought, the realm of empirical knowledge. In this field we have on one side the reference to a reality beyond, and, on the other side, its experimental verification. In this realm, the meaning of a statement, while not separable from its verification, is yet not identical with it. Similarly, in the theological field, the meaning of such a statement as 'God created the world', while inseparable from the statements in which the existential reference is more evident, is yet not identical with them. Still less is the meaning of 'God created the world' to be identified with the existential attitude and policies of a man who lives as if he believed this to be true.

A similar treatment to that given above of the theological doctrine of the Beginning might be given to the doctrine of the End. Here it would be conceded that the future in which we believe the Last Things to lie is not clearly conceivable, yet we must retain the notion of its 'futurity' as approximating more closely to the truth than any other. At least it is clearly more apposite to say that God's final victory lies in the future than to say that it lies in the past!

Before we leave the doctrine of creation, with its ineradicable moment of mythology, there is something more to be said on this doctrine and on the chapters in Genesis which tell of man's creation. There does appear to be another aspect of the matter of the creation, than that on which we have touched already. The development of modern science, with the evidence which it has supplied about the primitive beginnings of our race, would suggest that the story of man's creation and fall as recounted in Genesis are not accurate, if they are treated as accounts of historical events. Yet from the facts of man's existence today, as seen by faith, certain historical events in the past, in their barest schematic outline may surely be inferred. Thus, quite apart from the mythical conception of *creatio e nihilo*, if man now exists, in all his singularity of intellect and existence in the divine image, then there must have come a moment in time when man began to be. And whether this startling and new thing came to be in one way or in another, yet there must have been a moment when all at once it began to be, even if an imaginary spectator could not have told at what moment man became human. Similar considerations would suggest that there must have been a first sin, though this may not have been what theology calls the Fall, and though man did not sin in the exact manner recounted by the Genesis story. If intellect, existence in God's image, and human sin are all so strikingly singular as we believe them to be, then, whether a hypothetical observer could have noticed their coming into being or not, these things must have happened at some definite point in the past time series. If this be the case, then we can say that there is a schematic truth about the Genesis story, which is distinct from the mythical doctrine of creation, about which we have hitherto been speaking.

4. The collapse of mythological concepts

One of our important suggestions has been that all thinking about God must employ inadequate, and in that sense mythological, concepts. But we must not allow this conclusion to delude us into a complacent belief that, where all is mythological, all is equally acceptable. We cannot, as it were, sit back and declare the whole project of demythologizing to be a mare's nest. For it appears that certain mythological concepts may prove their own inadequacy to be so radical that in the course of time they become altogether impossible. And it would seem that there are at least two ways in which this collapse of mythological concepts can occur.

The first cause of the collapse of a mythological concept is its increasingly manifest failure to do justice to the reality which it claims to describe. Bultmann would as an instance quote the concept of sacrifice as applied to Christ's work.[1] While not agreeing with this verdict, I might suggest another instance of the collapse of a mythological concept, or series of concepts.

Very early in the church, the apostles attempted to give an interpretation of the place of Christ in the universe in terms of the concepts of election, adoption, and exaltation to a place of divine honour. It must be pointed out that all these concepts are thoroughly mythological. There can, however, be no objection to them on this score, for, as we have seen, some element of the mythological is necessary in all judgements which attempt to deal with the transcendent reality of God. But very soon the Church found it necessary to use other mythological concepts, in particular the concept of pre-existence, whose task is approximately to indicate the place of Christ on the side of God in contrast with us men.[2] That these concepts heighten the tensions in

[1] *K.u.M.*, I, pp. 20 and 41.

[2] In his learned and suggestive book *Christology and Myth in the New Testament*, Allen & Unwin, London, 1956, Geraint Vaughan Jones maintains the opposite thesis to that put forward here, seeking to reverse the historical verdict of the church at this point. Referring to the doctrine of pre-existence as mythical, he seeks to demythologize it, reinterpreting it in terms of what he believes to be the non-mythological Christology of the Synoptic Gospels (without the birth-narratives) and the Book of Acts. Believing in the fundamental Christian doctrine of the Lordship of Jesus, he is satisfied that he can do justice to it within the framework of an adoptionist Christology. Vaughan Jones discards the notion of pre-existence and the notion of co-creatorship, and declares that Christ's Sonship of the Father 'may be regarded as the result of divine "adoption" (as in the *kerygma* of Acts) or as election, without any loss to the full affirmation of faith, for it means a mutual knowledge so complete that the mind of the Son expresses the mind of God; a Sonship involving such unity with the Father that the Son is wholly drawn into the divine nature as the divine nature is drawn into the life of the Son' (p. 144). We cannot agree with Mr Vaughan Jones that these concepts of election, adoption and exaltation are non-mythological.

He chooses an analogy from human creativity to illustrate the discontinuity of Christ with the rest of mankind to which the New Testament title of 'Kyrios' gives expression. In human creativity, without miracle, he says, we have something quite new brought into existence in the world, something, especially in the field of art, which is once-for-all and unrepeatable, something belonging to the noumenal sphere, which enters into the phenomenal realm. Using this analogy (pp. 190 ff.) he essays to depict the Incarnation as an act of divine

Christology and, in particular, that they make it harder to do justice to the full humanity of Christ, must be admitted. And yet surely we must feel that here we have a more adequate mythology than that of the book of Acts, and that the mythology of Paul and John and the Author of Hebrews is replacing the less adequate Christology of the speeches of Peter.[1]

In view of this conclusion it might be better to describe this task of replacing a collapsed mythology by a more adequate one, not as *de*mythologizing but as *re*mythologizing.

There is, however, another way in which certain mythological concepts may become discredited. Let us again cite an example. The advance of scientific knowledge, whether we like it or no, has had the result that many phenomena, which men used to ascribe to the agency of demons, are now expected to have another explanation.[2]

creativity emerging from the noumenal being of God himself. Now certainly, on p. 196 Vaughan Jones affirms that the emergence of human creativity is only an analogy of the newness and discontinuity which entered the world in Christ, yet it is hard to avoid the conclusion that in fact it is more than an analogy for him. He claims that those categories which mark out man as discontinuous with the rest of nature are applicable to Jesus, and if Jesus, as we believe, was fully human, this will be true. But what is vital to faith, and here is of supreme relevance, is that discontinuity to which universal human categories are not applicable. And of this no account is here given, save that Jones declares that the resurrection affirms Jesus to transcend the natural order, and to stand on God's side as well as on man's. An approving quotation from Berdyaev might be taken to indicate that Jesus is held by Mr Jones to be a created being facing both man and God (p. 194). Accordingly, it is hard to see how Jones has the right to claim that he has logically arrived at his desired conclusion, given on p. 201, where he says, 'So the divine participation in struggling agonic history and in human experience is affirmed by the Christmas stories, and in them creation is subsumed into the being of the Creator, who descends into the human scene in order to experience it from within and redeem it.' In fact, while one must be grateful to Mr Vaughan Jones for a vigorous and honest facing both of the New Testament evidence and the extremely puzzling problems he encounters, he has not shown us any very convincing reason why we should reverse the verdict of the Church, which declared Adoptionism to be a thoroughly unsatisfactory form of Christology. The notion of pre-existence, though confessedly inadequate, secures the truth so central for the New Testament, and so vital for faith, that Jesus, as Lord, stands on God's side over against man, his creature.

[1] It must be remembered also that Peter's audiences were Jews, and that the whole argument of the early Church against the Jews turned on their conviction that Jesus was the Messiah, the fulfilment of the hope of the Hebrews. When Paul and John were writing, the whole Gentile background against which the gospel had to be preached had become visible. Here were peoples who had no interest in the Jewish Messiah. It was only natural that now the cosmic significance of Christ should become more manifest to the first missionaries of the gospel.

[2] A friend of the writer, in the process of psychological analysis, experienced a violent abreaction, in which his strong immediate impression was that a powerful and evil demon had been cast out of him, and was thrown violently to the ground. He could even locate the place where it fell, on his right side.

Even if we still believe in demon possession, we must admit that the realm of the demons has been considerably curtailed by the advance of science; and we must admit that while there may still be such a thing as demon possession, the hypothesis that there is, is definitely in part an answer to problems of a scientific character, and is to some degree verifiable or falsifiable by scientific method.[1]

This second type of the collapse of mythological concepts will accordingly only occur in the fields where certain phenomena appear which are subject to scientific examination, such as may be found in the field of psychology and para-psychology. The sphere of the transcendent, to which such methods of scientific examination cannot apply, will be untouched. Science can tell us nothing about the concepts which we should apply to God himself, nor has it any power to cause their collapse.

It would no doubt be Dr Bultmann's opinion that the concept of miracle, as it has usually been understood, has suffered a collapse of this second type. We have already treated of this subject in a special chapter. The claim is made by the apologists of miracle that it belongs both to the historical or mundane sphere as a datable event, of which it could be said that either it did, or did not happen. And on the other hand, they also would affirm that it belongs to the transcendent sphere, in that its true significance is not grasped until it is seen as a special act of God.

Our argument against Bultmann here was urged on philosophical grounds, since we maintained that this rejection of miracle was due to a faulty philosophy. Yet we are not prepared to say that every miracle story told about Christ narrates plain facts which must be affirmed to have happened as recorded. For, particularly in the Fourth Gospel, there do appear to be miracle stories, where it may not unfairly be said that the evangelist seems interested almost wholly in the preaching significance of the story, and hardly, if at all, in its reference to actual historical occurrence. In Bultmann's own language, these stories seem more intent on telling me what God intends to say to me now than in bearing witness to what happened. Here then, while in principle

But intellectually he was convinced that it was not so; what had happened was that a part of his own subconscious self had been disclosed to his awareness, and the powerful feelings of dread were gradually replaced by others of a not unpleasant kind. In the old days such a man would have said, 'I know there are demons, for a demon has been cast out of me!' Yet this would have been only a mythical expression of what really happened.

[1] It must be observed that if, and in so far as, demons actually exist, the concept is not mythological!

rejecting Bultmann's views on the question of miracle, we are prepared to concede that in relation to particular miracle narratives he may be right.

We must now for a moment revert to the question of the demonic. For it is not only in relation to the phenomenon of demon-possession that we are confronted by this problem.

One of the most attractive suggestions of the demythologizing theology, has been the interpretation of the demonic element in human life which it offers. This the demythologizers claim to be a mythological expression of a universal fact of Christian experience, that when men treat as of absolute value any power less than God, such as money, or the life-force, or race, they inevitably fall into a desperate bondage under it. As Bultmann has said, 'This sphere tyrannizes over the man who makes it the foundation of his life, who "lives according to it", who allows himself to be seduced into basing his life on that which is visible and at his disposal, instead of basing it on that which is invisible and not at his disposal. . . .' It is true that this teaching is not an original discovery of Bultmann's, for other writers such as Paul Tillich[1] and Theophil Spoerri[2] have written impressively in this vein. But Bultmann has certainly treated the theme powerfully, not only in his theological writings, but even more so in his sermons.[3]

We are left with the question in our minds, Is there nothing more in the demonic than this? Here it would appear that a true demythologizing might be possible, since the question is whether our own religious experience demands some other explanation than that offered by the demythologizers. If there are actually demons, they do not belong as God does to the sphere of the transcendent, and so do not need to be described by inadequate concepts as he does. If science can show that this hypothesis is not necessary to explain obscure types of mental illness, can reflection on our own religious experience go some way towards persuading us that there are not conscious superhuman forces of evil at work in opposition to God?

If this were so, then we would be within sight of the collapse of the concept of the demonic. If it be said, however, that the Christian doctrine of God as creator demands that the doctrine of the demons be not literally understood, since this would introduce an intolerable dualism into the universe, then we must ask whether the problem of

[1] Paul Tillich, *The Protestant Era*, Nisbet, London, 1951 and *Systematic Theology*, vol. I, Nisbet, London, 1953, *passim*.
[2] *Die Götter des Abendlandes*, Furche Verlag, Berlin, 1931.
[3] See ch. VIII, pp. 176 and 178.

evil which is left when all demythologizing has been completed, is not just as serious a challenge to belief in God the creator as a belief that Satan and his angels exist?

Frankly, I must confess that while there is much suggestiveness and power in the Bultmannian demythologizing account of the demonic, I cannot make up my mind whether there is more in the demonic than he believes.

If the belief in the demonic has to submit to demythologizing, then one of the most important doctrines of Christ's work may require rethinking and restating. This is the doctrine of Christ's work as victor over the forces of evil, for these have often been represented as demonic in character. Now our interpretation of this Christus Victor Theory will vary very much according as we believe, or do not believe, that there are personal superhuman forces of evil at work in the world, which received in some way a decisive defeat by the death and resurrection of Jesus.

Mr Vaughan Jones has pointed out that there has been a good deal of slack thinking and talking about the decisive victory fought on Calvary against the forces of evil, and much loose pulpit use of the figures of D Day and V Day, which has led to the conception of all history since then as consisting of mopping-up operations against the forces of evil. Mr Jones concedes that Emil Brunner, who introduced the D Day figure that Cullmann has also used, goes far towards correcting any possible false impression that might be received from his words, by emphasizing that the battle continues with apparently undiminished severity. Evil, continues Mr Jones, is evidently not one in the way that Hitler's armies were organically one, so that the closing by Montgomery of the Falaise Gap in 1944 seriously weakened their powers of resistance all along the line.

If the concept of the demonic, literally understood, should prove inevitably unrealistic and untrue to Christian experience, then we might here have a further example of the collapse of a misleading mythological concept on theological grounds.

5. Bultmann's antithesis between cosmological and existential judgements

In the pages of Bultmann we frequently meet an antithesis between cosmological and existential judgements. While this is closely related to the antithesis between mythological and existential judgements, it is worth drawing special attention to it, since it enables us to draw an important distinction between two elements in cosmological judgements, one of which is transitory and the other eternal.

In the first essay in *Kerygma und Mythos* we read the following sentence: 'The true intention of myth is not that of giving an objective world-picture. Rather is it an expression of the way man understands himself in his world; the interpretation that myth requires is not cosmological, but anthropological, or, better, existential.'[1]

It is indeed true that the genuine intention of myth is not cosmological in the sense of offering a detailed account of the structure of the physical universe. But all theological statements have a cosmological significance, inasmuch as they claim to express more than individual feeling, and to be judgements about reality. The Doctrine of God, the Doctrine of Man, and the Doctrine of Christ cannot but imply at the same time a Doctrine of the World, the *kosmos*, and the relations between all these magnitudes.

On the other hand, whatever statements of faith are made about Christ, or God, are inevitably made in concepts which are inadequate, and sometimes particular concepts thus used pass completely out of date. Vaughan Jones reminds us '. . . According to the popular cosmology of the ancient world, space was not "empty", but peopled by invisible beings. It was the strange world of which there are suggestions in Colossians, Ephesians, and late Jewish angelology. This world space was essentially mythological space, for it was represented as a cosmos ruled by the seven deathless cosmocrats, the world-rulers of Ephesians 6.12. In it planets became elements (Gal. 4.3-9) and the elements were equated with demons.'[2]

Now it must surely be maintained that in the cosmological statements of, let us say, Paul, or any other New Testament writer, there are the following two elements. First, there is the intention to affirm the lordship and reality of Christ; and, second, there is the expression of this lordship and reality in relation to the beings of the mythical cosmology of his day. While we admit the collapse of belief in the Cosmocrats, yet the cosmological intention of reality in Paul's thinking is by no means to be discredited with the passing of the cosmocrats or the other denizens with which the fantasy of the first century peopled the universe. One element in this cosmology is therefore utterly out of date, and the other has permanent value. The cosmological is thus not wholly convertible into the existential, and a new expression, which will still in some degree be mythical or inadequate, must be found to

[1] *K.u.M.*, I, p. 22. [2] Op. cit., p. 78.

satisfy that intention of reality which Paul described in terms that are now impossible for us.

Further, there is some indication that Paul himself, and here he is doubtless typical of other early Christian writers, does not really lay very much emphasis on the cosmological imagery which he uses. There is here a clear parallel with the use which Christian thinkers make of the terms of contemporary philosophy; as Barth has said somewhere, there is a 'fundamental lack of seriousness' about the detail of the imagery used. Vaughan Jones has drawn our attention to the 'gods many and lords many' (in contrast with the one God and Christ), and the weak and beggarly elemental spirits of the universe. And the whole emphasis of Romans 8 is not on the details of the cosmology of principalities and powers, but on the fact that 'whatsoever gods there may be' they are not powerful enough to separate us from the love of God in Christ.

This point must not be pressed too much, so that we underestimate the difficulty of reinterpreting some of Paul's mythology. But there is surely some help for us in this consideration, that there are two elements in his cosmology, one of which is eternal and the other has long since passed away. And that Paul's major emphasis is not upon the transitory but on the permanent.

6. Paradox, profound or bogus?

For some time now the term 'paradox' has been fashionable in theology, and there has been much puzzlement as to its real place within this discipline. Dr Ronald Hepburn asks in his book, *Christianity and Paradox*, the question, When is a contradiction not a mere contradiction, but a sublime paradox, a mystery?[1] While certain theologians have seemed to take delight in the contradictory, as Tertullian did with his 'Credo quia absurdum', we can see that Dr Bultmann is not of their number, since the contradictions which he claims to find in mythical statements in theology are in his opinion grounds for believing that these formulations must be superseded by other ones. It will be remembered, further, that we have here denied on one ground or another the truly contradictory character of most of the examples chosen as contradictions by Bultmann. Yet because we have said that we are forced, in theological statements about God, to use concepts, and then to deny their adequacy, in our opinion there must be a

[1] *Christianity and Paradox*, p. 17.

certain element of paradox in theology,[1] and we have therefore an obligation to offer to the sceptic some justification for our conviction that we are not embarking on a series of self-stultifying contradictions.

We would, of course, agree with him that sheer contradiction has no legitimate place in Christian theology, and that therefore there is nothing to be said for Barth's definition of sin as 'an ontological impossibility'.[2] For an ontological impossibility is that which cannot exist, and sin obviously does exist. To say as Barth does is, then, to break the law of contradiction, and while this violence to reason may express a justified horror at the mystery, and indeed the unintelligibility of sin, to call it an ontological impossibility is an expression of emotion rather than of thought.

How then are we to differentiate legitimate paradox from contradiction? By the suggestion that paradox, when legitimate, is always aware of its own provisional character, and convinced that the appearance of contradiction does not amount to the reality. The apparently contradictory positions must both seem to be well founded, and thus must both for the moment be held, in the conviction that a quick resolution of the difficulty will be premature, and that thus elements of the truth will be lost.

It will be remembered how, in the writings of Professor Karl Heim, a poly-dimensional scheme is elaborated. Heim tells us that one of the first signs of the dawning of a new dimension will be that in the dimensional scheme as hitherto elaborated, an apparent contradiction occurs. But when the full facts of the case have been understood, it is realized that what seemed contradictory, is not in fact so, since when the new dimension is fully disclosed, the apparent contradiction is resolved.[3]

Without committing ourselves to Heim's ingenious scheme, we may use this as an illustration of the legitimate use of paradox in theology. It would appear that there are two kinds of legitimate paradox in this discipline, according as we are aware that we cannot expect to resolve this apparent contradiction within the limits of our present life, or as we have reason to hope that we may do so.

[1] Yet in so far as we are conscious of the inadequacy of our concepts, we are saved from actual paradox, which would only arise if we first claimed that they were adequate, and then denied it. Our use of personal categories to describe God is essential to our faith, for they are the least inadequate. Yet all the while we are aware that he is our Father *in Heaven*, i.e. that he is not as other fathers are.

[2] K. Barth, *Dogmatik*, III, 2, p. 162, Zürich, 1948.

[3] Karl Heim, *Christlicher Gottesglauber und die Naturwissenschaft*, Furche Verlag, Hamburg, 1949, p. 149 (Eng. tr.: *Christian Faith and Natural Science*, SCM Press, London, 1953, pp. 145-6).

In any case it will be clear that this distinction between paradox and contradiction cannot provide us with a universal yardstick by which both sceptic and believer can come to an agreement as to which paradoxes are bogus and which are genuine. For in every case the decision must be made as to whether we are compelled by the facts of the case to accept provisionally two positions which appear mutually contradictory. And the decision that we can surrender neither depends on our evaluation and interpretation of this experience and that, and this evaluation, depends in turn upon our existential outlook upon life. And in such matters we may indeed be able to reason with the sceptic, but can offer him no outright proofs. Such radical paradoxes then as legitimately appear in our thought about God, have justification only in so far as we have not sight to replace the partial vision of faith.

7. A norm for theological thinking?

Bultmann has asserted that there is a norm for theological thinking, a thinking which is neither the thought of science, nor yet mythical thinking.[1] It is, he says, the thinking which we employ when we say 'I love you', or 'I ask you for forgiveness'. As will appear from what follows, we are in general agreement with him on this point, and our own position will have to be expounded in some detail. That is, we agree with him so far as to say that the kind of thinking suited to dealing with inter-personal human relations is more suited than any other type of thinking to deal with our relation to God.

Bultmann however defines his own position more precisely by saying that the patterns of inter-personal relations in general and the patterns of legitimate thought about them have been laid down by Martin Heidegger, and he takes the further step of saying that the patterns of thinking about God (for theology as a scholarly discipline) have thus at the same time been laid down by Heidegger, who has made the same claim for himself. We have shown in an earlier chapter our reasons for questioning both of these conclusions. Further, the only attempt in detail which Bultmann has made to dovetail a piece of theological thinking with the ontological thinking of Heidegger, has proved so unconvincing, that the fruitlessness of this general project is self-evident. On the other hand, and without reference to Heidegger, Bultmann has given us several expositions of what, in his opinion, the character of existential theological thinking is. Here, too,

[1] *K.u.M.*, II, p. 187.

we have been convinced that a breakdown has occurred, since Bultmann's expositions, in our opinion, failed to break out of the circle of subjectivism. We saw, further, that his views entailed such radical separations between faith and knowledge, that such a breakdown was inevitable.

In spite of this, we are convinced that Bultmann is right in believing that the paradigm of personal relations gives us the most adequate analogy for our talk about God. We do not believe, as he does, that here is a language which with complete adequacy and with no trace of the mythological or inadequate can be used to describe our relations to God and our knowledge of him, yet we are sure that he is most adequately spoken of in personal terms. And our main reason for so believing is that he has revealed himself primarily in such terms to the men of the Bible under both dispensations, in the Old Testament and in the New.

By this conviction we are encouraged to make our own attempt to use the personal analogy to describe the human encounter with God and human knowledge about him. Standing as we do at the conclusion of this book, we can only offer in brief a homespun project of interpretation, in which no attempt is made to pierce to ontological levels or define the horizons of human possibility as Heidegger does in his work. But the claim is made that whatever the inadequacies and errors of this project, it does avoid the radical separations which mark Bultmann's essays on 'What is the Meaning of Discourse about God?' and on 'The Christological Confession of the World Council of Churches', and bring them to rapid confusion.

8. 'Knowledge-of' and 'knowledge-about': the outline of an alternative theory to Bultmann's

It might seem presumptuous to tackle so huge a philosophical theme in a few concluding pages. But Bultmann's mistakes are so much bound up with his errors in the field of epistemology, that those who criticize him are surely obliged to offer at least the outlines of an alternative epistemology of the personal. To give one example, his declaration that events known by other persons are irrelevant to the present encounter of faith[1] implies a wrong estimate of the relationship between knowledge about God and the direct knowledge of God, or acquaintance with him, of faith.

Therefore, at the risk of some repetition, I shall set down rather

[1] *K.u.M.*, I, p. 44.

more systematically than elsewhere in this book the outlines of a theory which seems more in accord both with the Biblical witness, and with common sense. While so doing, it is only fair to acknowledge the motive which lies behind some of the remarkable—and illogical—statements that Bultmann makes, especially in his essay 'What is the Meaning of Discourse about God?' The motive is the desire to respect the honour and the transcendence of God.

In talking about our knowledge of God, we must acknowledge frankly the difference between this knowledge and our knowledge of other, human, persons. It will at least be universally admitted that human inter-personal knowledge is a better analogy here than our knowledge of things! Let us accordingly consider our knowledge in relation to other human beings. It is clearly of two very different kinds.

(*a*) The first kind, which we may call 'knowledge-of,' or personal encounter, is so near to us, and so important in our life, that it is taken for granted, and often curiously misunderstood by the theorists, and, as it were, approximated to the second kind, which we shall describe as 'knowledge-about'.

This first kind of knowledge, 'knowledge-of', is prior to the second, 'knowledge-about'. Not always necessarily prior in time, for I can know a lot about a man before I meet him. But prior in many senses, one of the chief of which is that the great proportion of our knowledge *about* persons is ultimately derived from our own, or other people's knowledge *of* these persons. 'Knowledge-of' cannot occur without an increase of 'knowledge-about', and these two kinds of knowledge are extremely closely interwoven in our experience.

The question may actually be raised whether 'knowledge-of' is knowledge at all. For it contains in it just as important elements of action, or will, and feeling. My activity in relation to the 'thou' is at once acting, feeling and knowing. Certainly, if the 'spectator-attitude' is an essential of knowledge, then 'knowledge-of' is not knowing. In this activity my attention is, with my action, directed towards the 'thou'. But surely this is knowing *par excellence*, as our use of language indicates when we ask, 'Do you know so-and-so?' This means at the least, 'Have you met him?' If I know him, then he also knows me. In this encounter of which we have been speaking, every look in my eye, every gesture of my hand, every word I say is itself a knowing. But at the same time it is an action in face of the 'thou', and an expression of feeling, be it affection, interest, suspicion, fear, reverence, or merely attention.

This encounter has its own immediacy; it is dependent on the 'thou' over against me, but it is not mere immediacy. It is nearest to immediacy when I meet for the first time a stranger about whom I know nothing. But when I meet an old friend or acquaintance, it is already enormously enriched by memory, by what I know about him, and by what we have already experienced of each other. It may also be enriched by knowledge passed on to me by others who have encountered him, though this can never take the place of my own encounter. 'Knowledge-of' is thus one aspect of a two-sided whole. It also feeds 'knowledge-about' and is nourished in turn by it. It is certainly not propositional, but it is undoubtedly knowing.

Now we come to the second kind of knowledge, 'knowledge-about'. This is commonly thought to be always propositional, but while it can be formulated in propositions, and often is so, it may be expressed in actions—for example in the elaborate preparations made for the reception of royalty, and in other cases by gestures or other actions indicating fear, or reverence or hatred. One person may communicate by such non-propositional means to a second person his knowledge about a third person. Normally, however, 'knowledge-about' is expressed in propositions, and thus communicated from person to person.

It is clear that epistemologically other persons become the objects of our thought when we think about them and know about them. This has no effect upon their status as persons. They remain persons, even when known or known-about, and as persons they remain free, except in the epistemologically quite irrelevant situation where a man uses knowledge about another man in order to blackmail him, or the like. Even when I know that my neighbour has made a promise, my knowledge of this does not give me control over him in the way that I can control a thing. For it is precisely as a free person that he has bound himself, and as a free person that he feels bound to keep his promise. Things neither make promises, nor do they keep them. Knowledge about a man may be used for good or for evil. It may be made the means whereby I assault his dignity as a person, as when I belabour the public by propaganda, or subliminal advertising. But 'knowledge-about' does not in any way diminish the freedom of sovereignty of the person thus 'known-about'. For example, however good I know a man to be, however thoroughly I may be assured that if I ask his forgiveness for any injury done to him, he will forgive me, yet that does not absolve me from the obligation of making this personal request of him. I cannot by-pass the dimension of 'knowledge-of', which is the privilege of persons alone. Only when he has personally assured me of his forgiveness, have I the right to know that I am forgiven, since he has given me that right. In the last resort I must apply myself to the 'I-thou' relationship with him.

It is sometimes said by writers of the existentialist school that God is the Subject that never becomes an object. Bultmann nowhere uses this language, for the good reason that he thinks that both these terms are utterly inadequate to existential thinking. But there is a kinship between this statement and Bultmann's assertion that statements about God are both senseless and wicked. If the person who says that God is the Subject that never becomes an object, means that by being known he would submit to the control of man, then we must retort that this is palpably false. Even human beings do not become objects in the sense of falling under our control, when epistemologically they become our objects. Nor, *a fortiori*, does God!

But if by saying that God is the Subject who never becomes an object, theologians are talking in epistemological terms, then also they are wrong. For this would mean that we could never know *about* God. In this case a direct and incommunicable 'knowlege' *of* him might be possible. But it would be utterly unlike any other knowledge that we have. And preaching, witness, theology and the Christian Church would not exist, for all these imply, and seek to communicate, knowledge *about* God. And more, the statement, 'God can never become an object', taken epistemologically, seems to be nonsense, for it both asserts that nothing can be said about God and says something about him.

As we have seen Bultmann's mistake is similar. He is opposed to statements about God, on the ground that they imply a neutral platform from which we may say one thing or another about God, according as we find it illuminating.[1] Statements about God do not, however, imply this supposedly neutral, but really rebellious will; they imply only an epistemological abstraction, and this is necessary for any statement which is to claim a trans-subjective validity.

In opposition, then, to what Bultmann's views seem to imply we may say, quite clearly and confidently, that God both desires that men should know about him and speak about him, even when this knowledge precedes a direct knowledge of him. And he desires most of all that they should have knowledge of him by faith, by personal acquaintance, and that, knowing him, they should bear witness to him.

[1] *G.u.V.*, I, p. 26.

In relation to other human persons, knowledge of them by acquaintance is, as I said, the primary knowledge, which feeds, as it were, our knowledge about them, and this latter is communicable to others. But our knowledge *of* others can never be transmitted. It comes to us, so to speak, as a gift of grace, which only they can give to us. There is an analogy here with our knowledge of God.

There is a further characteristic of our knowledge of human persons which depends on the fact that personal being is known in a history. The personal qualities of a man do not reside in him as redness or hardness resides in a pencil; they are not to be discovered by the same kind of sense experience. If I say that John is conscientious, kind, forgiving, charming or insufferable, these things are not to be discovered by touch or sight. They are, rather, 'indicator' words, giving approximate hints to the hearer. But if the hearer asks me, 'What do you mean when you say that John is charming?' I find myself engaged in telling him a story, the story of certain events in which John's history and mine, or that of some third person, are intertwined. 'This is what John did', I will say, and the narrative of his history will convey better and more subtly than any accumulation of descriptive terms just the sort of man John is. Man is a being with a history, and in this history he reveals himself. The story of his history is his own story. Yet he is not just a history, but a being whose mode of existing is historical.

Now suppose that I come to meet him, knowing something about him, but not yet having met him. I approach him as a being with a history. He is mysterious to me, known about, and yet unknown by acquaintance. I make, as it were, an adventure of approach to him, and he continues to 'write his history' by the I-thou responses that he makes to me. But my waiting over against this mystery, this personal confrontation, which the Germans describe by the word *Gegenwart*, leaves both him and me free. Neither of us can forego this patient waiting and readiness for each other, if we are to know each other.

Surely the relationship between God and the believer has its points of similarity with what happens here. And though I have developed these remarks about our knowledge of human persons, and dare now to claim that there is an analogy here with our knowledge of God, yet this is offered, not as a piece of natural theology, but because I believe that the kind of revelation which is recorded in the Bible gives me a certain authority to do so.

As our knowledge of a man's past history may immensely enrich our personal knowledge of him today, so with reverence it may be said that the history of God with men in the past may be appealed to when he approaches them today to give them knowledge of himself by faith. Can it be denied that this whole way of speaking is characteristic of the Psalms,[1] where God is continually appealing to Israel's knowledge about him from the past. Is it not characteristic of the whole Bible?[2] Did not God speak to Moses as 'the God of thy father, the God of Abraham, the God of Isaac, and the God of Jacob'?[3]

Christians believe that in the life of Christ God approached mankind in a unique manner, in an I-thou confrontation. This was no theophany, visible to all and sundry, for the facts of that life were visible to a great many people who saw in them no revelation of the Father. To those who received faith, however, both his contemporaries and later generations, the story of Jesus' life and the manner of his death have been immensely important, for in the light of faith these historical facts are seen to be the disclosure of the heart of God.

For Bultmann, however, the facts of the life of Christ are of very minor importance, since not past history is revelation, but present confrontation. True, past history as such is not confrontation. But if this past history was the history of God with men, then does not the God whom we hope to meet today stand illumined by this past history. Of course Bultmann is right in telling us that we must not confuse the acceptance of the truth of certain statements about past events with personal faith; but such a narrative of past history is of decisive importance for my faith today since that faith cannot be independent of God's past revelation through historical events to the men who were its original witnesses. And I would suggest that an epistemology of the personal, of the kind suggested above, is implied by the historical Biblical record of revelation. Further, I would claim that only along such lines of thought can the extreme tensions between faith and knowledge, and between revelation and history be avoided, which rend amidships and sink so disastrously the vessel of Bultmann's theology.

[1] E.g. Ps. 105. [2] Deut. 32.1-14; Heb. 1.1. [3] Ex. 3.6.

Appendices

Appendix A

FAITH AND HISTORY

WHILE this book was preparing for the press, Dr Macquarrie kindly permitted me to see the proofs of his latest book, *The Scope of Demythologizing*, SCM Press, London, 1960.

Here he restates his position on the relation of faith to past events. Faith is not, he says, dependent on the researches of the historian, because in the gospel 'there is a minimal core of historical factuality which cannot be reasonably doubted' (p. 93). This answer does not seem much different from Kähler's and Althaus' solutions to the problem, and with it I would agree, though I am less sceptical than Macquarrie about the assured minimum of our knowledge about Jesus.

I must, however, reformulate more precisely my view which he criticizes on p. 97, that faith is not positively dependent on the results of historical research, but that it is vulnerable to the possibly negative conclusions of historical research (p. 150). Macquarrie will agree that faith is not built up on the foundation of facts which the most negative historical critic can accept, but upon a general acceptance of the witness of the New Testament, which includes both a claim that certain things happened, and that in them God revealed himself. On the negative side, my assertion of vulnerability is meant to make it clear that faith would be vitally stricken, could it be shown by historical research that Christ had never lived, or had been either a mere political revolutionary, or a bad man. Macquarrie, I take it, agrees with this general thesis, while asserting that it is inconceivable that such a result could be established by historical research, a conclusion from which I would not seriously demur.

What I am concerned to maintain is the vital importance that certain past events of history should actually have happened, and that they should have had a certain character, even apart from the deeper significance which faith sees in them as divine revelation. It is here that Bultmann's declaration that 'almost nothing can be known about the life or personality of Jesus', separates him from Macquarrie's much more reasonable position.

I must disagree, however, fundamentally with Macquarrie as to the reasons why this substratum of historical factuality is necessary for faith. (See Appendix B, p. 223.)

Appendix B

THE WORK OF CHRIST

ON p. 93 of his *The Scope of Demythologizing* Dr Macquarrie makes it clear that he ascribes to Bultmann—and himself agrees with—that view of Christ's work of which Prenter accuses Bultmann.

Macquarrie holds that it is important that we should believe that Christ actually lived and died, for if he had not, we could never have known that such a life and such a death were true human possibilities. But surely this does not carry us decisively beyond the position of Yorck von Wartenburg. Nor can it be a fair account of Bultmann, whose teaching is that without Christ philosophers can *know* what authenticity is, but cannot, as they vainly believe, achieve it (*K.u.M.*, I, pp. 34-37). For Macquarrie the reverse seems to hold; unless we know that Christ lived and died we cannot know that this kind of living and dying is a true human possibility. But, once we know this, it seems that we can achieve it by our efforts. But surely the true importance of historicity for faith is that only if Christ actually lived and died can his life and death be raised above the status of mere human ideas and fantasies, whose sole value might be to act as symbols of human possibilities which would lie within man's own native powers. Historicity is here essential because it alone can provide the vehicle of a divine act of revelation, forgiveness and salvation which we could not perform for ourselves.

Appendix C

A SERMON BY H. W. BARTSCH

(This sermon is translated by David Cairns from the German *Die Anrede Gottes* by H. W. Bartsch, by kind permission of the author and his publisher Herbert Reich, Hamburg.)

Now if Christ be preached that he rose from the dead, how say some among you that there is no resurrection of the dead? But if there be no resurrection of the dead, then is Christ not risen. And if Christ be not risen, then is our preaching vain, and your faith is also vain. Yea, and we are found false witnesses of God; because we have testified of God that he raised up Christ, whom he raised not up, if so be that the dead rise not. For if the dead rise not, then is not Christ raised; and if Christ be not raised, your faith is vain, ye are yet in your sins. Then they also which are fallen asleep in Christ are perished. If in this life only we have hope in Christ, we are of all men most miserable.

I Corinthians 15.12–19.

THE people in Corinth, to whom these words were sent, were certainly not worse Christians than we are. They laid some store by their faith, certainly more than most of us do by ours. It meant for them liberation from all the fear under which they had lived in heathendom. It had brought to them the certainty that they had been adopted by God, whether they were slaves or free men, rich or poor, sinners or just men, Jews or Greeks. And God's Kingdom would come soon, so that all these differences which had caused them to suffer, had lost through this faith their significance. Their faith was a happy and liberating faith.

But at one point this faith found its limit. If death came, then the Corinthians believed that all was lost. That meant that life was at an end, and there was no further hope. We do not rightly know why this was their belief, what difficulty so held back their faith, that it could not liberate them from this domination by death. But this is where Paul attacks them. It is just here, he says to them, that your faith shows what it is worth. Everything else is lost, if this enemy still retains his power, when he still opposes himself to the power of God. Paul says to them that they have not rightly understood the message of Easter, if it has not given to them the certainty that they have received the gift of a new life after death also.

It is worth nothing that the Corinthians should obediently and believingly accept the fact that Christ is risen. It is of no value, when they repeat the Creed, and really assent to it when they do so, unless it means for their life and their death this final and conclusive liberation from all servitude.

And so it is still with us today. It is not important that you should with astonishment, but believingly, accept the story of Easter as true. That will do neither you nor anyone else any good. And it is of no value that you should believe in the resurrection of the dead, as if this had made you superior to the Corinthians. It *is* important that the Easter story should give to you the final limitless liberation from all other powers, that you should be able to stand under the Lordship of God, and of him alone, knowing that nothing can take you out of his hand.

In order, then, that you may hear the message of Easter rightly, as a word spoken to your life, let us hear once more the word of Jesus' passion and death as a word to our own life.

We think, all of us, that we know very well what suffering means. One can speak with whom one wills, there will never be any lack of complaints. Everyone has grounds for complaints; we don't need to start counting the reasons why. It's the same with the farmer, as it is with the displaced person; the business man and the worker, too, have plenty of reasons for complaint. And yet all these things, even if they include the most frightful sufferings of this world, do not compare with the frightful suffering that meets us in Christ's passion. The very thorn that makes the ache in every suffering is there in the passion of Jesus.

It was not the whipping and the blows, not all the incidents that the hymns of the passion describe in detail, it was not the contempt of the people, who demanded his death, it was not the physical sufferings of his crucifixion, which were the cause of his passion. The deepest agony comes out in his cry, which rings out to us across the centuries, 'My God, my God, why hast thou forsaken me?' That God forsook him in this hour, that he really hung powerless and helpless there on the cross, that was his agony.

He really could not have obeyed that sneering challenge, 'Come down from the cross!' He could not have done it, and even if he had asked for the legions of angels, they would not have come, for God did not hear him any more. So he really was delivered into the hands of the men who mocked him. They were right with their mockery, 'He put his trust in God. Let him deliver him, if he takes pleasure in him!' But God did not help him.

And here is the heart of all our complaints and our sufferings, in so far as our complaints are not mere childishness—and some of them are just that. But this is the heart of our suffering, when our troubles really make us despair. We feel ourselves delivered over to disease and danger, to suffering and death, because we have lost the sense that God protects us, because we feel ourselves forsaken, just as Jesus did on the cross. And thus other powers and cares and sufferings get a stranglehold upon us. When an unemployed man sits with the few pence that the unemployment bureau pays him, in his hand, and does not know how he will feed his family with it, then the suffering that makes him despair lies just in the fact that God does not feed the hungry, and that he cannot make fresh red cheeks with a few crusts of bread. And when a sick man groans on his bed, and the doctor can't help him any more, then the dreadful thing is that even God can't help any more, that all help is at an end. And perhaps the despair of the homeless and their homesickness, whose fate today seems to us so desperate, culminates in the thought, which they can hardly repress, 'God has forgotten us, he doesn't care for us any more'.

And now the passion of Jesus gives us in him a man who stands beside us, who had just this experience, yes, even down to the most terrible of deaths, the experience of being deserted by God, and of being delivered into the hand of those who hated him.

If we have rightly understood this, then we rightly understand also what Easter means, what it signifies for us.

It is not of importance that then, once upon a time, a man rose from the dead, as if we should open mouth and ears before this miracle, stand gaping at it, and believe it. More than one such story of raising the dead is told in the New Testament, and yet none of these stories was able to prevent Jesus uttering his cry of dereliction. The man who remains sceptical of the story of the resurrection of Christ, and will not believe this miracle, should not think that he has decided everything. He has not heard at all what God wants to say to him here. And if you believe in this story, don't think that you have decided everything. The Corinthians believed it, and Paul cried out to them, 'Your faith is vain!'

No, everything depends on our hearing what God is saying to us, to you and me, in this story. The disciples, too, thought that it was all up with Jesus, they all forsook him. And now, suddenly, it became clear to them, that God had declared himself to be on the side of this crucified Jesus. The man who can't believe the story of the resurrection, must just believe that God awakened this faith in the disciples in some other way, that God, the living God, declared himself in the midst of death to be on the side of his Son.

And so our ears are opened for what God wants to say to us. He says that right in the midst of dereliction, in the deepest contempt, he is on the side of those who are forsaken and despised by all. He says to you, too, that he is on your side, when you are just as much deserted as Jesus was then on the cross, that therefore you need never cry again what Jesus there cried, 'My God, why hast thou forsaken me?'

It has pleased God to say this to you in this story, which is proclaimed year by year at the festival of Easter. That is why this story remained alive, when others grew dim and were forgotten. That is why this story is the ground of the hope of countless Christians, in which they lived and died. That is why the cry of victory, 'Christ is risen', is the cry with which the Lordship of God is proclaimed over all powers and principalities. He does not look back to something that happened once upon a time, but he calls you to look forward without fear, because he takes the thorn from all your troubles, the last bitterness from all your sufferings. Now it can never happen again that you are delivered into the power of anything that might make you afraid, for where he stands, even the pain of the greatest sorrow does you no harm. He will soon turn to good your cross, your anxiety, your suffering; yes, he has even control over your death!

And that is what the apostle was getting at in his letter to the congregation in Corinth. If there was any power that was able to seize them out of the hand and protection of God, then all their faith was mere self-deception, then in truth they were more miserable, more to be pitied than other men, for their faith was vain and worthless. Only if there was no barrier that separated them from the Lordship of God, was their faith true, only then had they rightly understood the Easter message.

And therefore we are not concerned today with the belief in an old story from the past; we are concerned only with the revelation of the power and goodness of God which has made all other powers unable to harm us! It is our concern to know that nothing can happen to us but what he has foreseen and provided for. If we know that, then the new life has come to us also with this message of Easter, then are we truly already risen with Christ.

BIBLIOGRAPHY

Althaus, Paul, *Das so-genannte Kerygma und der historische Jesus*, Gütersloh, 1958, Eng. tr., *The so-called Kerygma and the historical Jesus*, Oliver and Boyd, Edinburgh, 1959.

Ayer, A. J., *Language, Truth and Logic*, Gollancz, London, 1936.

Barth, Karl, *Kirchliche Dogmatik* III.2, Zürich, 1948.

Bartsch, Hans Werner, *Die Anrede Gottes*, Hamburg-Volksdorf, 1954; see also *Kerygma und Mythos*.

Braithwaite, R. B., *An Empiricist's View of the Nature of Religious Belief*, CUP, London, 1955.

Brown, James, *Subject and Object in Modern Theology*, SCM Press, London, 1955.

Brunner, Emil, *Der Mittler*, Tübingen, 1927, Eng. tr., *The Mediator*, Lutterworth Press, London, 1934.

Gott und Mensch, Tübingen, 1930, Eng. tr., *God and Man*, SCM Press, London, 1936.

Das Gebot und die Ordnungen, Tübingen, 1932, Eng. tr., *The Divine Imperative*, Lutterworth Press, London, 1937.

Mensch im Widerspruch, Berlin, 1937, Eng. tr., *Man in Revolt*, Lutterworth Press, London, 1939.

Offenbarung und Vernunft, Zürich, 1941, Eng. tr., *Reason and Revelation*, SCM Press, London, 1947.

Dogmatik I, Zürich, 1946, Eng. tr., Lutterworth Press, London, 1949.

Dogmatik II, Zürich, 1950, Eng. tr., Lutterworth Press, London, 1952.

Bultmann, Rudolf, *Jesus*, Berlin, 1927.

'Die Geschichtlichkeit des Daseins und der Glaube', *Zeitschrift für Theologie und Kirche*, 1930, vol X.

Glauben und Verstehen, vol I, Tübingen, 1932, *Glauben und Verstehen, vol II*, Tübingen, 1952, Eng. tr., *Essays—Philosophical and Theological*, SCM Press, London, 1955.

Theologie des Neuen Testaments, second ed., Tübingen, 1951, Eng. tr., vol I, SCM Press, 1952, vol II, SCM Press, 1955.

Essay, 'Neues Testament und Mythologie', in *Kerygma und Mythos* I, written 1941, published in *Kerygma und Mythos* I, 1948, Hamburg-Volksdorf, Eng. tr., *Kerygma and Myth*, SPCK, London, 1954.

Essay, 'Abschliessende Stellungnahme Bultmanns', in *Kerygma und Mythos* II, Hamburg-Volksdorf, 1952.

Bultmann, Rudolf (*cont.*)

Marburger Predigten, J. C. B. Mohr, Tübingen, 1956.

Jesus Christ and Mythology, Eng. tr., 1960, SCM Press, London.

de Burgh, W., *Towards a Religious Philosophy*, London, 1937.

Collingwood, R. G., *The Idea of History*, Oxford, 1946.

Craig, A. C., *Preaching in a Scientific Age*, SCM Press, London, 1954.

Gogarten, F., *Entmythologisierung und Kirche*, Stuttgart, 1953, Eng. tr., *Demythologizing and History*, SCM Press, London, 1955.

Haug, Hellmut, article in *Zeitschrift für Theologie und Kirche*, 1958/2, 'Offenbarungstheologie und philosophische Daseinanalyse'.

Heidegger, Martin, *Sein und Zeit*, Halle a. S., 1927, Eng. tr., SCM Press, 1961.

Hepburn, R. W., *Christianity and Paradox*, Watts, London, 1958.

New Essays in Philosophical Theology, no. 12, 'Demythologizing and the Problem of Validity', SCM Press, London, 1955.

Jones, Geraint Vaughan, *Christology and Myth in the New Testament*, Allen and Unwin, London, 1956.

Kähler, Martin, *Der so-genannte historische Jesus and der geschichtliche biblische Christus*, 2nd ed., Münich, 1956.

Kerygma und Mythos edited by Hans Werner Bartsch. Herbert Reich, Hamburg-Volksdorf, vol I, 1948, vol II, 1952, vol III, 1954, vols IV and V, 1955. Eng. tr., of vol I, *Kerygma and Myth*, SPCK London 1954.

Lackmann, Max, *Vom Geheimnis der Schöpfung*, Stuttgart, 1952.

Macquarrie, John, *An Existentialist Theology*, SCM Press, London, 1955.

Article in *Expository Times*, November, 1956.

The Scope of Demythologizing, SCM Press, London, 1960.

Malevez, L., *Le Message Chrétien et le Mythe*, Brussels, 1954, Eng. tr., *The Christian Message and Myth*, SCM Press, London, 1958.

Ramsey, Ian T., *Religious Language*, SCM Press, London, 1957.

Russell, Bertrand, *Mysticism and Logic*, Allen and Unwin, London, 1918.

Ryle, Gilbert, *The Concept of Mind*, Hutchinson, London, 1949.

Schumann, F. K., Article in *Kerygma und Mythos*, I, 'Die Entmythologisierbarkeit des Christusgeschehens'.

Spoerri, Theophil, *Gotter des Abendlandes*, Berlin, 1931.

Taylor, A. E., *The Faith of a Moralist*, Macmillan, London, 1930.

Tillich, Paul, *The Protestant Era*, Nisbet, London, 1951.

Systematic Theology, vol I, Nisbet, London, 1953.

de Waehlens, *La Philosophie de Martin Heidegger*, Louvain, 1946.

Warnock, G. J., Essay VI in *Logic and Language*, OUP, London, 1953.

INDEX OF PERSONS

www.ingramcontent.com/pod-product-compliance
Lightning Source LLC
Chambersburg PA
CBHW071847090426
42811CB00029B/1944

9780334047568